LIMINAL COMMONS

LIMINAL COMMONS

Modern Rituals of Transition in Greece

Angelos Varvarousis

BLOOMSBURY ACADEMIC
LONDON • NEW YORK • OXFORD • NEW DELHI • SYDNEY

BLOOMSBURY ACADEMIC
Bloomsbury Publishing Plc
50 Bedford Square, London, WC1B 3DP, UK
1385 Broadway, New York, NY 10018, USA
29 Earlsfort Terrace, Dublin 2, Ireland

BLOOMSBURY, BLOOMSBURY ACADEMIC and the Diana logo are trademarks of Bloomsbury Publishing Plc

First published in Great Britain 2022

Copyright © Angelos Varvarousis, 2022

Angelos Varvarousis has asserted his right under the Copyright, Designs and Patents Act, 1988, to be identified as Author of this work.

For legal purposes the Acknowledgements on p. xi constitute an extension of this copyright page.

Cover design by Adriana Brioso

All rights reserved. No part of this publication may be reproduced or transmitted in any form or by any means, electronic or mechanical, including photocopying, recording, or any information storage or retrieval system, without prior permission in writing from the publishers.

Bloomsbury Publishing Plc does not have any control over, or responsibility for, any third-party websites referred to or in this book. All internet addresses given in this book were correct at the time of going to press. The author and publisher regret any inconvenience caused if addresses have changed or sites have ceased to exist, but can accept no responsibility for any such changes.

A catalogue record for this book is available from the British Library.

A catalog record for this book is available from the Library of Congress.

ISBN: HB: 978-0-7556-3889-5
PB: 978-0-7556-3890-1
ePDF: 978-0-7556-3892-5
eBook: 978-0-7556-3891-8

Series: In Common

Typeset by Deanta Global Publishing Services, Chennai, India

To find out more about our authors and books visit www.bloomsbury.com and sign up for our newsletters.

For Anastasia and the ancient junipers of Gavdos.

CONTENTS

Foreword by Massimo De Angelis	viii
Acknowledgements	xi
Chapter 1 INTRODUCTION	1
Chapter 2 COMMONS, CRISIS AND LIMINALITY	9
Chapter 3 LIMINAL SUBJECTS OF COMMONING	45
Chapter 4 COMMONS IN EXPANSION	81
Chapter 5 BEYOND CLOSURE AND OPENNESS	113
Chapter 6 TRUST, ALTRUISM AND SOLIDARITY	137
Chapter 7 EPILOGUE: RITUALS AND TRANSFORMATIONS	173
Bibliography	189
Index	200

FOREWORD BY MASSIMO DE ANGELIS

In her important 1990 book *Governing the Commons*, Elinor Ostrom studied hundreds of cases in which communities around the world came together and self-organized in the governance of shared natural resource systems, be these forests, grazelands or rivers. The crux of her work rests on a selection of commons cases that have lasted for long periods of time, in some instances for hundreds of years. She, therefore, was able to develop her formational principles, which she argues are essential for the commons' sustainability and resilience over time. There is of course much value in studying commons' endurance, especially if we are interested in learning ways to create commons-based systems and institutions that endure and have the capacity to contrast the hegemony of capital, concerning the ways we reproduce socially through cooperation.

But what would commons' endurance mean in a world inundated with multiple constantly evolving crises, which often worsen the conditions for social reproduction?

For commons systems to endure in our turbulent world, flexible, engaged and creative adaptations are required, in order to have a plurality of ways to challenge the main source of those crises: capitalism. In turn, for the subjects making up and participating in these commons systems, such creative adaptations imply transformative processes whereby participants necessarily search for and find meaning through their participation, and challenge their known systems of perceptions, forms of communication and ways of being-in-common, a transformative journey that generates a new sense of what is worth living for.

Our world is one whose massive and multiple crises open many fronts and insecurities that create fractured subjectivities, which are either torn from a context that threatens their social reproduction or mesmerized by a precarious present and an always more uncertain future. Reconstructing this world requires new transversal sensitivities that at a minimum seek to articulate the three dimensions of what Felix Guattari called 'the three ecologies': the psyche, social relations and non-human natural ecologies.

But how can this new sensibility be developed?

There is no transcendental machine that would allow us to do that. Only in the immanence of doing things with others we can hope to change the world around us as well as our own subjectivities. Thus, the current multiple crises are not only the source of our anxieties and desperations; they also constitute the contexts in which new subjectivities are formed. These perplexed subjectivities are able to pool resources and people together in necessarily new and creative ways as an alternative to the rigidities of the old world, folded in many nested contexts. Precisely because the crises are multiple and their presence is felt in an even larger multiplicity of contexts, the creative efforts seeking a way out are emerging as a vast, decentralized archipelago of commons experiments, a process that facilitates transversal social learning that may create temporary solutions to different aspects of the current crises of social reproduction while at the same time giving rise and circulating new 'traits' of being in common while socially cooperating with others.

In our times, commons endurance thus does not only require the enduring of singular commons à la Ostrom. It also requires the endurance of a commoning practice deployed in a vast array of contexts, the endurance of a multitude of temporary, ephemeral commons whose transformative function as a whole is to seek ways to address different crises in different contexts and create new subjectivities. In the context of a commons literature that in the last couple of decades has seen the definition of the commons to move beyond mere natural resource systems, and by taking stock of the intense seasons of social upheaval in Greece after the 2008 crisis, Angelos Varvarousis' book turns its gaze into this constellation of temporary (or transient) commons, which he calls liminal commons.

Varvarousis approaches the crisis and liminality from the perspective of how individuals and collectives experience the uncertainty of the in-betweenness, of threshold spaces that both separate and connect – spaces that processes of commoning turn into liminal commons. Liminal commons are thus social systems that catalyse a transformation of the subjects in particular moments of crisis, with a corresponding intensity of perturbation. The subjects of the liminal commons are liminal subjects, subjects whose identities have been deterritorialized by the changing conditions posed by a world in crisis. Crises thus produce a disarticulation between higher scale social systems and the microsystems experienced by subjectivities. However, through commoning they are entering in relations with one another in performative, repetitive and norm-recreating activities, thus giving rise to liminal commons to meet specific needs and desires in everyday life while at the same time (re)construct identities and new subjectivities.

Building from important contributions on liminality in anthropology and social theory, Varvarousis' contribution is extremely timely and precious to those of us who seek to understand the possibilities of 'lines of flight' away from the organizational pattern of the capitalist-dominated social cooperation. Commons that seem to appear and disappear with great rapidity may be seen as an unimportant manifestation of failed social experiments. This book instead makes us see them as ephemeral baubles of a turbulent 'liquid' surface of a society in transition, an energy often generated and visible amid multiple crises, be this the Greek economic crisis as discussed in this book, or the building of community relief efforts in the aftermath of natural disasters such as hurricane Katrina in 2005, or the mushrooming of mutual aid networks in the context of the current pandemic.

Each bauble creates its liminal commons, a temporary space-time dimension in which subjectivities pierce hegemonic forms of social cooperation with their self-governing creativities, and in so doing they are in turn shaped by the autopoietic twirls of the new commons. With the disappearance of each bauble, new subjectivities with new experiences and sensibilities re-enter the larger social sphere, thus creating the condition for new processes of transformation. Liminal commons are thus often the result of upward waves of social movements, or, seen in another way, they generate subjectivities that give rise to new social movements.

The idea of the liminal commons as put forward by this book opens up an important area of research and political reflection on the relation between these transient commoning processes in the context of the crises of social reproduction and the possibility of an enduring social transformation, ultimately resting on the production of new institutions, systems and subjectivities attuned to a commons-based mode of production.

ACKNOWLEDGEMENTS

A book about transformations and transitions couldn't be anything but a self-transformation journey in itself. In my view, though, self-transformation is never an individual process but it is always nested in some form of community, ephemeral or more permanent. Indeed, this book is the outcome of the work of several micro-communities whose origins are lost in the past, and tracing them now is an impossible task. The idea of doing something on transient communities started when I was studying urban planning as an MSc student at the Department of Architecture of the National Technical University of Athens in 2008, the same year when the 'revolt of December' took place in the streets of Exarcheia – my neighbourhood – and beyond, an event that temporarily transformed the centre of the city into an archipelago of ephemeral encampments and other experimental forms of being-in-common. It was the summer of the same year when I decided to turn my academic lenses onto a series of ephemeral summer communities, communities that were formed in June or July and usually end at the beginning of September in order to self-organize, inhabit and collectively manage public beaches often in remote islands. Being part of both movements, I started to observe that there is a loose connecting tissue between these seemingly unconnected transient commons and that there is something bigger in this process of temporarily coming together that begs for more systematic attention and research.

This initial observation constitutes that symbolic beginning of the ten years research process that informs the chapters of the present book, and as the magnitude of the time frame and the number of the communities involved entail, compressing my gratitude for those who have played an important role in making this book possible cannot be done by way of a list of names. Some people already know that I owe them a lot, while others, who may have contributed – even unknowingly – in this effort with a small gesture, a smile, a sharp comment or a revealing insight at an unanticipated moment, will forever be the anonymous shadow co-authors of this text.

I am writing these final lines sitting at the office of one of the most important figures of my educational life: my beloved teacher Dina Vaiou who has always been a source of inspiration and transformation for me for more than fifteen years now. Dina, an emeritus professor of urban studies at the National Technical University of Athens (NTUA), was always enthralling me with the clarity of her thought, the modesty of her expression and her attention to aspects that I would never have noticed without her help. I will always be grateful to her.

Of course, since this book draws a lot on my doctorate work, my main supervisor Prof. Giorgos Kallis couldn't be out of this list. Every supervisor wants the best for their students, but Giorgos' contribution has far exceeded the expectations that any learner can have of his or her mentor. Giorgos' interest in my work was instrumental in changing my life direction, abandoning my previous life and diving into the depths of the academic world. In every step of my research, his influence on the evolution of my thought and the refinement of my arguments has been very significant. Besides this, Giorgos has become a true friend, with whom I have shared unforgettable moments of companionship and commoning: sharing a house, harvesting olives, playing sports, enjoying fiestas and many more. Our relation, through the learning ritual of the PhD, has turned into an enjoyable long-term collaboration and friendship. As I have already told him, I would never exchange him for any other supervisor.

I also want to deeply thank another mentor, Dr Christos Zografos. My relationship with him started when we shared a meal at Can Masdeu, a renowned peri-urban squat in the outskirts of Barcelona. Since then, our relationship has gone beyond the typical tutor–student dynamic and evolved into a deep friendship. With his careful and kindly formulated comments, Christos has always been an invaluable source of support, inspiration and refinement for my theoretical ideas and arguments. His humour, calmness and sharp ideas have been critical in the completion of this effort.

My friend Theodoros Karyotis has also been a key person in the completion of this book, as he undertook the complex task of copyediting the text to improve its flow and cohesion. Without his contribution, the book would not be as enjoyable to read and the thread of my argument not as easy to follow.

There are two people who, without even knowing it, have played a crucial role in the elaboration of the theoretical framework of this book. The first person is Pola Bousiou, a film-maker and social anthropologist whose work first inspired me to incorporate the concept of liminality into my work. Her book *The Nomads of Mykonos*, documenting a peculiar group of individuals who were 'performing liminalities' in 1970s Mykonos, resonated a lot with my own experiences of equally peculiar 'modern rituals' in a different Greek island I had been visiting for fifteen years. It was due to this theoretical encounter that I came up with the idea of the 'liminal commons' in the first place.

The second person is Stavros Stavrides, whose work has been a constant source of inspiration throughout my studies. When I first came up with the idea of the liminal commons, I went through the literature for relevant theories. Stavros' 'threshold spatial analysis' was an intellectual endeavour that instantly became a permanent point of reference, but also motivated me to work patiently towards extending it and complementing it.

Massimo De Angelis is undoubtedly the architect of the book series 'In Common', whose younger member to this date is my own *Liminal Commons*. I want to deeply thank Massimo for his continuous support throughout the publication process and his invaluable comments on how to further improve the overall argument of the book. I hope this book series can mark the beginning of fruitful collaboration among its contributors and perhaps can enact new possibilities for the formation of an international group that works and pushes towards a world of the commons.

I also want to thank all those both in Bloomsbury and in Zed Publications who helped me with the review and publication process of the manuscript. Kim Walker, Melanie Scagliarini, Olivia Dellow, David Avital, Tomasz Hoskins and Nayiri Kendir all helped me very much and were very supportive in the various phases of this complicated journey.

This book is partly dedicated to the memory of our beloved Silke Helfrich who left us too soon, only a few weeks before writing these lines. My relation with her was very important since Silke, even more than a great scholar and activist, was the person whose kindness and way of life could very much prefigure the commons-based society we strive to build.

I owe a special thanks to all the members of the research groups that I either participate as an active member or I have collaborated with throughout the years of my research on liminal commons. First of all, I want to thank the members of our research collective Research and Degrowth who have supported my work in multiple ways and constitute the pillars of our academic commons: Claudio, Federico, Giacomo, Filka, Marta, Aaron, Panagiota, Brototi, Marco, Francois, Christian, Fulvia, Diego, Irina, Gustavo, Viviana will all find fragments of our discussions in the lines of this book. Second, I would like to thank Penny Koutrolikou and Eirini Micha who together with Dina Vaiou constitute the 'Urban Mutations' group at the Department of Architecture of the NTUA. Also, a special thanks should be directed to the P2P research collective of the city of Ioannina in Epirus; we had the opportunity to exchange a lot during these years on how to think and strategize about the commons. I would also like to deeply thank the members of the 'Islands of Hope' team, Panos Petridis, Giorgos Tsitsirigos, Chrysostomos Galanos and Maro Pantazidou, with whom we have collaborated in many different projects during the ten years that this research lasted. Especially Chrysostomos has conducted a substantial part of the fieldwork that is related to the quantitative analysis presented in the fourth chapter and thus a great part of the empirical information that informs this chapter derives from his work. I also owe a special thanks to Georgia Bekridaki, a very recognizable member of the Greek social and solidarity economy movement who helped me a lot with networking and with mapping the nodes of the incipient Greek commoning movement.

Most importantly, I would like to thank all those who have dedicated their time and energy to respond to my questions, who accepted being interviewed and who filled out questionnaires. I would also like to thank all the collectives who trusted me to participate in their assemblies and the rest of their activities. I have learned a lot from this involvement. I would also like to thank all those who denied me access to their assemblies and who refused to participate in our survey because they made me reflect on the limitations and ethical ramifications of being at the same time an activist and a researcher.

Finally, I would like to thank my partner and all my friends who have been there to support me and who have tolerated my bad mood in periods of disappointment and stress. I would also like to thank them for both the nice and the difficult moments we shared in this period. Eleni Karafylli is the cornerstone of both my balance and well-being. With her inexhaustible care and kindness, she is the type of person who always helps you to believe that a better world is not only desirable but also possible. In addition, her unparalleled design skills gave shape to all the graphs and illustrations presented in the chapters of the book. Vasileia Dereli has been there since the first steps of this effort and her presence was catalytic for making up my mind to change direction in my life and work on the topic seriously. I also want to deeply thank Ilias Papadopoulos, my mentor in life and an expert in the art of 'inhabiting the threshold'. He is a sort of human being who always strives to change and never fits in the same uniform. Lorraine Leete, a passionate advocate of migrants' rights in Lesvos, has been a key person during my two years' stay on the island and helped me a lot with all her comments on my manuscript. Mariw Jaidopoulou Vrijea has always supported this work both emotionally and scholarly. Zografia Karekou supported me throughout the first years of this research with her sharp critical comments, but also with her caring character. Cristina Biliouri through her unfettered creativity has also been an important source of inspiration for this work. Finally, I would like to thank my good friends, Achilleas, Fillipos, Gerasimos, Marina, Anna, Telis, Thanasis and Vasoula, simply for being amazing.

Last but not least, I would like to thank my family, Anastasia Paschoudi, Argyro Varvarousi and Giannis Varvarousis, for the unconditional love and support; I owe them a lot more than what can be expressed in a few lines.

Chapter 1

INTRODUCTION

In 2009, Lesvos Island – now one of the most notable epicentres of the global refugee crisis – was a practically unknown spot at the outer edge of the European Union. Refugee flows were not absent at the time but the locals, as well as the rest of the world, were still unaware of the phenomenon. Indeed, migrants were arriving in Lesvos in large numbers even before 2009, but they were kept out of the sight of the locals as well as the international press. Their journey was rather standardized: from the coast of Turkey to the coasts of Lesvos, then directly transferred to the infamous detention centre 'Pagani' where they often remained for many months in detention. From there they were transferred by army or police buses to vessels in order to continue their journey by sea. Pagani detention centre, an ex-warehouse for storing fertilizers and other chemicals, was completely unsuitable for hosting people. Its rooms consisted of three windowless walls whereas the fourth side was made out of steel bars, looking just like a cage completely exposed to the elements. In these rooms, more than 100 or even 200 people were stacked, deprived of minimally humane conditions such as the right to walk outside the main room they were detained. And yet, this institution was functioning in the shadow of the EU, the Greek state and, most notably, the local community.

Until 2009, just a handful of activists on Lesvos were aware of the situation and were working on making the overall phenomenon visible to the locals and the rest of the world. At the beginning of the same year, together with activists from the EU and Turkey, they started discussing the possibility of organizing a Noborder Camp, a seven-day grassroots initiative to support and empower migrants on the island. The main argument against the organization of the Noborder Camp among the local activists involved in these discussions can be summed up by the following questions: Why put so much effort and energy to organize something that will be so impermanent? What can the foreign activists involved in the camp genuinely offer to our local struggles? Why not focus on organizing locally and on a more permanent basis? No doubt, all of these are legitimate questions, *especially in a world in which endurance is synonymous to success.*

The voices in favour of organizing the camp prevailed in the end and the event took place in August 2009. The structure of the camp was decentralized, with activities spreading in multiple locations inside and outside Mytilene, the capital of Lesvos. The main campsite of the Noborder Camp was built a few kilometres outside the city and offered all the basic amenities for making collective living possible. The activists also constructed an info point, a solidarity kitchen and a medical centre in Mytilene's centre.

During the week that the camp lasted, a peculiar daily *ritual* spontaneously emerged. A few days prior to the official opening of the event, a cohort of both local and foreign volunteers who had arrived earlier to help with the preparations decided to march towards Pagani detention centre. When they arrived in front of the 'cages' of the centre, they stood in front of the imprisoned migrants, but instead of following their familiar repertoire of actions (shouting slogans, clashing with the police forces, etc.), they remained frozen in front of the shocking sight. Most of them burst into tears. On the other side of the fences, the view of the frozen activists sparked an uprising inside Pagani, with migrants shouting for freedom and help. After this incident, the volunteers continued to march to Pagani almost daily. This marked the beginning of a highly impactful interaction between the activists and the migrants, an intense dialogue that continued throughout the days of the camp, leading to the escalation of the migrants' mobilizations inside the detention centre.

The camp marked *a transitional moment* in the history of the island and had a tremendous impact on the society of Lesvos and the lives of the migrants of Pagani. Its consequences exceeded by far the very issue of migration, as they touched upon other aspects of the social, political and economic life of the island. In addition, this temporary experience of *commoning* gave birth to a series of more stable commons and to several more stable solidarity structures in its aftermath. The info point, which through the continuous presence of the 400 or more activists in the centre of Mytilene, gradually turned into a place of sharing knowledge, political ideas and most importantly stories, laughter and tears. The people of Lesvos had the opportunity to gain insights on the situation of their island, with many of them openly expressing their compassion towards migrants as well as their willingness to become part of the movement. As a result, when the camp was over the local community of activists was much larger and stronger.

The collective effervescence of the Noborder Camp quickly spread in other political arenas; the pro-refugee movement *and all other* local social movements were empowered and popularized in the aftermath of the camp. It is important to note that the experience of the camp was transformative for almost everyone involved since *they all had to overcome their own identity boundaries*. Finally, the most evident win of the camp was that Pagani centre shut down just a few months later, as a result of the steep escalation of the migrants' continuous uprisings. For the first time during their detention, they knew that someone was witnessing their continuous struggle and transferring it to the world outside the 'cages'. Similar to many *rites of passage* around the world, the Noborder Camp finished with a massive celebration in the central square of Mytilene with locals, migrants and foreign activists dancing side by side.

This book is dedicated to forms of *temporary commoning* such as the Noborder Camp described earlier. Refugee camps, climate camps or summer camps, occupied squares, self-organized street parties or festivals are sites that involve intense moments of *commoning*, in which people are pooling and sharing resources and efforts for a limited period of time. What outcomes and effects do such commons have? What attributes and processes determine the effectiveness of such temporary commons? And what can be the role of such collective performances in broader societal transformations?

Research on the commons is primarily focused on enduring, long-lived systems, from centuries-long institutions managing aquifers or forests to years-long community gardens or open software. Stability and reproduction over time are seen as the sole markers of the 'success' of the commons. From the older Ostrom's rules for managing the commons to the very recent Bollier's and Helfrich's patterns of commoning, researchers search for fundamental attributes that contribute to the sustainability of a commons over time. What about commons, though, that are by their very nature short-lived, yet have major impacts on commoners and environments? How do we make sense of such commons?

At this point, it is important to remind ourselves that with the exception of the work of Elinor Ostrom and her colleagues, the discourse of the commons was virtually non-existent in the 1990s; radical thinkers were certainly unfamiliar with it, and the commons were absent from discussions on societal transformation. The financial crisis of 2008, which was soon transformed into a broader multidimensional crisis of legitimation of the fundamental structures of Western societies, was a milestone in attracting attention to the commons as social systems alternative to capitalism. This interest culminated with the introduction of the term 'commoning' by historian Peter Linebaugh as recently as 2008, as the term marked the different content that the commons would acquire in contexts of crisis. The commons were no longer treated as things or resources but as processes that are made and remade according to needs and to the social, economic and spatial relations that commoners invent and try out. Commons happen.

This shift from the commons as resources to the active verb of commoning, which prioritizes socio-spatial relations that are always in flux, offered us the opportunity to use the language of the commons to talk about a series of phenomena we either could not theorize before or had been theorizing in different terms. This shift revealed that commons, or rather, practices of commoning, can be encountered almost everywhere – in the public space, in schools, in slums, within families, in factories, in streets and in many other places. Similarly, the commons can be found in social movements and political struggles, in periods of emergency or even in contexts of remote island vacations; the (re)production of the commons has become a synonym for the collective (re)production of life itself.

In modern societies, the commons range from long-lasting social systems to precarious and temporary arrangements; thus, they can acquire different roles in social and economic life. The present book focuses mainly on the latter form of commons, which, despite their precarity, often acquire a highly symbolic function in society: *to facilitate transitions and to foster transformation at the individual, collective and even societal level.* I call these commons 'liminal' because they embody many of the qualities found in the intermediate phases of the 'rites of passage' that in archaic or tribal societies were performed to organize, symbolize and demarcate passages of different types: territorial, social status, time (harvest, New Year) or spatiotemporal ones such as the seasonal relocation of the entire tribe.

In contrast to the widespread belief that rituals are quickly vanishing from modern societies, repeated examples show that humans still invent and employ such collectively performed rites in order to prepare for, mark and symbolize transformation and transition – or even to explore the possibility of it. Even though they share many elements with the rituals performed in archaic societies, these new rites of passage tend to differ in many aspects, which are explored in detail in this book.

This work focuses on the transformative potential of the new commoning rituals that I call 'the liminal commons'. Liminal commons are transitional – yet not elusive – forms of temporary commons that despite their short lifespan are capable of creating and marking new realities that were previously unthinkable. They often start as the results of a specific crisis but also can spark generative processes of more stable commoning practices in their wake. Despite their impermanence, they can have deep and enduring effects.

I am aware that writing on and theorizing transformative processes is always a risky and controversial task since, at any level, changes are often temporary and can be reversed. Moreover, the transformation process itself is a contradictory and complex ad hoc process, which is difficult to capture and theorize. My work, thus, is inevitably prone to such contradictions, and I admit that it is but a preliminary attempt to capture some of the tendencies and mechanisms that characterize the manifold processes of transformation at large.

I had the opportunity to explore transformations in the context of Greece, an environment that in the last decade epitomizes flux and transformation through crisis. Over those years, the multifaceted Greek crisis has had devastating effects for great parts of the population; it has forced many people towards desperation, has increased social inequalities and has caused irreversible damage. This has been the 'ugly' yet absolutely real face of the transformative process of a multidimensional crisis. However, amid the ruins of the collapsed order, a series of new social, economic, discursive and cultural elements have emerged, which point to a more optimist scenario of societal transformation. The present work focuses precisely on these micro-changes.

In highlighting and analysing change, I do not mean to disregard the fact that structures are not easily transformed and that processes of transformation are lengthy and often incomplete. Yet, scholars only have the chance to choose and develop a small part of the issues they believe are important and necessary to study. Hence, in this work, I prioritize the exploration of micro-transformations and the role liminal commons play in them, rather than focusing on transformations that fail or are quickly reversed.

I acknowledge that the present moment is rife with fear and disappointment. The pandemic of Covid-19 cannot be characterized as yet another crisis causing a partial destabilization of the existing order in a limited geography; rather, it should be understood as a milestone event of global significance that can potentially lead to a 'post-human era' (Zizek 2020) and which calls for a re-invention of life at large. Yet, in many parts of the world, the crisis was already so intense that Covid-19 barely registers as a game-changing factor. The continuous pressure on the remnants of the welfare state, the pervasive threat of new world wars, the enduring economic crisis, the massive refugee flows from the Middle East and Africa and the continuous irreversible damage to the environment were already leaving very little room for hope.

Yet, while crisis breeds desperation, at the same time it opens up space for the reconstitution of everything. Even more, the escalation and blending of multiple crises demand new tools and modes for theorizing and making sense of the present. We can't afford to understand crisis only as a bad spell or an invincible impasse. Crisis should also be understood as synonymous with possibility. In this light, I propose to look into the multiple facets of the transformative potential of crisis. The pillars of this theoretical exploration are crisis, liminality and the act of commoning; their intersections and interactions are examined in the case studies included in the present book.

Chapter 2 is a theoretical one. It lays out the theoretical foundations that underpin the empirical part of this work. In other words, it is a 'threshold chapter'. It starts by exploring in detail the role of the commons and commoning at the dawn of the twenty-first century and then goes on to pose the research questions that guide this study. It then defines how the notion of crisis is used throughout the text and offers a critical engagement with the diverse theories on commons and liminality. The chapter ends with a preliminary attempt to define the basic characteristics of liminal commons and a detailed justification of why Greece has important things to tell us about this subject.

Chapter 3 is the first of the empirical chapters. It engages with issues of subjectivity and subjectification and relates findings from the field with broader theoretical discussions on the topic. The chapter draws on empirical research that took place between 2008 and 2014, related to the social mobilizations of the 2008 revolt and the 2011 'movement of the squares', both in Athens, as well as to many smaller events that took place between the two major events.

Chapter 4 delves into the issue of expansion of the liminal commons. It builds upon the observation that due to their contagious and metastatic character, liminal commons can become the expanding mode of commoning and give rise to a process of multiplication and expansion of existing ventures. This chapter draws on the unprecedented expansion of commoning projects in Greece in the wake of the 2011 movement of the squares and tries to understand why and how this expansion occurred.

Chapter 5 explores the issue of protection of the commons, which is approached here as a crucial dimension in the establishment and stabilization of the small or big differences that can be fostered within, through and because of commoning. The chapter engages with broader theoretical discussions on the topic and argues that the current debate is dominated by the polarizing dualism of openness versus closure. After deconstructing this binary opposition, the chapter develops a theoretical framework that brings to the fore strategies for the protection of the commons that go beyond the aforementioned dualism.

Chapter 6 is the last empirical chapter. It addresses issues of trust, motivation and membership turnover in the liminal commons by engaging with various theories, from classical commons studies to evolutionary theory and critical management. The chapter draws on an extreme case of liminal commons: Platanos Self-Organized Refugee Camp in Lesvos. The chapter explores the personal trajectories of participants and the transformations that took place through Platanos at the individual, collective and local levels.

The book ends with a final theoretical chapter on rituals and transformations, which offers final reflections on the issue of the transformative potential of contemporary commoning rituals, summarizes the theoretical discussion and attempts to weave the findings of the previous chapters into a robust argument. The chapter finishes by sketching out possible lines of future research for advancing and completing the theory introduced in this theoretical endeavour.

Chapter 2

COMMONS, CRISIS AND LIMINALITY

Why commons?

'Commons' and 'commoning' are two words that have relatively recently entered the public debate on people's alternative strategies of production and reproduction – and they have done so with emphatic dynamism. Interestingly, these two concepts do not concern a single audience. Rather, one can identify three different but interconnected audiences that, for different sets of reasons, have been influenced by this new or revamped vocabulary, or even have adopted it. I am calling it revamped because even though the commons have been the basis for social reproduction probably since the beginning of human social life, the debate around the commons was literally non-existent up until a few decades ago. At the dawn of the twenty-first century, however, both the use of the term and the debate around it have grown exponentially.

Who and why then is interested in the commons?

First, and perhaps most importantly, the commons have become part of the language of contemporary social movements and the various forms of grassroots resistance all over the world. These include the Zapatista movement in Mexico, which probably marked the tipping point towards a broad transformation of social movements globally, the 'Movimento dos Trabalhadores Sem Terra' or MST in Brazil, the KRRS (Karnataka Rajya Raitha Sangha) union of fishermen in India, the Via Campesina, the indigenous movements in Colombia and Nigeria against Shell Oil Company, 'Reclaim the Streets' and 'Guerrilla Gardening' movements, self-organized social clinics in Greece, Occupy movements in Spain, Greece, Egypt, United States, Turkey and elsewhere, as well as the squatting movement in Europe and beyond; the list of contemporary movements that have expressed their demands and their creativity through the incipient vocabulary of the commons and commoning is so long and diverse that it is impossible to include in a single book or map. The commons are used by these diverse movements to highlight the departure from purely dissident forms of mobilization and the incorporation of a series of more creative and constitutive practices in their repertoires of action.

Second, the commons and commoning have become part of the new 'mantra' of radical thinkers, who have discovered in these notions a new way for conceptualizing post-capitalist futures. These contemporary literatures often depart from new understandings of the processes of primitive accumulation or accumulation by dispossession, that is, the strategies used by capital and the state to destroy the commons and reassert their domination over local and global populations (De Angelis 2001; Harvey 2004). From this perspective, the commons and commoning signify the counter process through which labour's use value can be redirected towards the reproduction of societies rather than that of capital.

Lastly, the commons have come to form part of the language of a new business model that embraces the ideas of peer-to-peer production, cooperation, community building and even horizontality and self-organization. As economic elites come to realize that the rigid twofold ontology of the state and the market fails to guarantee profitability, they shift their strategies towards alternative economic models. For Jeremy Rifkin (2014), we are reaching the 'zero marginal cost society', where peer-to-peer and open businesses will surpass corporate capitalism. 'Sharing' lies at the heart of emancipatory commoning, yet at the same time it has become the core idea for the development of so-called Platform Capitalism, a model advanced by some of the most profitable enterprises of our time, such as Airbnb, Uber and Task Rabbit.

It seems that the multidimensional and enduring crisis of our times has opened a 'crack' that catalyses the development of diverse and often conflicting versions of the commons. As the commons and commoning are becoming a crucial terrain for the unfolding of future social configurations, all sides attempt to steer their development towards their respective desired directions.

But where does the dynamism of these concepts stem from?

In my view, it is precisely the malleability of these terms, their remarkable capacity to connect not only similarities but also differences, that renders them so attractive for the reconstitution of a world that appears to have entered an enduring and manifold crisis. This crisis, no doubt, has multiple facets. It is not only an economic crisis, a crisis of production and consumption, but also an ecological, moral and social one. And lately, it has also become a crisis in its more decisive form: a battle between life and death. The narrative that for over two centuries remained dominant in the Western world, mainly due to its connection with a socioeconomic system that has managed to provide a great percentage of the growing global population with the basics, is now more delegitimized than ever and seems to have reached an impenetrable impasse.

How to succeed in maintaining a healthy community and social development in a world in which cut-throat competition and social isolation prevail? How to deal with new forms of decentralized and immaterial labour through typically vertical and hierarchical systems of the corporate organization model? How to provide the necessary care work for the growing number of elders and of people affected by all sorts of health, social, economic and environmental disasters in a society that keeps commodifying almost everything? How to protect the last pristine environments on the planet and reduce species' extinction in a world that perpetually expands its commodity frontiers? How to set limits and give direction to the exponential growth of algorithms, data and machines, the 'big other' that defines and defies us, in a society that deifies technoscientific solutions to all sorts of problems? And how to seek novel ways of international cooperation, global justice and solidarity, which is needed to tackle the great global problems of our time, through political systems that still breed xenophobia, racism and clear-cut dichotomies in general?

The commons can indeed give a new meaning to old emancipatory ideas; describe ancient, pre-capitalistic forms of social production and reproduction; and offer a new language to contemporary social experimentations such as peer-to-peer production and solidarity economy. Furthermore, the commons are here to problematize and reinterpret a variety of social relations and institutions, such as family, language, friendship and community. Finally, they are here to put the major environmental problems of our times at centre stage by emphasizing that these problems are also part of 'our commons'; no exodus from the planet is possible for humanity.

In short, the main strength of the commons is that they can connect issues that up until recently were perceived as separate and independent: the sphere of production and reproduction with the sphere of politics and social movements; the ancient knowledge of indigenous populations with the contemporary social innovations of the Western world; utopian thinking with everyday practices; economy with culture; and the imaginary of progress with the right to autonomous institutionalization and self-limitation. Moreover, the commons can pose anew the question of the relation between the familiar and the other, to give new political and social depth to the vision of a world that contains many worlds, in which subjects, despite their difference, can relate to one another more on the basis of mutual recognition rather than competition.

The discussion on the commons has started and may play a catalytic role in seeking alternatives to the current societal impasse. Yet, despite its great importance, merely the presence of such discussion in the public sphere cannot mechanistically bring about the resolution of the major problems of our societies. In fact, due to its amplitude, the power geometries that traverse it and the fact that diverse audiences push it towards different and often opposing directions, the discussion on the commons may, after all, create as many problems as it resolves. For the time being, there are no final answers to these problems. Commoning is a learning process, so there can be no single theory to capture and foresee its future. On the other hand, theorization and reflection are necessary as there is no transcendental necessity in human history. What is perhaps needed is, on the one hand, a set of bold analytical tools that can shed new light on the most puzzling aspects of these problems and, on the other, new durable forms of sociality and novel institutions, which in their fruitful interaction with the aforementioned theories can inspire humanity to take action and escape the paralysing inertia it has been afflicted with in the last few decades.

Inhabiting crises

The word 'crisis' is omnipresent in almost all forms of narrative in contemporary societies and serves as a starting point for a great deal of writing, yet it has not been adequately developed at a theoretical and conceptual level (Roitman 2013). A crisis is usually understood as an error, a deformation or a rough patch. However, as Koselleck (2006) notices, the concept of crisis has been used to express different things in different periods. Historically, the concept of crisis has been used in numerous scientific and non-scientific contexts, including law, economics, theology, medicine, politics, history and the everyday experience (Roitman 2013; Koselleck 2006). It is originally derived from the ancient Greek verb 'krinein', which had various meanings: to separate, distinguish, examine, judge, decide, choose or explain. However, over a great period it was predominantly used in the medical context (Koselleck 2006). As a consequence, the concept was invested with an either/or connotation, evident thereafter also in contexts other than medicine. Thus, crisis has been used in the field of politics to force actors to choose between radically opposing alternatives. In the nineteenth century, the concept was introduced in the language of economics and acquired strong connotations of illness, imbalance or calamity (Koselleck 2006), which until today remain the predominant properties associated with crisis in the public discourse.

However, the most well-known historical reference to the concept of crisis is found in the Hippocratic School, when it used to denote 'the turning point of a disease, or a critical phase in which life or death was at stake and called for an irrevocable decision' (Roitman 2013: 3). While, on the one hand, this sentence, obviously, points to the previously mentioned radically opposing alternatives, on the other, it associates crises with processes of change and transition.

In consonance with this last observation, crises have been proposed as periods that can trigger social, temporal and epochal transitions and possibilities, especially in the field of history and philosophy (Koselleck and Richter 2006; Koselleck 1988; Foucault 1997). In these narratives, crisis obtains a generative and productive role; it is seen as capable of bringing into being new meanings as well as new forms of sociality, production and economy. This work builds upon this historical approach and analyses crises as periods that, by implying an ambiguous phase of possible transformations, can enable creative historical processes and thus cannot be reduced to mere decisive points of 'death or rebirth'.

In light of this dual nature of crisis (as both calamity and opportunity), one can ask the following questions: What is a 'real' crisis, and what is a 'failed' one? Can we speak of positive or negative crises? What happens when two or more crises intersect? And finally, how transformative can a crisis be when the 'normal' cease to exist?

In the contemporary literature on crises, one can come across two main strands: a first that demonizes crises by highlighting their devastating effects for the weak and the benefits for the rich (e.g. Klein 2007; Hadjimichalis 2017) and another one that mainly celebrates crises for the transformative opportunities they offer. Both strands are anything but new. On the one hand, crises were always been used instrumentally by the rich and powerful. Even in ancient times, wars began having a crisis in their background in cases in which the descending states or kingdoms declare war to shift the focus away from their inner problems or degradation. On the other hand, crisis was always invested with an expectation for change. Despite that fact that sinologists have debunked as inaccurate the urban legend that crisis in Chinese is written using the same character as 'opportunity' (Mair 2009), dozens of politicians, economists, executives, New Age therapists and even scholars still use this wrong assumption in their analyses and commencement talks. In addition, crises have inspired the production of a series of crisis-related concepts that emphasize the potentially transformative effect of catastrophes. Serge Latouche, for instance, one of the leading scholars in the field of degrowth, has repeatedly argued in favour of a 'pedagogy of disasters' meaning by this 'a decisive event that brings about a tragedy' that can operate as a 'jump-start out of the madness' (Latouche 2015: 122).

Janet Roitman (2013) in her thoughtful account on crises beautifully explained how both Martin Luther King and Barack Obama used the crisis in their influential speeches to characterize a moment in human history after which everything will be different and novel. Roitman argues that crisis is always constructed as an 'object of knowledge', a conceptual device that operates as a 'transcendental placeholder' and which is employed to open certain paths of action and inquiry while foreclosing others. Roitman continues that crisis should not be perceived as a decisive moment anymore since it has become rather a chronic condition. By focusing on the moment of the invocation of crisis and its implications, she makes an important intellectual effort to denaturalize the crisis narratives and subsequently open space for a path beyond the politics of crisis, one that she describes as the politics and analytics of anti-crisis.

Roitman's argument is convincing and well-articulated; however, crises are not only discursive statements (Khasnabish 2014) and even though the proclamation of a crisis can indeed be very efficacious for political elites, the harsh condition of *inhabiting a crisis* can truly disorientate people's lives, open cracks in dominant norms, and bring individuals and collectives together to reinvent themselves and their relationships. The manifold Greek crisis that has been the source of information and inspiration of this book has been approached through a series of different lenses. However, the vast majority of the accounts focus on the economic aspects of the Greek crisis (e.g. Tsafos 2013; Doxiadis and Placas 2018; Floros and Chatziantoniou 2017), the causes of the crisis (e.g. Douzinas 2013; Pettifer 2015; Papakonstantinou 2016; Hadjimichalis 2017), the management of the crisis (e.g. Varoufakis 2017), the discourses developed by the European Media on the topic (e.g. Tzogopoulos 2013; Mylonas 2019) or the future of the country after the end of the crisis (e.g. Holloway, Nasioka, and Doulos 2020). My aim instead is different. I am not focusing on the discursive aspects of the crisis but I am willing to explore how a process that was framed as a crisis (and was experienced as such through a series of devastating impacts) can spark creative and novel repertoires of action. In other words, my effort is to see how people can inhabit crisis in a constructive manner that potentially leads to new life paths. And I aim not only to do this on the level of the individual but also to explore creativity and positive response by larger groups and societies and transformations at the personal, collective, social and spatial levels.

Crisis as limit

Therefore, this book does not celebrate crisis, but it does not demonize it either. I do not doubt that as many scholars (e.g. Klein 2007) have convincingly shown, the ruling classes provoke or take advantage of social crises to impose politics of exploitation. I am well aware, moreover, that while new forms of production, sociality and economy may be produced through and because of crisis, these are often co-opted or subordinated by the dominant system, thus turned into parts of the new normality. In the worst-case scenario, these new configurations help the existing system of domination reassert its power. In a better scenario, they remain at the margins of society to constitute the necessary 'other', which serves mainly to define what is possible and what is not.

However, my research focus is precisely to explore the limit between the 'before' and the 'after' by simultaneously focusing on the experience of the in-between, as this limit is under continuous dispute and in extraordinary moments can be pushed towards different directions. Therefore, crises are opportunities not because they are de facto laboratories of positive developments but because they are sources of destabilization and, by extension, experimentation. Crises obtain their meaning only in juxtaposition with normality and normativity and hence crisis represents a limit.

But what kind of limit does crisis represent?

In the mainstream economic narrative, as well as in great parts of the mainstream discourse, crisis is understood as a bad spell – a period of aberration that temporarily intrudes in the otherwise linear, progressive process of social evolution. Common expressions employed to transmit such a view, for instance, the 'cyclicality' of the phenomenon, directly imply that crisis is something external to society. In this narrative, social-historical processes are destined to progressively converge towards a future, whose basic elements already exist in the present. Without a doubt, the imaginary signification that dominates this narrative is *perpetual progress*. Crisis, in this case, represents an alienated limit, one that has lost its transformative capacity under the burden of the iron laws of the transcendental historical movement forwards.

In another common narrative, crisis is understood as the end of the road, a place from which there is no return and no escape. Crisis, in this case, signifies an eschatological limit-end, which is inherently insuperable. In fact, this narrative cynically epitomized in the well-known Frederic Jameson quote that nowadays, 'it is easier to imagine the end of the world than to imagine the end of capitalism', has been increasingly gaining supporters over the last years. This is another conception of crisis as an alienated limit, one that cannot be inhabited creatively. In both aforementioned narratives, the concept of crisis is deprived of its capacity to bring forward critical responses to the question of 'what went wrong' and therefore to offer society the opportunity to rethink and reassemble its institutions and established social imaginaries.

Yet, there is a third manner to conceptualize crisis as a limit. It can take the form of a non-alienated limit-threshold. Contrary to all other existing forms of limits, thresholds offer the possibility to remain there, to inhabit them (Stavrides 2015). Thresholds are limits that do not only separate but also connect (Simmel 1994). The importance of this specific quality is that it allows a view in both directions. By inhabiting the threshold, one can observe what exists not only inside but also outside, not only in the past but also towards the future. By being able to critically examine the past, one can sketch, always precariously and incompletely, trajectories towards a desired future, even if this future always remains unpredictable. This experience of suspension at the thresholds affords the possibility of reflection, critical review and insightful visioning, thus bringing out the full potential of the concept of crisis, giving it the capacity to lay the foundations of a radically different future *ex nihilo* as Cornelious Castoriadis would say but not in nihilo or cum nihilo.

From Elinor Ostrom to autonomous Marxists and beyond

Commons may constitute the new beacon of radical thinking, and they have become a crucial element in the vocabulary of contemporary social movements and grassroots ventures all over the world. Moreover, crisis, when seen as a limit-threshold that creates a stage of suspension and experimentation, can be catalytic for the subversion of the dominant social structure and the emergence of new forms of sociality. Yet, the relation between such periods of crisis and the emergence of new commons remains unexplored. How can a study of crisis contribute to a better understanding of the processes of commoning and vice versa? Why is the aforementioned stage of suspension that usually follows crisis important for social transformation? Is crisis necessary for any social transition? When and why does a crisis come to an end, and what can it leave behind? Do commons that emerge in contexts of crisis and emergency differ from those that emerge and develop in non-crisis contexts? How does a crisis affect the social relations of cooperation and competition?

Rethinking Elinor Ostrom's work through crisis

Elinor Ostrom's 2009 Nobel Prize in economics was a milestone marking increased attention and appreciation for the commons. Ostrom (1990) researched the conditions under which collective forms of governing resources can work. Drawing on more than 1,000 instances of commons all over the world and crossing disciplinary boundaries, Ostrom concluded that more often than not communities self-organize and self-manage to control access and use of shared resources. The 'tragedy of the commons' (Hardin 1968), whereby open access destroys a common resource, is the empirical exception, Ostrom demonstrated. Together with her colleagues, she developed a theoretical research framework known as Institutional Analysis and Development (IAD) to understand and assess the variables that may cause the commons to succeed or fail. Her greatest achievement, 'Eight Design Principles for Successful Commons' (Ostrom 1990), remains to this day, at least for a particular current of commons thought, a landmark set of reference guidelines for the study of commons.

Undoubtedly, Ostrom's work armed those who oppose the logic of aggressive individualism (Stavrides 2016) and totalitarian statism with important arguments and thus contributed to the destabilization of economic orthodoxy, which simply views policy in terms of a dichotomous choice between state and market (Harvey 2012). Ostrom demonstrated that communities can develop rules that allow them to keep egoistic interests in check, and consequently she challenged the pervasive assumption that humans are naturally competitive.

Despite her innovative research, however, Ostrom never questioned two of the foundational pillars of economic theory. First, the assumption that natural elements, as well as tangible or intangible man-made creations, are mere resources to be allocated and managed. Second, the assumption that humans are 'rational beings' who always rationally calculate and choose what is more profitable for them. Thus, Ostrom's analysis disregards the fact that the very concept of 'benefit' is culturally and historically determined (Stavrides 2016) and therefore does not always translate into profit-seeking and cost-sharing. Moreover, by focusing more on institutions and less on actual subjects, her analysis fails to grasp the multiple, diverse and often contradictory human motives behind commoning.

Ostrom criticized the assumptions of conventional game theory, as she effectively showed that the conditions and rules that dominate these games differ from real-life processes (Ostrom 1990). She concluded that if subjects were allowed to talk with each other (or had cultural rules of sharing) then they could perhaps solve many common issues with ease. However, given the fact that her focus was not on subjects but on rules, she adopted a unifying and simplistic view of commoners. Hence, commoners were treated as if they did not have diverse possessions, power, skills, knowledge, political motivations, ideologies and so on. In her view, the commons are social systems exclusively preoccupied with the management of resources. They do not form part of social movements and do not interact with them; they do not embody goals that go beyond the economy and do not have any projective or prefigurative function. Ostrom's model corresponds to a rather homogeneous community consisting of rational individuals, who decide to set up a commons to better fulfil their needs.

When one studies the commons as systems that emerge outside the rest of the life of commoners and the particular spatiotemporal contexts in which it develops, one may assume that the motivations of the commoners can be accounted for with a linear model such as the above. The discipline of economics, for instance, commonly essentializes human nature, portraying humans as inherently profit-seeking, cost-sharing and selfish. However, other disciplines, ranging from psychology and history to philosophy and evolutionary studies, have shown that this depiction is ideologically loaded and misleading; it should thus be treated as an imaginary construction that accompanied the emergence of capitalist societies only. Castoriadis, for instance, speaks about anthropological types, that is, imagined types of humanity that allow a social structure to function (Castoriadis 2010), and argues that these specific images of humanity are historically defined and thus prone to change. Of course, these are sweeping generalizations that do not allow for a more nuanced and molecular analysis of actual social processes. However, they can be valuable for macro-analysis, especially when these analyses develop to explain periods when a particular kind of normality seems to dominate over its alternatives.

Periods of prolonged and enduring crisis, however, render these sweeping generalizations ineffective since manifold crises can shake even the foundational elements of a social structure. Crisis destabilizes not only economic systems or national and international apparatuses but also individual and collective identities, societal premises and truths, and even the very meaning of what has value and whatnot in a particular social context. This affects a lot what we expect from our participation in collective action or, in other words, from our participation in the commons. As dominant criteria of what is important and what is not collapse or are heavily challenged, a theory of commons grounded in motivations, subjects and goals that have ceased to be dominant and meaningful in the present society loses its analytical value and therefore should be modified and amended. Within crisis, *commoners are transitional subjects* who, in the process of commoning, bring along all their doubts and ambiguities. The commons become transitional social systems too; rather than being the product of rational calculations of isolated individuals, they become laboratories for the production of new forms of subjectivity, sociality and spatiality and are invested with fears and hopes for the transition to a post-crisis condition and the establishment of a new, more just normality. Hence, any theory aiming to make sense of the new commons that emerge in contexts of crisis cannot but challenge and expand Ostrom's original theoretical framework.

Crisis and the commons in autonomous Marxists' approaches

In contrast to Elinor Ostrom's work, crisis constitutes an important aspect in the more recent literature on the commons and commoning, deriving primarily from the work of autonomous Marxists. While Ostrom's focus is on the institutions of commoning, autonomous Marxists are primarily concerned with the political dimension of the commons, their emancipatory potential and their role in social transformations. Their analysis is often grounded in an understanding of the current global crisis as a sign of failure of the market and the state to provide the means of production and reproduction to great parts of the world's population, including those in the heartland of the global North. They argue that the wealth of this world, cumulatively produced over many generations, is being held hostage by capitalism. To that extent, they regard this pool of labour past and present as 'the common', which should be appropriated by those from whom it was expropriated (Midnight Notes Collective and Friends 2009).[1]

Against this background, Massimo De Angelis (2013) argues in favour of 'Plan C&D', namely 'Commons and Democracy'. Using crisis as a point of departure, he identifies four different scenarios for reshaping the world and concludes that only C&D is capable of challenging the current dominant social configuration and leading to social justice and human emancipation. In other words, departing from the assumption that the dominant system is perpetually in crisis, this literature attempts, through the commons, to give new meaning to the concept of communism, dissociating it from the statism and totalitarianism of the past. Antonio Negri and Michael Hardt, despite their divergence from the core autonomous Marxist framework of the Midnight Notes Collective, seem to agree with this formulation.

The work of autonomous Marxists gave new depth to the discussion around the commons and expanded the possible fields where the concept can be applied. The basic points of divergence between Ostrom's theory and the framework advanced by autonomous Marxists could be summarized as follows:

- First, autonomous Marxists have challenged the centrality of resources in the process of creating and sustaining a commons, a key element in the neo-institutional theory of collective action espoused by Elinor Ostrom and her colleagues.
- Second, they have stressed the centrality of social relations and the processual character of the commons by introducing the term 'commoning' (Linebaugh 2008), which stands for the institutionalized process of coming together over time to pool and govern resources (D' Alisa 2013). According to a new tripartite definition, the commons involve some kind of resource,

---

1. The Midnight Notes Collective was established in 1979 in the United States. It is a group of scholars and activists that has published many essays and books on topics related to gender, energy, geopolitics, enclosures, commons and commoning, class struggle and immigration. Among its members are eminent autonomous Marxists, such as Silvia Federici, George Caffentzis, Iain Boal and Peter Linebaugh.

the institutions that govern the resource and a community of commoners interlinked through the act of commoning.
- Third, they have linked the process of commoning with social mobilization by claiming that commons-based modes of production and reproduction can give additional materiality to movements (De Angelis 2013). This idea was inspired by the 'Occupy' cycle of mobilization – known also as 'the movements of the squares' – which combined forms of protest with forms of commoning. In turn, it inspired practice-based movements to link to the broader discussion on the commons and to identify with broader national and international social mobilizations.
- Fourth, whereas in Ostrom's approach the commons are regarded as 'nested' institutions between the private and the public, typically requiring support from institutions at higher levels to operate (Ostrom 1990; Steins and Edwards 1999), for autonomous Marxists the commons constitute the alternative that lies beyond and against the private/public dichotomy (Federici 2010; Hardt and Negri 2009; De Angelis and Stavrides 2010).
- Fifth, autonomous Marxists have opened up space for older emancipatory ideas, such as that of communism, to become influential again. Through the commons, these revamped ideas are now dissociated from both reformism and the violent occupation of state power. Instead, they relate to communitarian procedures of prefiguration and social relations that create communities of solidarity and sharing.
- Sixth, they have first proposed that the notion of the commons can be generalized and become the basis for metaphoric expansions beyond its original content; that is, the commons should not be perceived as systems relating only to the natural elements of earth, water and air but also to the fields of knowledge, information, DNA, language and values (Caffentzis 2010).
- Lastly, by situating the commons in the context of crisis, they have challenged the conception that the commons belong to the past and have, instead, argued that they are the 'cell' form of future social life (De Angelis 2013) that can abolish capital and state and become the central element of future social structures.

The commons are employed by autonomous Marxists to describe a universe of diverse and plural counter-hegemonic resistance against the state and the market, organized democratically and horizontally. In this respect, the commons are entrusted with the task of antagonizing the logic of capital accumulation, confronting the processes of capitalist enclosure and promoting a political plan for societal transformation. Following this logic, autonomous Marxists do not assess the success of the commons with regard to their sustainability only, as Ostrom did, but also concerning their political character and identity. In other words, this new literature marks a qualitative shift; *successful commons are not only those that can ensure a community's survival but also those that maintain a degree of independence from markets and the state, that do not fuel capitalist accumulation and that promote an anti-capitalist agenda.* The commoner thus becomes the subject of revolution and transformation, an equivalent to the worker in Marxian theory.

This new conception of the commons as the main vehicle for societal transformation beyond and against capitalism has led several thinkers of this current to adopt some highly polarized and therefore controversial terms to describe different aspects of commoning. Caffentzis and Federici (2014) speak of anti-capitalist commons to distinguish them from 'pro-capitalist' ones (Caffentzis 2010; Caffentzis and Federici 2011). Likewise, De Angelis uses the terms 'distorted commons' and 'commons fix' to describe those commons that do not conform to his idea of how commons should be (De Angelis 2013); Hardt and Negri (2009) speak of 'corrupted commons' to describe those processes, ventures and social relations that, despite having commoning at their heart, produce 'more of the same' and reaffirm capital and the domination of private property. Thus, it does not come as a surprise that some of these scholars dismiss the work of Elinor Ostrom either as inadequate and irrelevant or as neoliberal and dangerous (e.g. Caffentzis 2004).

To be sure, this ontology of 'good and evil commons' serves the important task of emphasizing the political and social dimensions of commoning and helps move the discussion beyond Ostrom's framework, which reduces the commons to their managerial aspects; nevertheless, I argue that the analytical value of this ontology is limited. First and foremost, this clear-cut ontology disregards what, in my view, is the most important aspect of commoning: its ability to connect what was unconnected. This is a process that can only develop through mutual problematization and cross-fertilization, and therefore an inherently contradictory process. Every commons has 'distortions' and 'corruptions', and every commons is pulled towards different directions by both 'internal' and 'external' forces. Commoning is a process of negation and affirmation, which destabilizes subjects, collectives and even societies to stabilize them again upon new foundations. This process is never linear or progressive, but it evolves in stages whose characteristics and duration cannot be predicted. However, the transition from one state of affairs to another cannot happen mechanically; *it must be prepared and processed in an in-between stage*. This usually takes the form of a stage of suspension, in which the remnants of the old order meet the aspirations of the upcoming one.

Throughout this book, an effort will be made to shed light on the extraordinary conditions of transition, which involve metamorphoses at the individual, collective and social levels. By focusing on transitions and not on an ontological perspective of good and evil, I aim to develop an analytical framework to explain such extraordinary moments of temporary commoning; by extension, I am not interested in defining evaluation criteria for the commons. Moreover, I opt not to demonize any of the available theories on the commons or ostracize contradiction and problematization from my analysis. My purpose is, rather, to create a theoretical threshold and a meeting point, where various theories and observations will come together to make sense of the very condition of 'transitoriness' and its qualities. Crisis is omnipresent in this effort. It refers to the destabilization that takes place on different scales: from the molecular level of the individual to the institutional level of complex societal apparatuses. The focus is theoretical, but the content is empirical, experiential and even personal. Thus, crisis does not operate as a point of departure and does not limit its scope to describing the capitalist impasses of our times. Crisis is both constitutive and constituent in the emergence, development and sustaining of the new commons that I have examined and which I call the *liminal commons*; it leaves its mark on subjects, spaces, times and all their intersections. This study aspires to analyse the fluidity of transitions without becoming a declaration of agnosticism. This is why, throughout this effort, the description of crisis and suspension is always accompanied by a study of both the before and the after. Hence, crisis and commoning are examined in their co-productive relation; none precedes the other, but both co-create and transform one another.

Liminality

The 'spirit' of this work resides in the careful examination of human experiences that emerge in contexts of crisis. To this extent, crisis is not approached from a macro-historical or genealogical perspective but is grounded in specific places and groups of people. My interest, thus, is to speak about the very condition of transitoriness and how individuals and collectives experience the uncertainties of the 'in-between'. To theorize this experience of suspension that often follows periods of crisis, I have been inspired by anthropological theories of the 'rites of passage'. Liminality is the core concept in these studies; it highlights the unsettledness, anxiety, hope and contradictions that each transitory period involves (Horvath 2013; Thomassen 2014). Liminality refers to the 'in-between' stage in rites of passage, in which the subject(s) have lost their established identities but have not yet obtained concrete new ones.

Throughout the history of social thought, liminality has proven to be a very flexible concept, one that has been used for the conceptualization and exploration of various phenomena, both personal and social. Yet, the potential of the concept has not been thoroughly exploited (Thomassen 2014). Originally, it was exclusively used in the study of rites of passage in archaic (or tribal) small-scale societies (Van Gennep 1960 [1909]) to describe the intermediate phase of those rituals when the 'liminal entities are neither here nor there; they are betwixt and between the positions assigned and arrayed by law, custom, convention, and ceremonial' (Turner 1977). Thereafter, the concept has been used to push the limits of social and political theory to different directions (Thomassen 2009; 2014), including the study of the commons (Stavrides 2015; Varvarousis and Kallis 2017).

Arnold Van Gennep introduced the concept of liminality in an effort to offer a meaningful classification of all existing rites in his classic book Les Rites de Passage, published in 1909. He explored different types of rites of passage: territorial, in social status, in time (harvest, New Year) or spatiotemporal ones such as the seasonal move from one place to another for the entire tribe. Starting from the importance of transitions in all societies, he was the first to detect an underlying pattern that characterizes almost all rites of passage consisting of a tripartite ritual form: separation, transition and incorporation. In the stage of separation, the subjects are being stripped from their previously established identities, in the second they pass through the ambiguity, anxiety and uncertainty of the 'in-between' and in the last stage they are incorporated again in their social milieu with new, transformed identities. He named the intermediate stage liminal and subsequently the first stage pre-liminal and the third one post-liminal. He claimed that this ritual form has universal applications and illustrated this hypothesis by using an impressive amount of detailed ethnographic data from places as diverse as Indonesia, Russia, Greece, India, Morocco, sub-Saharan Africa and Australia.

Although Van Gennep himself intended that his 'rites of passage' scheme applies to both individuals, cohorts of individuals and even to entire societies, his work concentrated, almost exclusively, on the study of individual 'life crises' transitions. In addition, even if Van Gennep's work was dedicated to transitions and he was the first to point 'liminality' as an indispensable part of each process of transformation, in his work one can find only a few examples about the very experience of transitoriness that characterizes liminal periods. His preoccupation instead was to prove the universality of the tripartite structure of the rites of passage and less to delve into the emotions, contradictions and potentialities that each of the different stages involves.

Although his work was an attempt to describe concretely acted out rituals of passage, and liminality was a concept invented to conceptualize their middle stage, it seems that he was aware that he invented a concept that belonged to something 'bigger' (Thomassen 2014). Actually, Van Gennep knew, both implicitly and explicitly, that liminality could have a much broader application, and despite his limited attention to this aspect in his book, he knew that the concept can capture 'something essential about the imprecise and unsettled situation of transitoriness' (Horvath 2013: 10). In fact, Van Gennep's framework can be seen as an alternative to Durkheim's concurrent analysis of rituals and the role they have in every society (Durkheim 1967). Indeed, whereas Durkheim approached rituals simply as the vectors by which individuals become socially determined as acting and thinking beings, Van Gennep showed that it is inadequate to conceptualize rituals simply as needs of a particular social order, and he argued in favour of a theoretical framework that allows a shift in focus from the individual to the collective level and vice versa in their fruitful interaction in and through liminality (Thomassen 2009). This allowed Van Gennep to recognize that rites of passage do operate not only as processes of unification and undifferentiation but also as processes of differentiation of age groups, genders, status groups and personalities (Thomassen 2014). Such a theoretical framework that acknowledges the dynamics between the individual and the collective level may prove vital in the analysis of processes of commoning since too often commons studies argue for the primacy of the social or the collective over the personal and regard the individual – both epistemologically and methodologically – as an opponent to combat.

The most influential scholar in the study of liminality is undoubtedly Victor Turner, who rediscovered the concept after it was underplayed for more than half a century, primarily due to the lack of translations of Van Gennep's work, but also due to intra-academic power relations (Thomassen 2009). With his work, Turner (1967, 1977, 1988) gave new depth to the concept and pushed its limits beyond its original use by removing it from the context of archaic, small-scale societies and situating it in the contemporary world. He was also the first to 'liberate' the concept from its structuralist and functionalist content by applying it in the study of social processes in general (Thomassen 2014). Turner paid particular attention to the study of the actual experience of liminality and was one of the first theorists who directed scholarly attention towards 'embodiment'.

Turner (1977, 1982, 1988) realized that liminality is useful not only in conceptualizing in-between periods and spaces but also in theorizing the reactions of humans when exposed to extraordinary experiences. He emphasized the multiple and often contradictory psychosocial qualities of 'inhabiting the threshold', including the potentially liberating dimension of the liminal experience. For this reason, he introduced the term 'communitas', which signifies any collective experience in which people distance themselves from mundane structures and their social identities and may attain a sense of equality (Turner 1978). Turner distinguished communitas from community since the former signifies a 'modality of social relationship' and the latter signifies 'an area of common living' (Turner 1991 [1977]). Originally, he linked communitas with social phenomena such as pilgrimage or what he calls 'liminoid experiences' (Turner 1982), which may include charivari, extreme sports, fiestas and parties, carnival or a visit to a museum.

Nevertheless, communitas can offer important insights into the study of commoning practices. Stavros Stavrides, in his book Common Space (2016: 59), argues that 'what a discussion on the equalizing experience of communitas can offer to a problematization of the commoning practices is the means to understand a community of commoners as a community which develops in its members a feeling of the sharing of qualities which are common to all'. Even though Turner's work remained largely apolitical, he was the first to propose liminality as a possible tool for an emancipatory theory, as he explicitly acknowledged that liminality could be both the cause and the outcome of an instant dissolution of what he calls 'social structure' (Turner 1991[1977]) and that 'social dramas' are 'units of aharmonic or disharmonic social processes, arising in conflict situations' (Turner 1988).

In the wake of Turner's work, liminality has been used in myriad different ways across different disciplines, ranging from religious studies to economics, tourism, arts, geography and even management.

Oftentimes, the concept of liminality has been used in ways that divest it of its original content, which involves the resolution of a personal or collective crisis and therefore a change in status and a transition. This has led to a loss in dynamism and analytical value of the concept since under this perspective it could signify almost anything. Homi Bhabha's (1994) usage of liminality, for instance, is quite reductive, as he merely associates it with a positive expression of cultural hybridity.[2] For others, liminality is just a synonym for marginality (Garsten 1999; Harjunen 2003; Pritchard and Morgan 2006).

The majority of these studies use liminality in a sweeping manner, as a concept to theorize any 'betwixt and between' situation or object, any in-between place or moment, a state of suspense, a moment of freedom between two structured world views or institutional arrangements (Thomassen 2014). It is also quite common for such studies to assign positive connotations to the concept, such as a celebration of difference, novelty and innovation that stems from the dissolution of the rigid taxonomization that once characterized the social sciences.

This shift was actually prompted by Turner himself, with his introduction of the concept of 'liminoid' to theorize mere breaks from normality that can happen in the contemporary world and which do not involve any kind of transition. I believe, however, that for liminality to become a useful concept in the study of the relation between crisis and the emergence of commoning initiatives, it should regain its original dynamism, linked with the condition of transitoriness. Liminality has the potential to open up spaces for thinking about the contingency inherent in every period of crisis; this is precisely its merit in the analysis of such processes.

The important questions that arise, then, are: Do liminal periods always come to an end? Is it possible to indefinitely extend liminality? What kind of outcomes can be expected from liminal periods?

Scholars have argued that perpetual liminality is possible, especially in the context of (post)modernity, in which liquidity and fluidity become the cornerstones of human existence (e.g. Szakolczai 2000). In a similar vein but without using the language of liminality, political philosophers and post-structuralist scholars have argued in favour of processes of constant re-identification as the sole source of human emancipation. 'Liquid modernity' (Baumann 2013), a term that signifies the impossibility of constructing an identity durable over time

---

2. Retrieved from Thomassen (2014).

and space in contemporary societies, has been either condemned or celebrated by opposing schools of thought; some argue in favour of constant transition and others emphasize the value of structure, fixed 'resistance' identities (e.g. Castells 2004) and order.

In my study of crisis and transitions, I am not following any of the two sides. At first glance, a study of crisis that celebrates liminality as a perpetual condition can be attractive, as it highlights possibility and contingency. Nevertheless, after a more careful look, it appears inhuman; life cannot be meaningful without a sense of identity or points of reference. A perpetual crisis is alienated and deprived of its transformational potential. On the other hand, as Goethe reminds us, 'all transitions are crises', in the sense that crisis is an important prerequisite for most, if not all, transitions. Hence, throughout this book, liminality is used in a flexible but not boundless manner. Liminality indeed implies the dissolution of order and negation of identity. However, liminality is always a formative period, too; it is the period when new identities – or even institutions and social structures – can be born.

When, in his essay 'Bridge and Door', Georg Simmel (1994) theorizes the dual character of these archetypical artefacts, he is actually trying to illustrate the contradictory nature of the human being, who 'always has to separate and cannot unite without separating'. 'Human is the limit being who has no limit', Simmel writes. In his view, humans need to create boundaries around them, boundaries that can protect them and offer them a sense of 'being-at-home'. However, he argues that humans would never build boundaries if they were not able to cross them. This view is not merely theoretical but is informed by the actual experience of the threshold and the very act of both crossing and inhabiting a boundary. Likewise, the theoretical effort expended and the examples used here are focused on and informed by the actual experience of crisis as it is lived by real subjects. Crisis then becomes the constitutive and constituent element of this crossing from one state of affairs to the other and from one type of social order and structure to the next one. The condition of liminality signifies and informs this act of crossing. Crisis and liminality can be encountered in different acts of crossing that unfold at various levels and scales, from individual and group transitions to societal ones. Of course, crossing scales is not an easy task and the creation of theoretical tools to be applied in multiscalar situations should be approached with care and caution. However, bringing together levels of reference that are usually kept apart appears to be a worthwhile effort.

The basic idea put forward in this theoretical work is that flux and movement never stop. Institutions, collective practices, places, subjects and entire societies never stop changing and hence are in constant transformation. However, the pace of change is not constant and cannot be maintained at its highest level for prolonged periods. A return to what can be called 'normality', which can be either real or perceived, is important for individual subjects, groups and societies at large. Normality here is never an accomplished or rigid state, but rather an expression of the individual and collective desire for stability and a sense of being-at-home, to use Simmel's metaphor. Normality, thus, is an impossible limit that is first and foremost imagined but is also characterized by stability in social relations, institutions, economy, law and politics. However, in almost all the aforementioned scales, normality neither is univocal nor lacks diversity; it is shaped through dominant narratives, established power geometries (Massey 2013) and techniques of governmentality (Foucault 1991). In other words, normality is shaped through normalization. Thus, normality, crisis and liminality are not absolute terms but relative ones, which try to conceptualize spatiotemporal stages in which transformations have different intensities. Wars, natural disasters, pandemics, economic crises, big social movements and most important intersections of the above are elements that challenge normality and create conditions of crisis. Crisis opens a stage of suspension, a liminal stage in which new forms of sociality are formed and tested. Normality returns or at least attempts to do so; yet, it will never be the same as before, as elements that were created within, through and because of liminality create new relations between the known and the unknown, the normal and the 'other'.

Social structures, social imaginary and social normalization

Throughout the history of the social sciences, several theories have been developed around the concept of 'social structure'. The word 'structure', however, is always used to designate the sum of relations and articulations in a specific society (Deleuze and Guattari 2012 [1988]). Social structures are composed of socioeconomic stratifications (e.g. classes), social networks, institutions, systems of law, as well as norms and beliefs; they are mediated by forms of coding and decoding. While social structures are porous systems that are always susceptible to transformation, they often oscillate between phases of stability or normality and phases of collapse and transition. For Greek-French philosopher Cornelius Castoriadis, a central element that creates coherence in a particular social structure is what he calls the 'social imaginary'.

The social imaginary for Castoriadis is the *magma*[3] of social imaginary significations and of the images and schemes that are created in order to support it in a particular society (Castoriadis 1975). Those social imaginary significations are the outcome of the creative capacity of society itself, and they are imaginary because they are not real (they cannot be derived from things) and they are not rational (they cannot be constructed logically) (Castoriadis 2010). Social imaginary significations are 'embodied' in specific institutions, a term which for Castoriadis denotes 'the entire set of tools, language, skills, norms and values [...] everything that, with or without formal sanctions, imposes ways of acting and thinking' (Castoriadis 2010: 46). Thus, the social imaginary *is the shared collective imagination distilled in specific institutions, which operates as the 'glue' that holds a society together by being a representation of it*. In each society, it is the social imaginary that determines what is real, worthy, possible, acceptable or desirable. However, not all social imaginary significations are explicit in every society; rather, some of them 'can be grasped only indirectly and obliquely' (Castoriadis 1975: 143). Whereas for Castoriadis the individual imaginary has its locus in the unconscious, the social imaginary has no explicit locus, but it is 'the invisible cement' that denotes almost nothing and connotes almost everything (Castoriadis 1975).

Castoriadis argues that each society's distinct social imaginary creates a dominant anthropological type (Castoriadis 2010), that is, the type of human 'needed to make it function'. In this regard, Castoriadis theorizes social structures as systems that are characterized by some form of organizational, informational and cognitive closure, although those entities are 'subjected to disruptions' (Castoriadis 2010: 49). In his view, disruptions are always the result of a continuous creative social process that produces new meanings and social imaginary significations

---

3. Magma is a concept used by Castoriadis in analogy with the notion of Gestalt in psychoanalysis. It signifies the indefinite sets of social imaginary significations that constitute the social imaginary. However, this magmatic social imaginary is irreducible to the sum of the imaginary significations that compose it, as it cannot be reconstituted analytically or by any means of order (Castoriadis 1975; Mountian 2009).

capable of replacing the older ones and therefore self-altering the social imaginary and the social structure at large.

While Castoriadis chooses to emphasize the creative dimension of the production of the social imaginary as a society's collective work, Michel Foucault focuses more on the role of power in the creation of normality in a specific social structure. He calls this process 'social normalization' (Foucault 2009). He emphasizes that this project of normalization is not univocal and is not promoted by a single force but involves various mechanisms that, in his own words, 'develop from and below a system of law, in its margins and may be even against it' (Foucault 2009: 56). Through discipline and taxonomization, social normalization separates the normal from the abnormal; at the same time, it prescribes an optimal model of social and spatial relations, forms of behaviour, social roles and imaginary significations and attempts to get individuals, movements and entire societies to conform to this model.

Liminal commons

Commons, community and identity

The commons are often imagined as small-scale ventures in the farmlands, in which peasants come together to collectively cultivate their crops; as fisheries in which fishermen jointly define the rules of management; as complex systems of collective irrigation or as social systems for the management of alpine meadows and vital water resources. More recently, the commons are imagined as digital communities that produce digital goods, as urban and peri-urban gardening projects, as housing squats and even as manifold commons (Bresnihan and Byrne 2015), that is, commons that involve multiple activities and intra-common relations. The underlying principles that characterize all these forms of commons and constitute the criteria for their success or failure are their capacity to endure over time and to create strong community bonds among their members.

A clearly defined community is the cornerstone of Ostrom's analysis of the commons while endurance is the most important measure of success. Ostrom is interested in long-term commons only, and throughout her work, she tries to identify the institutions that may allow them to persist over time. In this respect, fixed communities are deemed better than open ones, because within fixity people can better incorporate and follow specific norms and principles, which according to Ostrom are essential elements for successful and enduring commoning. The 'rational individual', which Ostrom uses as the privileged unit of her analysis, has a 'natural' tendency towards free-riding. Hence, those who do not follow specific norms of behaviour are considered violators and punished through systems of graduated sanctions. Community and identity – as well as community-as-identity – become synonyms for the commons, while relations of proximity and control are often envisaged as the sole source of coherence, sustainability and taming of human profit-seeking egoism.

On the other hand, the anti-capitalist commons of the more politically oriented literature on the commons are often associated with the image of 'emancipated communities' that are barricaded in 'liberated strongholds' and are always ready to fight and defend themselves against the hostile outside (Stavrides 2013, 2016: 228). 'Consciously constituted communities' (Midnight Notes Collective and Friends 2009: 11) are formed on the basis of antithesis to capital, which gives shape to a coherent project with the ideological function of prefiguring the cooperative society that the radical left strives to create (Federici 2010: 2). Hence, social centres, anarchist squats, occupied factories, workers' collectives and the other (re)productive ventures that fall into the category of anti-capitalist commons may be open in terms of ethnicity, gender and perhaps class origin and religion, but they remain homogeneous or with a tendency towards homogeneity regarding their political identity and the stance they should have against capital accumulation. As with Ostrom, the criteria of endurance against corruption and co-optation by capital and of coherence-through-collective-identity-formation remain the predominant factors of success or failure for anti-capitalist commons.

Stavros Stavrides has identified the problematic use of the terms 'community' and 'identity' in the literature of commons and has tried to produce theoretical responses to them. He argues that if the commons are constituted on the basis of a necessary closure, community and identity, they will operate as exceptions. Under specific conditions, exceptions can actually fuel the systems of domination and normalization rather than challenge them (Agamben 1998; Stavrides 2016). He calls this commoning 'enclosed' and emphasizes that 'institutions of commoning established in a stable and well-defined community may very well look like the dominant institutions in the ways they regulate people's rights and actions' (Stavrides 2016: 41). By extension, Stavrides criticizes both the logic of clear boundaries as defined by Ostrom and the logic

2. Commons, Crisis and Liminality   33

of anti-capitalist commons as conceived by sectors of the autonomous Marxists.

Stavrides' work is oriented towards political transformation and emancipation, and his arguments are built upon the assumption that if the commons are to contribute to human emancipation, they must 'tend towards an openness of sharing: self-managed cooperation which is open to newcomers, knowledge "production" which is not limited to those who understand it, create it or "finance" it and festive and joyous events which do not separate consumers from artists' (Stavrides 2016: 3). To explore the possibility of permanent openness for commoning practices, he offers a counterimage to the image of an enclosed spatiality, the image of a potential 'city of thresholds' (Stavrides 2013; 2015). This city of thresholds is the spatial equivalent of an emancipating project based on the negotiation between different but open identities in the process of collectively inventing the future (Stavrides 2013). He illustrates his arguments with examples ranging from the 'Juntas de Buen Gobierno' of the Zapatista movement to social housing experiences in Athens and the Occupy movement. His analysis is rich and theoretically elaborate, and he builds bridges with the work of Foucault, Ranciere, Benjamin, Agamben, Hardt, Negri and other major theoreticians. Besides the theoretical and projective value of his work, however, in his latest writings, Stavrides has tried to ground these abstract ideas in practice; to that end, he has developed a set of institutional proposals on how the commons can remain open, called 'the institutions of expanding commoning' (Stavrides 2015; 2016). Stavrides invites us to abandon the very concept of community because it implies some sort of homogeneity and exclusivity; instead, he prefers to use the concepts of 'communities in movement' and 'public sphere', drawing basically on Zibechi's work on Latin America (Zibechi 2010) and Ranciere's concept of a possible 'common world' (Ranciere 2006).

The value of Stavrides' work resides in that he offers an image of how common space can operate as both a source and an outcome of emancipatory practices, and thus he contributes to overcoming the conception of the commons as mere systems of resource management. Moreover, he relates commoning with the tendency of the human being to cross the borders towards freedom, to rephrase Simmel's words; this is important, as it expands the research agenda, previously focused on the more static issues of preservation and defence of the commons. In addition, he offers a beautiful 'thought-image', in his terminology, about how an emancipating spatiality of commoning could be envisaged. Lastly, he also offers a basic but partial set of rules on how the commons can remain open and welcoming to newcomers. In my opinion, his books are also a wonderful and refreshing read.

However, Stavrides' work has more limited analytical value in explaining real-world commoning processes, because the author intentionally chooses to emphasize and explain only one of the two opposing and contradictory tendencies that any human being, group or society possesses – the tendency to open towards the unknown and the 'other' and the tendency to create their own cosmos and protect it from what is regarded as external to it. Stavrides chooses to stress the continuities that may be created by erecting bridges towards otherness, but he does not pay enough attention to – or even downplays – the discontinuities that may appear, and do appear, in this process. His focus, thus, is more normative and less analytical. His theory offers insights on *how to* keep commoning endlessly open and not on *how do* actual commons try to regulate the relations between the inside and the outside.

This one-sided approach may bring to mind the previously mentioned literature that celebrates liminality and associates it only with positive shifts. Such a celebration of liminality doesn't take into account central aspects of the liminal condition as described by Van Gennep, for whom liminality always dissolves existing structures and gives birth to more stable ones. Most importantly, however, such a conception is a far cry from how, in actual human experience, relations are established between the self, the intimate environment and the entire world. Van Gennep himself was the first to notice that liminality must somehow come to an end (Van Gennep 1960 [1909]), while more contemporary thinkers on the field argue that 'human life ceases to be meaningful in perpetual liminality' as 'without a return to normality and background structures that one can take for granted (at least until they are shaken again), individuals go crazy and societies become pathologic' (Thomassen 2014: 216). If considered concerning human experience (and if liminality is to be taken seriously, it must engage with human experience) and not as a theoretical metaphor about potential emancipatory practices, a state of permanent liminality may resemble what Bateson, in his effort to define schizophrenia, called the 'loss of frame'. A last point, particularly important for a work on the commons, is that Stavrides' inherently 'expanding commoning' contradicts the majority of studies of the commons. Ostrom insists that individuals have an inherent tendency to enclose their common world and invigilate it from others; she goes on to claim that, according to her studies, this is a universal phenomenon (Ostrom 2009). Even if one claims that this perception of universality is an outcome of the limitations of Ostrom's theory, her specific biases and the way she selects the commons under study, it is still difficult to argue that permanent openness and endless transformation are or can become the essence of human beings.

Commons and temporality

A thorough study of the theories on the commons will reveal a peculiar gap; none of them pays any attention to time. Commons in all cases appear timeless and their examination is usually narrowed to their material, geographical, organizational and spatial characteristics. While this might seem strange at a first glance, there is a good reason why it happens: stability and endurance are seen as the sole markers of success in the commons. This naturalization of perpetuity as the ultimate goal of any commons leaves no space for time to be explored as a meaningful parameter in their development. Hence transient commons can only be understood as failed commons.

While this focus on stability and endurance is certainly worthwhile since these two qualities are indispensable for claiming the commons as an alternative system of governance and provision for contemporary societies, my argument is that we should also look beyond them. The prevalent focus on stability, endurance and instrumental outcomes may miss important effects that even seemingly 'failed' commons can have. How do we make sense of commons that despite their short lives had major effects on commoners and environments? How do we make sense of the symbolic alterations and investments that experiences of temporary commoning can have on places and collective memories? And lastly, how do we make sense of the different stages/phases of a commoning project if time is excluded from the equation?

On the other hand, this a-temporal approach is not prevalent only in the commons' literature but is also apparent in many other social science fields. One can distinguish two major approaches to the study of temporality in social science. The first approach, similar to the commons theories, examines its subject of research in an a-temporal and linear manner, as if events and processes unfold in a continuum in which all periods and moments have similar importance and density. The second approach studies critical moments and events as if they lie outside time, as exceptional periods in which the 'objective' structures and deterministic explanations evaporate completely. This often leads to an idiosyncratic 'transitology', which begs for highly subjective (if not elusive) explanations and which usually ends with a mandate for a 'methodological exceptionalism' (Dobry 2015: 94). Despite their obvious differences, both approaches do not try to incorporate time as a meaningful parameter and they either neglect or ostracize temporal dimensions from their analyses. In contrast, my intention is to avoid this polarization and develop a theoretical analytical tool for studying transitional processes without either neglecting their specialness or forgetting that they are still embedded in specific spatiotemporal contexts that need to be taken seriously into account by theorists.

Hakeem Bey's temporary autonomous zones

I am not aware of any concrete studies in the field of commons that try to understand and analyse the merits of temporary commoning. However, Peter Lamborn Wilson's (widely known as Hakeem Bey) book on temporary autonomous zones (TAZs) (2003, Autonomedia), a controversial bestseller of the 1980s and 1990s, can be regarded as a precursor to my theory on liminal commons. Both his work and this one have an explicit focus on the study of temporary experiences of collective action and both try to decouple this transitoriness from failure, as it happens with most theories of collective action. However, despite these important similarities, Hakeem Bey's TAZs differ substantially from liminal commons in many senses.

In the various chapters of the book, Bey gives many different clues about what a TAZ is and what is its function in contemporary societies. These scattered fragments of definition create a rich 'chaos-ontology' of the TAZ that sheds light on its different aspects. Yet Bey consciously avoids giving a single comprehensive definition since his aim is not to create an essay but a 'poetic fancy' and his rich, original terminology is 'not meant to define areas but to suggest tendencies' (Bey 2003: 106). In one of these fragments, Bey claims that a TAZ is 'a guerilla operation which liberates an area (of land, of time, of imagination) and then dissolves itself to re-form elsewhere/elsewhen, before the State can crush it' (Bey 2003: 99). His starting point is what he calls 'the closure of the map', a historical development that refers to the absence of *terra incognita* in the modern world. Since there is no outside on earth and since every *topos* is mapped, albeit roughly, by the 'Expert' State that is 'omnipresent' and 'all-powerful', we can't claim 'permanent solutions', Bey argues. Hence, the project of revolution is impossible and waiting for it is undesirable. The only viable opportunity to experience the likes of revolution nowadays, Bey continues, is to look for a temporal outside or, in other words, a temporary autonomous zone.

2. Commons, Crisis and Liminality 37

TAZ's lifecycle is simple: it strikes, dissolves, in order to strike back again. Its aim is rather straightforward too: it is a 'bootstrap operation' that enables individuals to experience autonomy, freedom and ecstasy, which can have a transformative effect on them. 'One cannot struggle for what one does not know' (Bey 2003: 96), Bey claims and subsequently assigns to TAZs an educational role. In his effort to specify the kind of transformations that TAZs can bring about, Bey singles out three directions: first, TAZs create the conditions for surpassing the 'misery of the family' and entering the 'prodigality' of the band; second, TAZs operate against the 'clock-work universe' and the 'death of the festival' and thus incarnate the 'right to the party' by unfettering the festive attributes of insurrection; lastly, TAZs transform individuals from passive consumers to active 'rootless cosmopolitans', a category that includes all sorts of wanderers, 'psychic' travellers, gypsies, 'X-class artists', in short, nomads.

Bey also assigns to TAZs a triple topology: in time, space, but also in relation with each other. TAZs belong to the moment: 'as soon as the TAZ is named (represented, mediated), it must vanish, it will vanish, leaving behind it an empty husk' (Bey 2003: 99). Bey argues that there might be some TAZs that can live longer but this can happen only if they go unnoticed and remain invisible (from the omnipotent State). In general, TAZs represent the peak experience and as usually happens with peak experiences they can't last for long. Despite their precarity, TAZs have an actual location in space; they are not virtual. Their spatiality varies; they can take place almost everywhere, in ships and urban centres, in hilly enclaves in the countryside and also in beaches and other interstitial spaces. Their scale also varies; they can be monadic but they can also involve entire populations and bigger lands as in the case of the 'Republic of Fiume',[4] the last 'pirate utopia' in Bey's words. TAZs are elusive and disappear, but what keeps them in a sense 'alive' and operates as a 'support system, capable of carrying information from

---

4. The Free State (or Republic) of Fiume, perhaps the first modern TAZ according to Bey, refers to the temporal occupation of the city of Fiume (now Rijeka in Croatia) by a peculiar army called the 'Arditi' led by the controversial Italian poet Gabriel D' Annunzio that lasted about 15 months. According to Bey (although Bey's writings are disputed by some historians), the central principle of the constitution of the new state was the music and daily life there was a mix of pure aestheticism, hedonism, and wild partying. Bey also mentions the multicultural and open character of the Republic of Fiume.

one TAZ to another', is the 'web'. The web is a chaotic alternative to the ordered 'net'. Whereas the net is a totalitarian apparatus that tries to capture and taxonomize information, the web develops in its cracks and tries to break this classification which leads to hierarchy. The web is horizontal, anti-hierarchical and only facilitates info exchange. It is as if the net is the instrument of the state that contributes to the aforementioned 'closure of the map' and as if the web is the instrument of the TAZs in their effort to break this uniformity.

Hakeem Bey's work is a literary masterpiece and a very lively account of temporary 'peak' experiences; it's not by chance that it attracted so much attention among certain audiences over time. The study of TAZs should be inscribed and understood in the context of the wider studies and writings on 'nomadology', a particular field of postmodern thought originally propagated by Gilles Deleuze and Felix Guattari. Eminent in this field is the argument that societal transformation cannot be the outcome of a polar political opposition since every time you move the one side, the other one – the mirror – operates a similar move (Deleuze and Guattari 2010). The whole idea of the 'war machine', apparent also in Bey's TAZ, is to win the war without even giving a battle, only through multiplicity and metamorphosis, which is its 'pure strategy' (Deleuze and Guattari 2010: 5). Yet whereas Deleuze and Guattari's work is highly elaborated on the philosophical level trying to destabilize 'royal science', psychoanalysis and the foundations of existing knowledge more generally, Bey's project focuses on the value of temporary emancipatory experiences and constitutes a moral call for more amoral and transgressive actions that liberate individuals from 'any restriction and limit' – an effort perhaps to rewrite Lao Tzu's *Tao Te Ching* for the contemporary nomad-anarchist.

TAZs have many similarities with liminal commons, but also substantial differences. Both focus on temporality and transitoriness and depart from an understanding of the transient as failed, and both value the potential transformative effect that temporary experiences can have on individuals. However, the similarities stop somewhere there. TAZs represent an 'intensification, a surplus, an excess, a potlatch', which individuals can experience either alone or (preferably) collectively. In contrast, liminal commons focus explicitly on temporary experiences of egalitarian cooperation and self-organization and not on mere breaks from normality. Bey's focus on individuals restricts his account from offering any insight about the relations among the practitioners of TAZs, their forms of organization and regulation of their internal relations. TAZs are completely unregulated, a form of salto mortale in the depths of individual freedom. This is both their scope and essence. Also, while TAZs destiny is to disappear in order to reappear somewhere and somewhen else, liminal commons aim to operate as transitional structures, which eventually facilitate the creation of more stable commoning projects. Moreover, while TAZs belong to the broader realm of 'lifestyle politics' (Portwood-Stacer 2013) or in the narrower one of 'lifestyle anarchism' (Bookchin 1995), focusing therefore on liberating temporary experiences as a matter of lifestyle choices, liminal commons are better suited in the field of the study of the commons and liminality; they often start as outcomes of crises rather than individual choices. Lastly, liminal commons do examine not only transformations that happen at the individual level but also those that happen at the collective, local or even the societal one.

What is a liminal commons?

Imagine this:

- A group of volunteers rushes to a border island in which refugees arrive in thousands and state authorities are absent. Without knowing each other, without even speaking the same language, these people quickly set up first aid, cooking and sleeping infrastructure in order to cope with the situation and manage this infrastructure in common.
- Amid an economic crisis and overstressed by austerity measures, another group of thousands, if not millions, of people decide to occupy the central square of a city centre. Their desperation, anger, disorientation and loss of income are so strong that these people decide not only to demonstrate but to transform the occupied public space into their new home. To do this, they establish procedures of space-sharing and management in which everyone has the right to participate.
- After a big earthquake, a suburb of a major city in the global South has been partially destroyed. The authorities and global NGOs are nowhere to be seen, and a certain degree of self-organization is needed. People, without necessarily knowing each other and without having any communal bonds, decide to set up local commissions to cope with the impact of the disaster.
- On a remote beach of a beautiful Mediterranean island in which no infrastructure exists, people of every age, ethnicity and background decide to spend their holiday in a self-organized and self-

sustainable way. In order to survive, they dig wells, create spaces of gathering that belong to all, plant vegetables and lay down the rules for sharing available resources and managing waste. They know that after a few months everything will be over, but they still invest part of their time in commoning activities.

The previous examples are all instances of commoning because people pool resources and labour to create common goods or to jointly manage their shared space, infrastructure and waste; what is more, they do so without any recognizable leadership or top-down hierarchy. However, in all these examples, neither long-term sustainability nor the existence or formation of collective identity are considered important necessary prerequisites or even goals. What is needed, however, for this common doing to take place is effective communication of the differences among all the diverse subjects, who do not share common codes, norms, habits and knowledge. Such a stage for the negotiation of differences is often experienced as an in-between space (Stavrides 2016) because only a space that resists identification can remain open to all. Liminality, thus, as the concept that signifies a condition of in-betweenness and loss of identity, becomes the cornerstone of this heterogeneous organization and the driving force behind the effective communication of difference. A willingness to open up their previously stable identities is required of those who participate in this common doing.

This opening up of identities can differ from person to person, from one group to another and, most importantly, from one context to another. In our examples, while in the cases of refugee arrival, earthquake and austerity, identity destabilization is the outcome of a generalized crisis that affects everyone, in the case of self-organized beach commons, identity destabilization is triggered by a desire for contact with the 'other' and is mediated by a conscious gesture towards otherness. Thus, liminal subjects, that is, subjects who have problematized or collapsed identities, constitute the backbone of liminal commons. Those subjects are open and can therefore be inventive and vulnerable at the same time; they may suffer from uncertainty or they may use this uncertainty to create their lives anew.

In liminal commons, the 'glue' that brings actors together is the practical production of the common. Community in liminal commons is a fluid and temporal arrangement created to share and sustain this common doing; it is characterized by great instability and high membership turnover. Both the manifestation of individual identities and the formation of collective identities are discouraged in liminal commons because they are recognized as obstacles in the process of commoning. Liminal commons unfold in contestable spaces or in spaces susceptible to contestation, such as public spaces. The space of liminal commons is a crisis-scape that transforms according to rapidly changing needs and emergencies. There are very few predefined shared values in the process of creating and sustaining a liminal commons, and they are often narrowed down to the belief that all participants are equal and have equal rights of participation in decision-making; this often leads to the adoption of horizontal structures of organization.

The institutions that are performed during this kind of commoning, which define what is to be shared and how, are also characterized by fluidity. Liminal institutions are not fixed but precarious; they emerge and perish quickly, according to whether they prove functional or not. They aim at unification rather than exclusion of the diverse potential commoners, and they promote the non-antagonistic coexistence of different perceptions.

Liminal commons are not only the outcome of a specific kind of crisis, that is, economic, social or environmental. They are also processes that are formative of new crises at various scales – from the micro-scale of the individual to the macro-scale of an entire society. 'Crisis is contagious', as Turner said, and this corresponds to the actual becoming of the liminal commons. Liminal commons can not only 'transmit' crisis to the individuals who incidentally take part in the incipient forms of collective action emerging in the respective processes of commoning, but it can also affect the surrounding environment by expanding crisis and its transformative potential to places far beyond the traceable periphery of the actual common space. This kind of expansion often follows a rhizomatic pattern (Deleuze and Guattari 2012 [1988]; Castells 2012). A rhizomatic expansion has no centre or periphery, does not begin from or end at a specific point and often resembles what is called punctuation in biology. Its nodes are either not connected or connected mostly through unforeseen encounters, following a decentralization–recentralization process (Zibechi 2010). The nodes of the rhizome are not stable but appear and disappear within a highly accelerating spiral; multiple nodes can be added to the rhizome without any previous control of whether or not they are compatible among them.

Liminal commons are transitional forms of commoning, primarily aimed at facilitating transitions. Such processes are often precarious and temporal, but they are indeed capable of creating new realities that were previously unthinkable. Thus, if a crisis is what poses the question, liminality can mark the period when tentative, often incomplete and contradictory answers are invented and put into practice. Despite the ephemeral character of those 'extraordinary' periods, such answers can have a lasting effect and may foreshadow the basic features of the emerging new structure, at least until this is shaken in its turn.

Liminal commons is an analytical category of commons and does not designate a preferable or desirable form. By extension, my aim here is not to totally displace Elinor Ostrom's theory or to discredit all other tools for the analysis of other types of commoning experiences; rather, it is to provide a new analytical framework for approaching a particular form of commoning, which until recently was off the radar of the burgeoning literature on the field. This work tries to remain equidistant from Stavrides and other advocates of permanent openness, on the one hand, and the determinists of necessary closure, on the other. My interest is directed towards studying forms of commoning that develop within crisis and emergency, and which can catalyse new transformations in rapidly changing conditions. I am aware that openness, a characteristic of such periods, will come to an end, that crisis will either give birth to new structures or will itself become 'the new normal'. I believe, however, that it is important to explore the experiences that emerge in this 'in-between' and examine how they affect the 'after' because it is within crisis that reflections, inventive ideas and new forms of organization are more necessary than ever.

Box 1. The Greek case and the research methods of the study

In recent years, Greece has often been at the epicentre of global attention for a series of reasons. For some, Greece represents the 'black sheep' of the European Union and probably of the whole of the West, as the country is routinely depicted as a corrupt state inhabited by lazy and untrustworthy people. It was the first of the 'tigers turned into pigs[5]' after the financial

---

5. In 2004, *The Economist* was praising the 'Celtic tiger' of Ireland for its economic growth, while in 2008 the IMF was similarly praising Greece for having a very healthy economic development, which they predicted would remain stable over the following years. Likewise, in 2008 Spain was celebrating the fact that its GDP surpassed that of Italy. Ironically, only 2 years later, all

crisis of 2008. After the movements of the squares in 2011, and along with the Spanish 'indignados', the global media started portraying Greece as the nucleus of a new culture of radical grassroots action and a social laboratory, where new forms of both governance and resistance are produced and tried out. In 2015, with the electoral win of Syriza, the endless negotiations with the IMF and the European Union, and finally the referendum, Greece was the centre of attention of modern politics. In late 2015 and early 2016, this attention intensified, since Greece became the epicentre of the so-called refugee crisis and Greek islands operated as the main points of entrance to the 'orderly' Schengen world. Of course, the pandemic of Covid-19 intensified all the above on an unprecedented scale.

These diverse depictions of Greek reality over the last decade are inaccurate and superficial, yet they are indicative of the multiple destabilizations and rapid changes that occurred in the country and which are codified here as 'the Greek crisis'. This book aspires to 'zoom in' on and explain the aspects of the Greek crisis that are related to the well-documented emergence and multiplication of the new commons. Before 2008, there were only a handful of such projects in the country; today, there is a wide spectrum of practices that have commoning at the heart of their activity, ranging from projects of the so-called social and solidarity economy to political and housing squats, social centres, urban space appropriations through commoning, social clinics and pharmacies, back-to-the-land self-sustaining experiments, self-organized refugee camps and squats and solidarity networks.

Why and how have these ventures emerged? What has fuelled their dispersion and multiplication? How are they organized? What can we learn from these experiences?

These questions constitute the guiding thread of this study, which officially started in 2013 and is still ongoing, but whose unofficial origins lie further back in time. The empirical content of this book is anchored in multiple qualitative and quantitative research techniques. The quantitative part includes a large-scale

---

these countries, together with Portugal, were repudiated by the international press as 'PIGS' (Kallis 2014).

face-to-face country-wide survey, completed by 404 individuals from 116 different ventures carried out between May 2016 and May 2017. The study covered a large part of the country, including the regions of Macedonia, Attica, Thessaly, Peloponnese and Crete. In many cases, these first-person structured interviews were followed by semi-structured or entirely unstructured interviews with participants of the projects under study. In this aspect, ethnography met quantitative social research methods. Approximately 600 hours of participant observation and interviews were completed in parallel with the survey project. Due to the unprecedented large scale of the study, its rigorous sampling strategy and the consistent use of the methodological tools it used, a certain degree of generalization of their findings can be claimed. However, several blind spots need further inquiry.

Also, over the years of my research, I was involved in five distinct commoning projects in Athens and Lesvos, conducting a total of forty life-story interviews and dedicating countless hours to interpersonal interactions and common activities. In this book, all names have been changed to ensure the anonymity of informants, aside from a handful of cases where interviewees explicitly stated that they wanted their real names to be used.

Chapter 3

LIMINAL SUBJECTS OF COMMONING

The main aim of this chapter is to explore the role of liminality in the formation of the subjects of commoning and of common space more generally. In the first stream of the literature on the commons, the one stemming from Ostrom's tradition, there is little attention to the commons as mechanisms of subjectification; the subjects of commoning are considered fixed and with given motives that are limited to economic reasoning. In contrast, in more recent literature, subjects are a central focus of the analysis. Yet there is little analytical work on how crisis affects individual, collective and spatial identities grounded in empirical data and specific case studies. This chapter aspires to contribute to this discussion by focusing on the period of the Greek movement of the squares. There is a dual purpose here. On the one hand, I am drawing on existing theories of the commons to identify their limitations concerning the subjectivities of the commoners; moreover, I seek to develop a theoretical understanding of how crisis affects the mechanisms of subjectification and normalization. On the other hand, I am exploring in detail how this generalized destabilization of identity formation processes has been manifested in the liminal commons of the indignant squares in Athens. Through the exploration of discourses, images and personal stories, I am unfolding the ontology of liminal commons in relation to space, kinds of social relations, expansive characteristics, inner dynamics, transformative capacities and contradictions.

The movement of the squares and the commons

The year 2011 was an important one. Urban uprisings took place in countries as diverse as United States, Israel, Greece, Spain and the United Kingdom. These were preceded by the mobilizations of the Arab Spring and followed by similar phenomena in the following years in Turkey, Brazil and Hong Kong. Despite their heterogeneity, their contradictions and their debatable repertoire of strategies, these unanticipated uprisings shook the governing elites (Stavrides 2016), disrupted the neoliberal status quo (Dikeç and Swyngedouw 2017) and challenged the social sciences (Arenas 2014).

One of the recognizable attributes of all these movements was the practice of encampment on public space, which was given central attention in the literature that tried to make sense of them. For Pickeril and Krinsky (2012), Occupy matters, most importantly, because it puts the issue of space at the top of the agenda and by doing so it reinvigorates the 'right to the city' debate. For Castells, while contemporary movements 'usually start on the internet social networks, they become a movement by occupying the urban space'; 'the space of autonomy is the new spatial form of networked social movements' (Castells 2012: 250). The centrality of space, however, has sparked vivid debates among scholars. For Marcuze (2011), the centrality of encampments led to a 'fetishization of space' that obscured the 'bigger picture' of social change. Kaika and Karaliotas (2014) underline the failure of the movement to implement broader democratic practices beyond the occupied squares. On the other hand, many have argued that encampments should be taken more seriously, as they created forms of *common space* that initiated new forms of living-in-common both during the mobilizations and in their aftermath (Stavrides 2013; Varvarousis and Kallis 2017; Castells 2012).

In effect, while the struggle for 'the common' (Hardt and Negri 2012) has become an important dimension in the literature on the movement of the squares, the content ascribed to the term is varied. Dikeç and Swyngedouw (2017) refer to the modalities of 'being-in-common' that emerged as urban commons during this cycle of insurgencies, emphasizing primarily their egalitarian organization, their prefigurative character and their role in the process they call 're-centring the urban political'. Departing from similar concerns, Kioupkiolis (2014) reflects on how the commons of 'indignant' squares reveal not only the strengths but also the limitations of the 'politics of the multitude' (Hardt and Negri 2005, 2009, 2012) and argues in favour of combining those politics with the politics of hegemony. For Hardt and Negri (2012), the 'struggle for the common' is one of the three basic characteristics that connect the different versions of the movement globally; the authors place special emphasis on the production of militant subjectivities through those experiences. Stavrides focuses more on the spatial dimension of 'indignant' occupations and stresses how those common spaces constituted forms of hybridization that were able to bring together 'incompatible and often opposing elements in the creation of 'unauthorized' combinations' (Stavrides 2016: 161). Finally, De Angelis argued that all contemporary movements 'in one way or another, to a degree, are forms of commoning' and also that 'struggles through commons are also now an increasingly visible form of struggle' (De Angelis 2014: 178).

From macro to micro: The merit of the empirical approach

Notwithstanding the rich literature on the connections between the movement of the squares and the theory of the commons, in most of the aforementioned accounts, the focal point is the link between the movements' commoning practices and the broader theory of counter-hegemonic politics; therefore, the exploration of the various elements of these commons hinges on their role in the anti-capitalist struggle. Most of these accounts constitute macro-observations and general theorizations and are rarely grounded in empirical work that can highlight the contradictions and the complexity of the field. As Paul Chatterton and Jenny Pickerill recently put it, 'still missing, are detailed empirical accounts of the messy, gritty and real everyday rhythms as activists envision, negotiate, build and enact life beyond the capitalist status quo in the everyday.'[1]

If the encampments of indignant movements were instances of commoning, what can they tell us about the broader theory of commons? How do they challenge Ostrom's theoretical framework?

There is a great deal of commons scholars who dismiss the theory of the institutional school and Elinor Ostrom in particular. Some denounce it as pro-capitalist and entrepreneurial and others as irrelevant for social change, while others yet do not refer to it at all. To be sure, Ostrom's work has gaps, inaccuracies and even mistakes. Nevertheless, it seems inappropriate to disregard her analysis because of her liberal leanings (Pennington 2012); after all, her work is the most detailed and empirically grounded on the field. There is a need, thus, not only for political manifestos and normative proposals but also for meticulous work to reveal Ostrom's inaccuracies and omissions and mend them through new theoretical propositions.

This chapter interrogates Elinor Ostrom's theory and explains why it is inadequate for approaching the commons of the movement of the squares. The core argument advanced here is that Ostrom's theory of subjectivity is simplistic and has limited potential in analysing liminal commons. The same is true for some theoretical efforts that came after Ostrom and draw on autonomous Marxism. Fixed identities and motives are challenged by liminal conditions and therefore different motives and

1. In Arenas (2014).

intermediate, incomplete and fluid subjects may appear – and should appear – if such commons are to function. Mechanisms of subjectification should be revisited and reconsidered. Crisis fuels this kind of commoning and becomes its cornerstone. Hence, for liminal commons, crisis is not merely a point of departure but a constitutive element.

The movement of the squares in Greece was one of the most dynamic and enduring among similar movements globally, especially concerning experimentation with commoning practices. The occupation of Syntagma (Constitution) Square lasted approximately three months, and some three million people passed through the square, about one-third of the Greek population.

Why and how did so many and diverse individuals decide not simply to temporarily gather in a public space but to occupy it and make it their new home? How has this experience marked the lives of those people? How was everyday life organized in the square and why was it organized like this? How was crisis imprinted on the encampment? These are some of the more specific empirical questions that inform this chapter.

The subjects of commoning in the existing literature

The subject in Ostrom's theory

The wording of Ostrom in the study of commons can be described as neutral. Ostrom studied the commons mainly as resources from a strictly scientific point of view. 'Commons is a general term that refers to a resource shared by a group of people', Ostrom insists even in her latest work (Ostrom 2007). Her work focuses on the institutions that, in her view, are preconditions of 'successful commons' and tries to develop a set of criteria for assessing that success. Her focus on the institutions of the commons and her choice to study the commons as systems remained constant throughout her work. This approach marked her research not only on what she calls 'common-pool resources'[2] but also on 'knowledge or information commons'[3]

---

2. Common-pool resources are natural or man-made resource systems that are sufficiently large as to make it costly (but not impossible) to exclude potential beneficiaries from obtaining benefits from their use (Ostrom 1990).

3. 'Knowledge commons' or 'information commons' are human-resource systems such as academic and digital libraries, open-source software or information technology.

(Hess and Ostrom 2007). Although she acknowledges that 'cultural commons', which include knowledge commons, differ from common-pool resources because 'participants not only share existing resources but also engage in producing those resources' (Ostrom 2010: 812), she insists that any study of the commons should be based primarily on modelling (Ostrom 2010). Ostrom acknowledged the fact that when people not only use resources in common but also create them, complexity increases (Ostrom 2010); however, she never delved into precisely defining the challenges that this increased complexity presents.

This analytical focus on the commons as systems of governance or models offered Ostrom a series of analytical advantages. It allowed her to create a robust theory about the rules that an enduring commons should abide by, and it enabled her to claim a degree of universality for some of her scientific outcomes (Ostrom 2009). Furthermore, it enabled her to challenge and reincorporate game theory in the study of action situations, to develop criteria for analytically structuring and separating those situations and, finally, to define a set of rules that could affect them (Ostrom 2010). More importantly, through this focus she was able to arrive at her famous 'Eight Design Principles for Successful Commons', a landmark set of reference guidelines for the study of commons to this day.

Yet, in Ostrom's theory, one can barely find life stories of commoners, detailed accounts of who they are, why they pool resources and labour together, what are their desires, aspirations and needs beyond economic reasoning, and how commoning affects their lives, identities and social relations. Ostrom's approach is profound regarding certain aspects of the commons, that is, institutions, but very superficial about others, that is, motives, affects, aspirations and more. In her own words, 'the essential questions for any commons analysis are inevitably about equity, efficiency, and sustainability' (Ostrom 2007). Therefore, her analysis is useful in approaching management issues but inadequate for exploring the role of the commons in the transformation of individuals, groups, places and societies. The latter requires a shift from the distant systemic view to a 'close-up' perspective that focuses on the subject, a shift from the commons to commoning.

In Ostrom's analysis, it is the resource that poses the question of the common, while commoners are reduced to users who may manage it efficiently or less efficiently. In contrast, the second perspective described earlier presupposes a shift of focus towards the issue of subjectivity and intersubjectivity in the production of the common. The only references to subjects in Ostrom's theoretical framework concern their differences regarding free-riding and altruism. In this respect, she developed a typology of the possible profiles of commons users, where she distinguishes four different categories: (i) those who always behave in a narrow, self-interested way and never cooperate in dilemma situations (free-riders); (ii) those who are unwilling to cooperate with others unless assured that they will not be exploited by free-riders; (iii) those who are willing to initiate reciprocal cooperation in the hopes that others will return their trust; and (iv) perhaps a few genuine altruists who always try to achieve higher returns for a group (Ostrom 1999: 279). Ostrom's subjects are limited to economic reasoning, which is the prevailing issue in her analysis of the commons. This reduces people's motives for commoning to economic incentives.

However, this is not the only problematic aspect of her theory of the subject. An equally important problem is that Ostrom's subjects are clear-cut cases; they are either altruistic or free-riders, while intermediate categories also appear as fixed. These dualisms may be useful when approaching social systems through modelling and calculations, but they are not representative of the real subjects that produce the common. In fact, it is the very theory of rational choice that presupposes fixed identities (Horvath 2015). In real life, though, identities are not predefined, but they are constructed *performatively* in everydayness, through repetitive, habituated and normalized acts (Butler 1997). They never reach a level of completion that may allow us to take them for granted. There are different, contradictory and even opposing 'common senses' that inhabit the subjects of commoning (Garcia, Velicu, and D'Alisa 2017). In the process of commoning, subjectivities should be understood not only as points of departure but also as points of arrival that are susceptible to change.

This static view of the subject in Ostrom's framework is not only problematic from an experiential or an abstractly theoretical point of view, but it also affects the outcomes of the study of any commons. Fixed identities produce specific, predictable social relations; this is never the case in real commons but can exist only in the realm of modelling. For instance, if one assumes that in a commons, by default, certain individuals will always be free-riders, others will always behave altruistically and others yet will always occupy the same intermediate positions, then the commons becomes an ad hoc battlefield. Sealed identities such as those described by Ostrom imply hostility between them, as their rigid borders go 'hand in hand with a description of a potential site of fighting' (Stavrides 2013: 14). This perhaps explains, at least partially, why Ostrom's view on the commons is articulated predominately around sanctions, closed borders and systems of surveillance and not on techniques of communication and further interaction beyond what is essential for resource management.

The point here is not that Ostrom's typology is incorrect, and the aim of this chapter is not to replace Ostrom's model with another. Rather, this chapter aims to *warn against the naturalization of such categorical distinctions and the institutional fixity of subject positions among commoners*. Such subjectifications can – and do – indeed emerge in the process of commoning, but they always reflect particular *spatiotemporal* qualities that emerge in, through and beyond the common production itself, while they always remain incomplete and more often than not contradictory. Such spatiotemporal qualities are highly dependent on the particular kind of commons that we are looking at, the general social context where those commons emerge and evolve, as well as the trajectories of the actual commoners before they decide to participate in the commoning process.

Anti-capitalist commons and the figure of the 'dispossessed'

Previously, I have argued that Ostrom's theory of the subject is inadequate for capturing, first, the multiplicity of the actors of commoning and, second, the internal multiplicity and contradictions that traverse each subject. I will now shift my attention to the commons theories of autonomous Marxists, who may have moved beyond Ostrom's claims of the primacy of economic interest but, as I will argue, still base their commons upon dualistic and foundational oppositions.

Diverging from the mainstream Marxist tradition, autonomous Marxists have replaced the worker with the commoner as the privileged subject of communist transformation (Lieros 2016). In their view of the 'communism of the commons' (Hardt 2011), the commons constitute bottom-up responses to the continuous character of 'primitive accumulation' (see, e.g., De Angelis 2003; 2007; Federici 2010, Caffentzis and Federici 2014) and, therefore, their commoner is primarily associated with the figure of the 'dispossessed'. The dispossessed is an ever-suffering figure, who has developed awareness of the fact that capital accumulation is at the root of the ongoing enclosures and thus creates 'anti-capitalist commons' to counter it (Caffentzis and Federici 2014). Anti-capitalist commons are those that do not primarily produce for the market and are not 'profit-driven'. They are the transformative vehicles that can lead to 'the vision that Marxists and anarchists have aspired to but failed to realize: that of a society made up of "free associations of producers'" (Caffentzis and Federici 2014: 101). However, this image of the ever-suffering 'dispossessed' as the privileged subject of a commons-based communist transformation brings to mind an older aphorism from the *Communist Manifesto*, according to which the workers of this world have nothing to lose but their chains. In reality, historically the workers have had a different opinion and, also, much more than that to lose.

This literature offers a conception of the subject that is also static. It aspires to provide a new ontology of the subject of commoning, and, therefore, it creates this ontology's privileged figure. No doubt, commoners can be – and, to a certain extent, are – people who have been deprived of past rights and resources. My argument, however, is that instead of trying to identify the privileged subjects of commoning, it is worthwhile to focus on how diverse subjects with diverse, contradictory and even opposing traits can enter commoning and on how this affects their imagined, perceived and practised identities. In other words, I am proposing to focus on the mechanism of identity transformation, instead of looking for static criteria of identity affirmation. This discussion, however, cannot take place in abstract terms but requires a focus on particular places and subjects that are in movement and interacting with each other.

Crisis and subjectification

A multidimensional crisis does unfold not only as an aberration, as a deadlock or as an eschatological state of death or rebirth but also as a period that potentially entails a manifold metamorphosis in many dimensions. Within and through crisis, it is not only well-established elements of a particular social structure that are contested – economic configurations, apparatuses of governance, ideologies, anthropological types – but also intersections of them, including the long-standing dualisms upon which this social structure is built.

Crisis deterritorializes subjects from their familiar rigid and closed identity-territory and puts them in a state of suspension or, in other words, a liminal state, in which different and even opposing forces act together. There is no specific mechanism of (trans)formation, no single master of ceremony for the subjects of crisis, only a machinic process of mutual reflection between habits and ideas yet to pass and habits and ideas still to come, characterized by precarity, multiplicity and contradiction.

According to Rancière (1992:61), every process of political subjectification involves what he calls a stage of 'dis-identification' or 'de-classification'. What Rancière perhaps disregards is the fact that within a multidimensional crisis, such a stage of dis-identification may not lead to the production of a new identity, but subjects may remain in the in-between for much longer, sometimes forever. Therefore, the primary subject of a deep and multidimensional crisis is the *de-identified*, the non-subject of suspension that has entered liminality and tries to figure out how to handle it, possibly to take advantage of it and ultimately to evolve by getting rid of it. What is the value of such an observation for the new commons that emerge in and through contexts of crisis?

A discussion of subjectivities and crisis cannot remain at the level of the single human being but should also explore the collective, the social and the spatial dimension. According to David Harvey, 'the relations between 'self' and 'other' from which a certain kind of cognition of social affairs emanates is always [. . .] a spatiotemporal construction' (Harvey 1996:264). Likewise, for Rancière, politics is the process of political subjectification that centres on the rupture with previous subject positions and which has always a spatialized expression (Rancière 1999). Crisis thus does not only deterritorialize humans but also affects spaces, including flows of humans, commodities, infrastructure, land, energy and materials in general; most importantly, it affects the mechanism of space production and also the very way space is conceived and interpreted. Crisis is spatialized, often producing contested spaces, crisis-scapes that are not marked by a predominant identity anymore. Within crisis, it is not only marginal spaces that obtain an interstitial character, in both metropolitan centres and the periphery, but the crisis of spatial identity is transmitted in every possible direction – from the centre to periphery and vice versa. The forms of contestation vary, and contested spaces are not necessarily emancipatory or counter-hegemonic, even though this 'emptiness' also means possibility – at the very least, the possibility of 'some fresh air to breathe that flows through the otherwise asphyxiating landscape of the corporate city' (Brighenti 2013: 17).

Crisis blurs dichotomies, dampens clear-cut dualisms. Crisis reveals that the public and the private – as clearly defined opposing poles within a dichotomy – may have exhausted themselves as valid categories of enquiry in endless dialectical oppositions (Sohn, Kousoulas, and Bruyns 2015). Ideologies are also obfuscated in contexts of crisis. In the elections of 2019 in the European Union, for example, we have witnessed an unprecedented reversion, a blending of discourses and political positions that makes it difficult to figure out to which one of the traditional camps – left wing or right wing – candidates belong.

The implications of the crisis for the very way the commons emerge and evolve, perish or stabilize are profound. First, the massive process of de-identification of great parts of the population through crisis is experienced as a shocking trauma, which may lead either to solitude, depression, collective disappointment and violent reactions or, on the other hand, to the opening of a new 'intermediate' space between the 'I' and the 'we', a space where solidarity and creativity may arise to cure this trauma (Androulidakis 2016). Can this be the same 'we' that claimed 'we are the 99%' during the movement of the squares? Second, the deterritorialization of subjects from their familiar territorial identities, together with the collapse or blurring of clear-cut dichotomies and dualisms, can open new space for negotiation between subjects who were previously unlikely to come together. Third, as both state and market-based solutions to everyday problems – for example, those related to public health and transportation – are proven insufficient due to crisis, emergencies arise. In such situations, commoning is not always a conscious choice or the outcome of a well-thought-out collective decision. Commoning simply happens, and, in many cases, the borders of such emergent communities of commoners are not just blurred but non-existent. Contradiction becomes a core property of these commons.

The Greek memorandum trauma: The 'I' and the 'we' in a time of crisis

The Greek crisis in numbers

At first, the dominant narratives on and explanations of the Greek crisis were macroeconomic and financial, that is, it was viewed as a debt crisis (Hadjimichalis 2011). But as crisis evolved, more qualifiers were added: a crisis of mainstream politics or, as framed by more conservative media, a crisis of values and a humanitarian crisis (Androulidakis 2016). However, the Greek crisis cannot be described in simple terms. It is not simply an economic, social, financial, political, humanitarian and lately health one. It is a multidimensional crisis of everything that previously seemed *self-evident*, and, in this respect, it is an existential crisis (Androulidakis 2016).

3. Liminal Subjects of Commoning 55

In economic terms, the country's depression is the greatest ever faced by a developed nation, especially after the Second World War.[4] Even though it is difficult to express in quantitative terms the grim reality of the Greek population or the multidimensionality and depth of the 'crisis effect' in the country, I will list here some impressive economic and social indicators that demonstrate the amplitude of the phenomenon. In 2013, three years after the first memorandum,[5] 1.4 million Greeks were unemployed, 27.5 per cent of the total workforce, up from 7.2 per cent in 2007 (Matsaganis 2013). While the Hellenic Statistical Authority announced that in 2017 the unemployment rate had slightly decreased to 23.2, the General Confederation of Greek Workers stated that the actual unemployment rate was above 30 per cent on that year (The Press Project 2017). For 18 to 25-year-olds, unemployment increased from an already record-high 36.6 per cent in 2009 to 65 per cent in 2013 (EL.STAT 2009, 2013). Around 450,000 families had no working members in 2014 (Insurgenta Iskra 2014). For those that do have a job, things are not much better: the median monthly gross wage fell from €1,997 in 2009 to €1,048 in 2015 (EL.STAT 2015). Minimum salaries declined from €751.5 in 2009 to €586.1 in 2013 (Vaiou 2014) while in reality even this historical minimum is often violated. VAT increased from 9 per cent and 13 per cent to 24 per cent, while taxes on property,

---

4. Greece's peak-to-trough decline of GDP by 33 per cent (and still falling) is worse than the 27 per cent decline in the United States during the most acute phase of the Great Depression.

5. Rather than a direct effect of GDP decline, Greece's great depression is the outcome of austerity policies implemented to deal with public debt. Public debt increased from €141 billion in 2000 to €263 billion in 2008, yet, as late as 2008, international institutions were praising Greece for its economic performance. This was a debt-fuelled growth (Lapavitsas 2012). After 2008, a period of repetitive recessions commenced, increasing the cost of borrowing and rendering Greece's debt unsustainable. Unable to borrow from the private bond market, Greek governments reached a series of agreements ('memorandums') with the 'Troika' of institutions (EU, IMF and the European Central Bank) which led to austerity and cuts in public services (e.g. 36 per cent cuts in education). On average, pensions were reduced by 30 per cent and salaries in the public sector by 20–35 per cent (Hadjimichalis 2013). Public expenditure decreased, but because of the decline in economic activity caused by austerity, the debt kept growing and new debt was simply used to service old debt and interest.

including small property, increased by 514 per cent between 2010 and 2014 (EL.STAT 2014). On account of the above, the purchasing power of wage earners plummeted by 37.2 per cent (Vaiou 2014). City dwellers cannot even meet their basic needs, the number of homeless people had skyrocketed (Kaika 2012) and some 145,000 children faced food insecurity and hunger (PROLEPSIS 2013; Insurgenta Iskra 2014). One-third of the total population faced some sort of mental disorder (Androulidakis 2016). The number of suicides had increased by 62.3 per cent between 2007 and 2011 (EL.STAT 2012); almost half of those committing suicide in 2012 were economically inactive (Insurgenta Iskra 2014). Cases of major clinical depression increased by 248 per cent between 2009 and 2011 (Economou et al. 2013), while Athens has been called the 'City of Xanax' by parts of the mainstream press (LIFO 2016). Social cohesion is not simply threatened; it has completely broken down. And all of these changes preceded the pandemic of Covid-19, whose impacts on Greek society are not examined in this book and are yet to be explored.

How have all these rapid changes affected the Greeks?

The dominant social imaginary before the crisis

Any attempt at describing changes at the national level is risky and necessarily involves sweeping generalizations. Besides, a comprehensive description of the intricacies of the Greek social imaginary in different historical phases is beyond the scope of this book. Instead, I aim to selectively depict some historical aspects of the dominant social imaginary that are relevant to the arguments of this effort, focusing only on the period of Greek history known as *Metapolitefsi*.[6] My goal is not to describe any unifying Greek identity, as there is no such thing; rather, it is to provide the reader with background information on pre-crisis Greek society based on existing literature, to offer insight on what has been affected by the crisis and how.

Greece has been a subordinated country throughout its modern history (Androulidakis 2016). After the fall of the military junta in 1974, a project of large-scale transformation of Greek society was set in motion. This project was traversed by diverse and contradictory

---

6. The period starting with the fall of the military junta in 1974 and ending with the outburst of the economic crisis and the subordination of the country to the Troika in 2010.

tendencies. On the one hand, a process of democratization led to the emergence of a series of innovative institutions in Greek society. The institutionalization of equal rights between men and women, the legalization of communist parties, the extension of the right to vote to everyone over eighteen and the effort to reduce economic equality and create a Greek version of the welfare state introduced new social imaginary significations in the country, such as equality, freedom of expression and independence.

Yet, many aspects of the older prevailing social imaginary maintained their potency. Patriarchy, sexism, nationalism and racism were intertwined with Greek particularities, such as the predominance of the family as the basic socioeconomic unit and the hegemonic role of the Orthodox Church in social and political life (Tsiganou 1999; Papageorgiou 2017).

At the political level, the tendency towards radical politicization prevalent during the dictatorship years gave its place to a paradoxical political behaviour that combined high participation in electoral and pre-electoral politics with increasing individualization (Demertzis 1994). This occurred because politics became the sole means of securing and developing the economic and symbolic status of the individual and the family (Demertzis 1994). Politics thus was reduced to a bidding competition between the two large parties, PASOK and New Democracy. The state was reinforced in this process, but only as a redistributive mechanism that guaranteed the preservation of economic privileges of individuals and families (Demertzis 1994).

During the early 1990s, a project of modernization took place that altered the Greek social imaginary at large. Its main elements were the introduction of casino capitalism centred on the stock market, the imperative of economic growth and the effort to transform the country into a leading economic power in the Balkans (Douzinas 2013; Androulidakis 2016). Economic efficiency became the new mantra not only in the discourse of economists and entrepreneurs but also in the day-to-day life of ordinary people. The level of individualistic utilitarianism had increased so dramatically during those two decades that 51 per cent of the Greek population stated that they were unwilling to reduce their consumption levels even if this was necessary for the sustenance of future generations (Androulidakis 2016).

In brief, before the crisis, the social imaginary in Greece consisted of a mixture of newer and older social imaginary significations. Despite its incorporation in the European Union in 1981, in terms of its social imaginary Greece continues to be in-between the West and the East

(Herzfeld 2002). While liberal significations such as gender equality, freedom of expression, individual and national independence were introduced, traditional ones such as the family, orthodox religion, patriarchy, sexism and racism not only persist but, to a great extent, prevail over the newer ones (Tsiganou 1999; Papageorgiou 2017). In the collective imagination, the state has a central and instrumental role as a guarantor of economic prosperity. Political parties remain an important source of identification for the people (Androulidakis 2016). Economic growth and efficiency have become the milestones of this new social imaginary (Androulidakis 2016), and human prosperity is identified with the commandment for 'mandatory pleasure' (Douzinas 2013: 34) based on individual material consumerism. The previous collective representation of the country as suffering and subordinated is combined with its new representation as 'an economic tiger'[7] in the Balkan region, which reaches its peak with the organization of the 2004 Olympic Games in Athens.

The first cracks

Although the beginning of the Greek crisis is commonly associated with the signing of the 2010 bailout agreement, the first indications of a looming generalized crisis could be found long before the debt crisis (Dalakoglou 2013; Varvarousis and Kallis 2017). The 1999 stock market crash, when more than 100 billion euros were transferred from small investors to bigger ones, was the first major signal. The ensuing Olympic Games of 2004 with their grandiose construction projects and the continuation of housing speculation managed to maintain the hedonistic way of life for a few more years. At the same time, the benefits from the early 2000s growth were not evenly distributed (Kaplanis 2011; Dalakoglou 2013); the term '700 euros generation' was coined before 2008 to describe young university graduates with no access to well-paid jobs (Dalakoglou 2013). The number of undocumented immigrants soared and became a new source of inequality (Dalakoglou 2013; Hadjimichalis 2013). The last act in the supposed economic miracle of the 2000s modernization project was based on credit expansion, cheap migrant labour, the construction of public works and a real estate bubble (Kaplanis 2011). Socio-spatial inequalities

7. https://www.thepressproject.gr/article/62453/The-tigers-that-became-PIGS-and-the-new-plan-for-growth.

emerged with unprecedented intensity in the urban centres of Athens and Thessaloniki (Dalakoglou 2013). During the Olympic Games and in their wake, public space surveillance and control were intensified and very often led to extensive violations of the 'right to the city' (Lefebvre 1968; Harvey 2009; Petropoulou 2010). The rising demand for spaces of free expression, mainly on the part of the younger generation, was increasingly met with the intervention of armed riot police forces, which were often provocative (Petropoulou 2010).

In December 2008, the simmering social discontent came to a boiling point in the student-anarchist neighbourhood of Exarcheia in Athens (Vradis and Dalakoglou 2011), when a policeman murdered a high school student. In Athens and over sixty more Greek cities a revolt erupted and a long period of clashes with the police ensued (Hadjimichalis 2013). The increasingly inequitable and controlled urban space became both the site and the stake of the conflict (Stavrides 2013a). The December 2008 revolt evolved into a confrontational anti-modernization movement. The conservative government responded with new and more brutal crackdowns by the police and intensification of surveillance (Fillipidis 2011; Dalakoglou 2013).

The 2008 revolt was perceived in different ways by different parts of society. The fear cultivated by the media and mainstream politicians in their effort to denounce the events as antisocial was indicative of the distress of the dominant system (Douzinas 2013). On the other hand, the violent clashes in the streets gave rise to a series of collective practices that previously were marginal. If we follow Castells (1983) definition of urban social movements as movements that seek to give new meaning to urban space, the 2008 revolt was perhaps the first enduring social movement with such characteristics in contemporary Greek history.[8] As an enduring urban social movement, the revolt gave rise to diverse practices of urban commoning.

It is in this crisis context that a heterogeneous 'we', different than the 'I' predominant in the previous period, started to emerge (see also Stavrides 2013). The December 2008 revolt was not a politically neutral movement. After the initial clashes, the main body of activists was entrenched behind the gates of three university occupations (Varvarousis and Kallis 2017) of far-left or anarchist character. Hence, the gates acted as checkpoints

---

8. Similar characteristics had already been noted in previous more contentious mobilizations, such as the ones in protest of the Attica wildfires in 2007, but their endurance was not so great in comparison to the events of 2008.

that both symbolically and physically controlled who could be part of the movement and who could not. On the other hand, the centrality of urban space in the revolt created the opposite tendency. Urban space was not only the setting of the social movement but also one of the stakes (Stavrides 2013). However, this was not enough. As urban space became the main stake of a movement with an anti-hierarchical orientation based on the principles of self-organization and autonomy, urban space often became a temporal commons, simultaneously acting as a source of belonging. That belonging was different than the one denoted by the concept 'collective identity', as the latter signifies a 'we-ness' that resorts to a shared definition of the group, either pre-existing or constructed in and through collective protest (Taylor and Whittier 1992; Polletta and Jasper 2001). As the actors of the revolt themselves put it, 'we are simply those who have shared the streets and occupations of December.'[9]

Of course, this 'simply' is not accurate. Not everybody was able to participate in the events of the revolt; the revolt itself found limited approval among Greeks and was constantly disparaged by powerful institutions. However, it was through the revolt that the commons-related slogan 'self-organization in every neighbourhood' first appeared with intensity in many different places, in both Athens and beyond. Self-organization materialized in a series of projects that had commoning at their heart. Open local assemblies, new squats, occupied urban spaces and other more precarious forms of commoning appeared. According to Attika's Observatory of Free Spaces, free spaces were doubled during 2008 and early 2009 (Petropoulou 2010). Despite the ideological and political prevalence of anarchism and leftism, at the organizational level, the commoning experiments of December 2008 and its aftermath were characterized by a culture of negotiation, openness and inclusiveness, which, however limited, was much more prevalent than before. Whereas to that moment the Greek squatting movement regarded squats as 'springboards' or non-alienated liberated strongholds from where to launch political attacks against the alienated rest of society (Tsavdaroglou 2016), the projects started during and after the revolt were marked by the primacy of socio-spatial connections and negotiations over identarian mismatches. Back in 2008, this was an important innovation for the country.

In addition to this relative organizational openness, the 2008 revolt marked a major disruption of the normality brought on by three decades of political and social stability and economic prosperity (Goutsos and

---

9. Declaration of the Skaramaga occupation at 61, Patision (2009).

3. Liminal Subjects of Commoning   61

Polymeneas 2014). The break with normality was a core demand of the revolt; this was manifested in many ways, a detailed description of which is beyond the scope of this chapter. 'No Justice, No Peace'; 'No control'; 'Merry Crisis and Happy New Fear'; 'Discipline is over: Magic Life'; 'Fuck May '68, Fight now'; 'The Road to Normality is closed ... due to Revolt'; 'Death to Bourgeois culture, The War has started' – these were some of the main slogans of the revolt, graffitied on Athenian walls. The anti-modernization movement was an anti-normalization scream – in terms of Holloway (2005) – of the young generation. On the one hand, the revolt can be regarded merely as an attack of a particular oppressed social group against the oppressive status quo. But since – as Victor Turner has argued – crisis is contagious, that revolt announced and celebrated crisis; as manifested by the slogan 'Merry Crisis' mentioned earlier, the revolt was meant to affect various directions. It was not simply a unidirectional infection (from the rebellious youth to the conformist rest of society), but it also allowed 'unauthorized' encounters and broke the pre-existing protocol of collective action in activist circles. The December 2008 revolt inaugurated a perplexing period of contradictions, a liminal period.

The intensification of the economic downturn in 2009 and 2010 spread the crisis to wider parts of society. The 'memorandum trauma' opened a new plateau between the self-referential 'I' of the period of modernization and an ever-problematic and unstable collective 'we'. This intermediate plateau was the space where the tensions of 'what has been lost' met the aspirations of 'what can be next'. This period, thus, was marked by a collective effort at the level of the entire population to rethink their cosmos in material, organizational and symbolic terms. A period of suspension and crisis is inhabited by subjects in suspension and transition, liminal subjects. Perhaps the new commons created during the 2008 revolt shared certain attributes with the liminal commons described in the introduction; however, due to their destabilized but still strong political identity, they cannot be categorized as such. In any case, those commons were precursors of the liminal commons of the indignant squares, which ensued.

The liminal commons of occupied squares

The first rally

On May 25, the first mass rally was held in Syntagma Square, organized spontaneously through social media as a response to a banner in a Spanish indignant square that read, 'Be careful, don't wake up the Greeks!'. 'We are awake' was the answer. Around 200,000 people attended, without any central organization (Hadjimichalis 2013). Some three million people were involved in the squares in varying degrees during the three-month occupation; this represents an impressive one-third of the entire Greek population. The movement was not limited to Athens but spread to more than forty cities throughout Greece.[10] While the term *aganaktismenoi* ('indignant') was used in the first call for protest on May 25 – mainly due to its relation with the Spanish 'indignados' – its use was the subject of debate since the very beginning of the movement. Shortly after their initial publication of the call, the administrators of the Facebook page clarified that 'the word "indignant" is not connected with a particular repertoire of actions'. On the contrary, they declared since the very beginning that 'our aim is to protest peacefully and spontaneously'.[11] As my informants Georgia, Evgenia, Christos and Konstantinos all mentioned, 'aganaktismenoi (indignant) was not a term widely accepted in everyday talks or the general assembly, although it was occasionally being used'. The term *apofasismenoi* ('determined') was also used (Goutsos and Polymeneas 2014).

Very soon, however, 'the movement of the squares' became the real name of the movement, while the term 'indignants' was used mainly by the mainstream media and all those who tried to reduce the movement to a mere expression of indignation by a middle class that has lost its former privileges. The space of the squares became not only the setting of the movement but also its actual 'essence' and at the same time the 'glue' that kept people together throughout the three months of occupation. The term 'square' became a synonym for the mobilization and an all-encompassing notion that symbolized the alternative reality created in Athens after May 2011. 'There was only one square in Athens', says Georgia referring to this period. Space became the first and foremost source of identification for the movement (Goutsos and Polymeneas 2014); phrases such as 'we are those who are here' and 'the squares are us' were commonly heard both in informal discussions and in assemblary procedures.

The common space

Since the beginning, the movement of the squares unfolded as a space-commoning project. On the first day, after the majority of the crowd

---

10. 'Vima' Newspaper, 19/06/2011.
11. My translation from Greek.

had left, some protesters decided to stay in the square overnight rather than end the occupation. On the second day, some people decided to form the first groups that would facilitate and organize the incipient collective activities of this alternative day-to-day life. The first groups formed were the artist group and the general organizational desk; many followed in the next few days. Initially, the initiative for setting up such groups was taken by a small group of people. Some of them were already prepared for this, as a group of people associated with the 'Zeitgeist' movement had been trying to promote the occupation of Syntagma for three or four months before the actual encampment in May. As Giorgos, a man in his early forties, told me: 'Don't think that there was no preparation for this. I was at the Zeitgeist Movement, and we had set up an information desk at Syntagma since the previous winter.'

Over the next few days, a tent city was erected, followed by the introduction of new everyday rituals. Some of the new groups focused their organizational efforts on covering basic needs, offering first aid, facilitating communication or being the 'mouthpiece' of the movement on the web and social media. Some others had a more theoretical focus and concentrated on producing political texts or providing a space for discussion on a series of issues. Others yet were formed to enable free expression, to promote artistic activities or purely for recreation purposes. Some of those groups were more enduring and persisted throughout the three-month occupation, while others appeared and disappeared in a matter of hours. A few of them are still active today, ten years after the encampment!

It would be impossible to offer a precise account of the common infrastructure set up in the square since it was rapidly changing over time. What I am offering here is an indicative image of what I believe is a characteristic moment.

At the centre of the lower part of the square, there was a big medical tent with all the standard equipment for offering first aid: beds, oxygen, teargas masks, medicine and, of course, doctors. At another spot, there was the social kitchen, in which volunteers were cooking meals. Supplies for the social kitchen came mainly through donations; a placard characteristically read, 'we need food because a hungry bear does not struggle.'[12] At another spot, there was an exchange bazaar with books, clothes and other stuff. An area with laptops and other technological

---

12. It is a humoristic take on the popular Greek adage 'a hungry bear does not dance'.

equipment, named 'technical support centre', was also created. The artist group set up its own space as well. Other groups whose activity did not require specific infrastructure either were nomadic or simply communicated their meeting place through a poster. A handwritten sign detailed all the different groups and their meeting times, which were usually between 11.00 am and 6.00 pm. There were several groups, and some were not very stable. Some of the groups are listed here indicatively: the artist group, the social kitchen, the cleaning commission, the technical support group, the multimedia group, the translation commission, the legal support group, the protection commission, the time bank, the commission for the unemployed, the eco-village commission, the direct democracy commission, the social solidarity group and the health centre. The cleaning commission was intentionally dissolved by the decision of the general assembly, and the task of cleaning the square every night was assigned to everyone using it (Papapavlou 2015).

Besides the infrastructure used for group gatherings, the tent city consisted of more or less stable places of habitation. Tents for one, two or more people were put up peripherally and diagonally from the central infrastructure. The people living there also put hammocks, seats and even carpets and other furniture typically found in the realm of the private. The square was transformed into an open neighbourhood. To a certain extent, people tried to reproduce the everyday rituals usually taking place in private houses, albeit in ways that were often overcoming privacy and its associated social relations. The making of morning coffee or the cooking of a meal brought together people unknown to each other. At night, people were coming together to drink, discuss, sing and dance in smaller or bigger groups. Common space was secreted (Stavrides 2013) everywhere.

While practically oriented groups were active throughout the day, the more political ones, organized around various themes, generally met after 6.00 pm in various places across the square. In principle, group discussions had continuity, as the agenda of each day was, as a rule, defined the day before (Papapavlou 2015). As Konstantinos, a member of the education commission told me: 'In the beginning, we had a general discussion about the current education system. Then we started building a discussion with a specific flow. The first goal that we set was to prevent "survivalism" (επιβιωτισμός) from dominating the discussion. Then we expanded the agenda to how we imagine education and to other issues.'

The general assembly was held every day at 9.00 pm and most of the days lasted until midnight when the metro closes in Athens; it had an overarching albeit non-binding character for other commissions and groups. During the three-month occupation, turnout ranged from several thousand people in May and June to a few dozen in August. The general assembly was entrusted with many tasks, ranging from practical and organizational issues to broader political and even philosophical ones. The process was highly ritualized, and despite the volatile environment of the square, it operated as a point of reference that remained stable even under extreme circumstances. The exact procedure of the general assembly has been described in detail by scholars (see, e.g., Papapavlou 2015: 143–50 and Mitropoulos 2011: 62–74) and need not be repeated here. The important elements I want to stress here are as follows: first, the assembly was – at least in theory – open to everybody; all participants were able to not only speak but also coordinate and facilitate the process. Second, many participants adopted the hand gestures and other elements used in the equivalent processes of Madrid and Barcelona. Third, decisions were taken by vote; in case of equal votes between the alternatives, the decision was postponed until the next day. Fourth, the assembly was supported through various other commoning mechanisms of the square (e.g. food from the social kitchen) as it was considered the crossroads where all other commoning procedures intersected.

Syntagma Square became the real epicentre of the incipient commoning practices in the city. However, the common space of the square was not an isolated 'island' in the urban fabric. A series of popular assemblies were independently meeting in various Athenian neighbourhoods and subsequently sharing their conversations and outcomes at the general assembly of Syntagma Square. In turn, the outcomes of the general assembly fed back to the neighbourhood assembly, without binding it. Some of those assemblies were first convened during the events of 2011. Other assemblies, such as the 'Koukakiou-Thisiou-Petralonon' or 'Holargos', were reactivated after a period of inactivity on the basis of the popular assemblies formed during the 2008 revolt.[13] These assemblies became what we can call 'peripheral lungs' for the central occupation, breathing out their particularities and local perspectives into the central stage and reciprocally receiving 'material' back to the local level. This gradually evolved into a fluid and unstable network of interconnected commoning projects that were

13. In 2011, I was actively participating in the former, while during the 2008 revolt in the latter.

dispersed throughout the metropolitan space. This 'rhizome' (Deleuze and Guattari 2012 [1988]; Varvarousis and Kallis 2017) had no stable structure and was not characterized by the typical centre–periphery relation, in which practices in the periphery are regarded as 'annexes' of those in the centre. Every node of the rhizome was independent of others, yet all together constituted the common fabric of the movement. A process of decentralization–recentralization[14] of commoning flows developed in Athens in this period, one that resembles what Raul Zibechi (2010) has described in reference to recent social movements in Latin America.

The human composition and the diverse repertoires of action

Given the fact that millions of people passed through the square during the three-month occupation, any attempt to describe the human composition is either overly generalizing and thus analytically meaningless or piecemeal and thus incomplete. Different types of people of every age, social strata, political background and aesthetic preferences gathered in the square: everyone was welcome to be at Syntagma for longer or shorter periods, as a passer-by or as an everyday participant. The occupation was the most inclusive event in contemporary Greek history (Papapavlou 2015).

A look at the surveys published in this period is indicative of the diverse and perplexing reality of the movement. The percentage of participants aligned with left-wing ideologies was similar to the percentage of those aligned with the right wing and of those who declared 'no ideology' (Simiti 2015). According to Karamichas (2012), the vast majority of participants (81 per cent) were not previously 'activists': in the five years before 2011, they had participated less than five times in any kind of demonstration. For many (43 per cent), this was their first mobilization ever. Political organizations and parties were also present in the square, albeit discreetly, without manifesting their political identities. According to the ethnographic findings of Papapavlou (2015), the occupation of Syntagma contradicts conventional wisdom in social movement studies, which posits that in any social movement those who have greater experience become the most active participants. The study also contradicts academic analyses of Syntagma that emphasize

---

14. Or deterritorialization–reterritorialization in Deleuze and Guattari's terminology.

the central role of radical left activists (primarily Syriza and Antarsya) during the encampment (e.g. Hadjimichalis 2013; Karaliotas 2016). Unlike Spain and other instances of the Occupy movement worldwide, the Greek movement was characterized by diverse tendencies, as well as different and often oppositional political projects that unfolded simultaneously at the square (Simiti 2015). There is a long discussion on the 'two Syntagma Squares', the upper and the lower one (Karaliotas 2016; Hadjimichalis 2013; Vradis 2011; Leontidou 2012). In many accounts, this separation is presented as an absolute one. The lower square is portrayed as an 'equalibertarian' stage characterized by a 'left-wing, anti-authoritarian and anarchist politics' (Karaliotas 2016: 9) while the upper square is portrayed as the 'stage of the ethnos' where a nationalistic and xenophobic discourse based on 'Greekness' was deployed (Karaliotas 2016; Hadjimichalis 2013). Likewise, the politics of the upper square are presented as a form of collective verbal abuse (Sotirakopoulos and Sotiropoulos 2013) or as conventional politics (Vradis 2011), which, by evoking an alleged 'glorious past', often demanded a stronger and more effective state (Simiti 2015: 9). In contrast, the prevailing narrative on the lower square is that its politics embodied the claim for a radical change in the system of governance at large (e.g. Vradis 2011).

However, the landscape at Syntagma was extremely fluid, and the repertoires of action of different groups were not subject to such an absolute separation. In many cases, the two squares were diffused into one another. This happened in various ways. On demonstration days, everyone was moving from one part to the other, and when the police forces were attacking the square, the people were defending not just their part but the square as a whole. As many people and small groups were spending many hours or even days at the occupation, their desires on what to do were also in flux. In several cases, after finishing a discussion with their thematic commission at the lower part, small groups of participants were moving to the upper part, just to have a look and to shout out slogans. As Giorgos, who sporadically participated in the direct democracy group as well as in other groups, said: 'At night, the upper square was sometimes freaky and other times funny. I was annoyed by some practices, but on the other hand, I enjoyed going there to have a beer with friends and just shout.' The opposite also happened; people who adopted the discourse of the upper square tried to adapt themselves to the rules and procedures of the general assembly. On May 31, the general assembly decided to make the issue explicit, and proposals were made for the establishment of mechanisms for connecting protesters between the upper and the lower part. In short, the accounts that emphasize the divergences and differentiation among protesters at the square are valid. However, I find it more fruitful to examine how and to what extent those polarized attitudes managed to coexist and perhaps influence one other.

The role of liminality for subjects

Why did all those different people stay in the square for so long? How did people, despite their deep differences and oppositions, manage to share the space and jointly produce such a rich and enduring alternative everyday life? Why didn't this heterogeneity lead to violent conflicts, as was often the case in the Greek context in the past (Leontidou 2012)?

'Syntagma was inhabited by the in-between of people' (Papapavlou 2015: 149). The main aim of this chapter is to explore the role of liminality in the formation of the subjects of commoning, as well as the role of common space more generally. Liminality is a tool for conceptualizing the condition of 'in-betweenness', mentioned by Papapavlou in the quote earlier. However, it is important to clarify what kind of 'in-betweenness' liminality refers to. My argument is that at least *three types of in-betweenness* can be identified, both in public discourse and in academic literature: hybridity, interstitiality and liminality. Their differences have not been adequately theorized. *Hybridity* signifies the coexistence of different elements, cultures and identities in a single person, group or even society (Bhabha 1994). This coexistence is usually regarded as peaceful, and the role of power and conflict is underestimated. The in-between is a neutral space that accommodates differences. *Interstitiality* in Brighenti's words (2013) signifies 'emptiness'. It is the condition of in-betweenness that is the outcome of an uncompleted process of identification and characterization. Interstitial is the subject or the space that has been left out of the identification and taxonomization process and thus has not been identified yet. *Liminality*, instead, is the product of a negation, inversion, destabilization or even dissolution of a structured entity, such as a personal, collective or spatial identity. In contrast to the other two forms of in-betweenness, liminality is associated with temporality and transition.

In her work on the Occupy movements, Judith Butler notices that the objectives of the people gathered in different assemblies across the world vary, and thus no theorist can come up with a single account based on any discursive or pre-discursive reasoning (Butler 2015).

However, what she seems to identify as the connecting tissue between the participants in the squares movement is the exercise of 'a plural and performative right to appear' in public (Butler 2015: 11). As she points out, in the current biopolitical condition, 'precaritization' becomes the predominant modus operandi of contemporary society, and this heavily affects the psychic reality of the 'people' (Butler 2015: 11).

Through the project of modernization explained earlier, individualistic utilitarianism had become a basic element of the psychic reality of modern Greeks. Individualism, however, often coincides with the demand for personal responsibility, which, in this context, means that any and all outcomes are attributed exclusively to the individual. In the course of neoliberalism, however, this self-reliance is not materialized through a process of self-reflection and an effort to increase self-esteem but is based on an entrepreneurial conception of the self, which is measured by economic standards and criteria of market success and failure. Thus, in periods of widespread economic prosperity, this competitive isolation is often experienced as a personal reward for the risks taken by the person. On the other hand, in periods of widespread economic recession, it can be experienced as a personal failure, leading to heightened anxiety, fear and an intense destabilization of one's identity.

It is against this background that I am proposing to examine the alternative everydayness of Syntagma. Crisis had destabilized the subjects and their mechanisms and sources of identification. While a mass of youngsters and other underprivileged social groups such as migrants had undergone a similar process leading up to the 2008 revolt, in 2011 many more social groups were added. The statistics of crisis and economic degradation previously presented are striking: bosses and managers became unemployed; the middle-class shrunk; petit-bourgeois and small entrepreneurs returned to their family home to live off the pension of their parents; women suffered the most loss and oppression (Vaiou 2014). Those who had embraced – to a lesser or greater degree – the culture of the entrepreneurial self saw the very source of their existence vanish.

This destabilized reality was one of the central characteristics of the Syntagma encampment. The most emphatic examples were the placards reading 'we are nobody' and 'we do not like where we are going, but we will not go back', as well as the extended use of the Guy Fawkes' 'anonymous' mask, which became a symbol of protest not only in Syntagma but also in other countries. However, these insights can only superficially capture the reality of the squares. Everyday life in the square was full of images revealing a perplexed and destabilized social imaginary. In June, in a demonstration I attended with friends, I was a witness to confrontations with the riot police at a street near Syntagma, at the nearby Kolonaki district, one of the richest in the city. At some point, a group of anarchist-looking hooded youngsters tried to storm the police forces. A lady in her late forties dressed in expensive clothes and golden jewellery joined them and started to punch a policeman's shield with anger. When things calmed down, I found the opportunity to ask her how she came to attack the police. She answered, 'I have become like you, who do you think I am?.' In another informal discussion at the square, I met Nikos, a guy in his fifties who used to come to the square almost every day to help with the organization of various tasks. At some point, I managed to talk to him, and he told me his story:

> Once, I had a good job with a company, but now I am unemployed. I felt fear and desperation; my life was shaken. [...] I came to Syntagma just because I was very bored at home, watching TV without knowing exactly why. [...] I am a very active person, and I cannot just sit around. I kept coming every day until the end of July. There were many people like me at the square.

The process of de-identification and deterritorialization of the subjects sometimes took the form of an intentional negation and at other times the form of a forced negation. Some people were feeling ashamed about their previous choices and lifestyles, and this was reflected in their ways of expressing themselves, both in conversations with others and in the general assembly. 'I am ashamed to belong to the generation that brought Greece to this mess', said someone at the public assembly. 'You betrayed our past', some protesters in the upper square were shouting. While every phrase and every word can be interpreted in many ways, and such statements can signify different things for different people, together they weaved the reality of the squares: a perplexing reality. I had the chance to share this reality with a good friend who defines himself as an 'amateur anthropologist'. He did not miss a day of the movement. He used to say:

> I go there every day because the connections I see there are unbelievable. I am so happy that this is finally happening. Before the crisis, I felt uncertain about who I am, and I believed that I was the only one to feel that way. This made me think of myself as an alien. Now I see that everyone is like me, and I feel much more comfortable.

How does this destabilization of identity relate to commoning?

The rapid precaritization, to which Butler refers, brings about the destabilization of people's identities and beliefs. While this may create anxiety and fear, at the same time it motivates people to seek solutions to overcome the fear. This condition implies some sort of vulnerability. In her reflection on the events of the squares, Athanasiou (2014) argues that people in Syntagma were indeed seeking to remain vulnerable. By 'vulnerability', however, she does not refer to 'individual passivity but rather to the abiding potentiality of being affected, in the sense of both susceptibility to regimes of power and relational openness to others' (Athanasiou 2014: 3). It is exactly this 'openness to others' – as well as a generalized openness to otherness – that allows practices of commoning to flourish in conditions of crisis. Commoning in this sense does not only signify the forms of solidarity that emerge among individuals in the process of occupying and maintaining an ephemeral urban common space; it also signifies an exploratory shift away from individualism and the beginning of an experimental practice that understands individual well-being as part and parcel of the broader social well-being.

In this context, liminality is not only reflected in the personal perceptions and lives of individuals, but it is also inscribed in social and spatial relations and becomes the glue that allows people to interact and exchange as equals. Liminal subjects, thus, are not only those who have lost their sources of identification but also those who have lost their affiliation with sources of relative power and hierarchization. This is why commoning can appear like a viable solution for managing such periods. This was known by anthropologists who studied liminal situations, and this is the essence of 'communitas' in Victor Turner's work. Due to their ambiguity and vulnerability, liminal subjects are more open to new experiences, more willing to get involved in practices to which they were previously unaccustomed or even hostile. Liminality, thus, is associated not only with fear, anxiety and desperation but also with experimentation and creativity.

More than 2,000 individuals were registered with the Syntagma Square TimeBank within the first days of its operation. More than 650 people joined the artist group at the square (Papapavlou 2015). I heard the term 'creative orgasm' dozens of times throughout my stay at the square, and many people were repeating during the general assembly and other public discussions that what happens at the squares is simply 'magic'. People rallied to Syntagma to make their existence visible, but also to meet others, to share their concerns and to overcome and socialize their fear. 'Fear? What fear? It is gone', read an unsigned placard. Likewise, after the projection of a video of a self-presentation of different groups and commissions active on the square, one viewer comments: 'I feel more human than ever; thank you for showing me that I am not alone in this situation [. . .] a more humane society is cultivated in Syntagma every day and gradually proliferates all over Greece.'

The capacity of liminality to promote commoning is contagious. This implies that it is not necessary for potential subjects of commoning to have faced themselves the traumatic experience of being forcefully deterritorialized, as the widespread destabilization upends everything, to varying degrees. In other words, while liminality is a condition that stems from negation and destabilization of identity, subsequently it becomes *a practice* and gives birth to a generalized culture of putting aside existing differences and establishing connections among them. Liminality promotes patience, mutual respect, negotiation and tolerance.

These elements were the cornerstone of the experience of the Syntagma encampment. The most obvious examples can be found in the very practices employed in the general assembly and the rest of the groups and commissions. 'We are all responsible for the square', 'we do not deprecate or revile the speakers', 'the assembly should be tolerant' were some of the most repeated phrases with which the facilitators urged people to respect others. The use of the aforementioned hand gestures to express agreement and disagreement was indicative of this culture too. While these tools were not used spontaneously but were introduced by people who had experience in facilitation and had connections with other Occupy movements,[15] their wide acceptance for the first time in Greece was characteristic of this new culture. It is also noteworthy that, despite the coexistence of diverse and even oppositional discourses at the square, violent conflicts between protesters were avoided (Leontidou 2012). The existence of a specific team assigned with mediating and diffusing any arising conflicts just confirms this tendency.

> This culture that emphasizes common ideas over differences and seeks to align the individual with the collective can best be observed at the molecular level, that of interactions among individuals and within groups. In 2011, Konstantinos was a student of political sciences and an active member of the education group. He was a

---

15. From an interview with members of Amnesty International.

member of a radical left political organization and was used to the harsh antagonism among left parties, common at Greek universities. About the operation of the education group, he mentions:

> It was impressive how different our interaction with other political groups was at Syntagma. Of course, we were there as blocks, and we still wanted to influence the procedures and announcements of the education group. However, the process was open. We were forced to open up and discuss in a different, more respectful way, both with the people and with those who were our political opponents before.

For Maria, a humanitarian worker who used to live in London, people with an NGO background played a crucial role in the organization of this new and open form of discussion and decision-making; this is something that has been totally silenced in the literature on the movement of the squares. The presence of different people with diverse skills and experiences was a new phenomenon, as to that point the dominant culture within the Greek social movements had been one of tough competition between the different radical left and anarchist actors. At the level of regular and everyday interactions, one could also observe a similar tendency towards respect and sharing. It is indicative of such spirit that at moments in which the crowd density at the square was high, people would ask those nearby for permission to smoke.[16] In a country where the law against smoking in public spaces had been ignored in practice for more than one decade, this was a notable change.

The ontology and operation of the liminal commons

Liminal commons develop in the 'in-between' of the people and constitute a field in which gestures towards otherness are not only desirable but also necessary. This happens because liminal commons develop in highly heterogeneous environments. Crisis is both a constitutive and a constituent element of these commons, as liminality becomes the prerequisite and the outcome of their operation. In contrast to commons built around a specific resource to be managed or to commons created as forms of production and reproduction against capital accumulation, liminal commons are mainly created to facilitate transitions. In other words, liminal commons *are not ends* in themselves,

---

16. Mentioned also by Papapavlou.

but they are *passages* towards other more stable structures. Despite their precarity, however, liminal commons can produce outcomes at many different levels, such as the social, the political and the cultural.

The people involved in the Syntagma encampment created a common space to gather, to interact, to protest, but most importantly to explore solutions on what to substitute the delegitimized social structures with. The following phrase heard in the general assembly reveals the experimental and prefigurative character of the occupation: 'We are not here to reflect existing society; we are here to explore how we want society to be after the crisis.' To an extent, the significance of the square resides in the fact that it made this common exploration possible. The thematic groups and self-organized structures such as the medical centre and the time bank were all part of this project of rethinking and reshaping a particular public space, of turning it into a source of ideas and institutions for the transition to a new social structure. On the one hand, the space of the square was raised as the most crucial stake of the movement. When, during the large June demonstrations, police forces repeatedly tried to evacuate the square, people persistently re-occupied it several times within a few hours. 'Their space' was indispensable in their effort to continue their exploration. It was on this square that they had established their precarious everyday rituals and it was there that they had set up the infrastructure that made this exploration possible. Tellingly, the cooking service in many cases distributed meals to those who were hungry, so they would remain at the square (see also Giovanopoulos 2011).

Nevertheless, while the people in Syntagma were stating 'we are here', they were at the same time stating, 'we are everywhere.'[17] This leads us to another major characteristic of the liminal commons: their fluid and expansive character. In liminal commons, as in all other forms of material-based commoning, space is central. Yet, while in most theoretical accounts of the commons space obtains its significance through its boundaries, in liminal commons space obtains its meaning through expansion. For Ostrom, the commons are unimaginable without their boundaries, but also in De Angelis' theory, boundaries 'bind [the commons] as systems and thus give them the specific unity that allows us to call them by their names' (De Angelis 2017: 82). Boundaries are perhaps important if the commons are to persist over

---

17. For a detailed discourse analysis of the movement, see Goutsos and Polymeneas 2014.

time, but they can become an obstacle if the project aims to facilitate transitions and expand.

What makes the liminal commons an expanding mode of commoning? As the liminal commons develop in, through and because of crisis and identity destabilization, they resist demarcation by any prevailing identity. The absence of a defining attribute does not only allow diverse subjects to act in common but also allows newcomers to join in and contribute to commoning. Liminality becomes the motor of expansion. Indeed, when people in Syntagma were manifesting in many ways that they are 'the ordinary people', they were not implying any kind of exclusionary criteria about what is normal – and therefore welcome – and what is not. On the contrary, this declaration was an attempt to establish an identity so broad that it would potentially encompass everyone and which would practically be a non-identity. The same can be said of their affirmation that the space of the square is their sole source of identification. As Manuel Castells put it: 'By joining an occupied site, citizens could be part of the movement without adhering to any ideology or organization, just by being there for their own reasons' (Castells 2012: 10). In their extensive discourse analysis of the proceedings of indignant assemblies, Goutsos and Polymeneas (2014) found that space was central. This led them to argue that the identity of the movement was essentially constructed in terms of space. The space of the square was contested and rapidly changing; it was a liminal space. Accordingly, the identity of the movement also remained contested and liminal.

The above applies not only to the space of the liminal commons but also to their institutions. A first institution of the liminal commons is that commoners explicitly discourage one another from acting on the basis of a clearly manifested identity and self-characterization. What matters, then, is what people do, not what people used to be. In the occupation of Syntagma, this was a crucial element. As Nikos confided, 'what I really like here is that, although I come in almost every day and I meet the same people, nobody has asked me where I used to work or where I am from.' The tendency towards common doing is conducive to the expansion of commoning practices since it keeps potentially paralysing disagreements at bay.

A second institution of the liminal commons is the non-binding character of decisions. This has been pointed out by other authors in reference to the resolutions of the general assembly. The resolutions of the assemblies were geared not towards producing unifying proposals

(Papadopoulos, Tsianos, and Tsomou 2012) but towards exploring the limits of a possible consensus (Stavrides 2013b). Different opinions were allowed to coexist.

Third, as accountability is difficult to implement in such volatile environments, liminal commons must find ways to prevent power concentration. Role rotation, loose organization, rule flexibility and rejection of all kinds of representation are mechanisms that prevent such accumulation of power. For instance, when the authorities or the media asked for a representative, a spokesperson or a coherent political programme, the assembly refused to provide any (Papadopoulos, Tsianos, and Tsomou 2012). In this spirit, a man took the floor at the general assembly to declare: 'We are nobody because we will not allow anybody to put his own hat upon our movement.'

Surface expansion and internal multiplication

'Surface expansion' refers to the expansion of common space and the inclusion of new commoners in the commons. It may materialize either through the expansion of the original space in an enlarged continuum or through the connection of the original common space with other emerging common spaces that may appear and disappear elsewhere. The occupation of Syntagma had both. On the one hand, the occupation spread towards streets neighbouring the actual square. On the other, Syntagma was temporally connected with many similar common spaces, which emerged through the decentralization–recentralization process described earlier. There are both continuities and discontinuities in this process. Common spaces that emerge through surface expansion may involve similar dynamics or not. They do not necessarily employ the same strategies and decision-making processes, and they may be very different in terms of their content. Some may have healthcare or direct democracy as their core issue; others may have as a goal the creation of a new eco-community; others yet may be oriented towards providing information to the general public or occupying a public building. Nevertheless, these different projects are interconnected and cross-fertilized by sharing their views and practices.

'Internal multiplication' is a more 'discreet' and less externally observable mode of expansion. It refers to the inner multiplication of the commons, the reconstitution of the project on different framing processes, the expansion of its fields of activity, the multiplication of internal micro-projects or the involvement of members in more than one activity. This is a process of self-transformation. In Syntagma, this kind of expansion happened in all the aforementioned ways. In the first place, the shift from indignation to determination marked an important self-transformation that affected the actual activities. Second, the list of incipient micro-projects increased exponentially throughout the three-month occupation. Lastly, commoning became so fruitful and even pleasurable that soon many people moved beyond their familiar subjects and started to experiment with previously unknown fields. As Katia told me, 'as an economist, I started with the Citizens' Debt Audit campaign, but then I realized that I wanted to try more. In the end, I painted my face, I joined the artist group, and I even helped in cooking.'

An important aspect of this transformative process was the effect that Syntagma had on leftist and anarchist political organizations. Unlike in Catalonia (Conill et al. 2012; Fominaya 2017), the practice of commoning was marginal in Greece before the movement of the occupied squares and the December 2008 uprising, and was looked upon with suspicion by political parties, including anarchist or autonomist groups keener on direct confrontation than on 'creating a new world within the cracks of the old'. After 2011, however, Syriza, the left-wing party that would go on to govern Greece, founded and funded Solidarity4all, a network dedicated to the promotion of commoning projects. The Antiauthoritarian Movement (Antieksousiastiki Kinisi), a leading anarchist group, and Antarsya, a far-left party, also got heavily involved in commoning initiatives.

Some concluding observations on the liminal commons

Liminal commons are transitional forms of commoning that constitute passages to more stable structures. To do so, they resist identification and closure. However, we have to keep in mind that such theoretical constructions can reflect the lived experience in the field. Was Syntagma with its liminal commons completely open to everybody? Can we speak of absolute inclusiveness? Has the temporal suppression of dichotomies and oppositions led to the emergence of a stable culture that emphasizes the points of connection and non-violently negotiates the points of disagreement and differentiation? In brief, have the liminal commons as transitory forms of commoning been successful in bringing about the transitions they aspired to? These are important questions that warrant further research and reflection. For now, I will only offer some fragmented and preliminary insights.

The theory of liminal commons does not prescribe a preferable form of commoning. Besides their primarily analytical role, described in the introduction, the liminal commons can only be explained and used in relational terms. This means that as a theoretical construct, the liminal commons indicate real tendencies and cannot be used as a model to which reality must conform. The occupation of Syntagma Square is explored under this focus. Despite the widespread tendency to celebrate the movement of the squares for its openness and inclusiveness, evident in many academic accounts, one should also mention those aspects that do not fit in the theoretical arguments. While to a great extent in Syntagma the outcome of liminality was openness, this was not always the case. In several cases, gender imbalances and other implicit and explicit divisions and power asymmetries have been reported, concerning both the organization and the actual doing of commoning processes. Heteronormative conceptions of the political were part of the narrative of open democratic processes, which in many people's imagination was mixed up with the glory of ancient Athens (Athanasiou 2014). Feminists and queer collectivities such as the 'purple bench' raised this issue in the general assembly as well as in other thematic groups; therefore, to some extent, Syntagma's openness was not only a product of the liminal state of de-identification but was also claimed and attained through contestation. In a similar vein, while the temporal suppression of oppositions may have ensured a smoother operation for the encampment, it has not necessarily signified their resolution. On the contrary, in several cases, it masked differences and made them appear non-existent, while they were perhaps cultivated beneath the surface. As a favourite ancient Chinese quote goes, 'bringing about change costs a lot of effort over a lot of time.'

My intention is not to present absolute or unproblematized social phenomena. Accordingly, my focus here is not on whether the theory of liminal commons can fully describe the experience in the field – as I am convinced that it cannot – but on whether it can effectively capture some tendencies. Indeed, I believe that what happened at Syntagma was an unprecedented process that brought together different people, a process that not despite but precisely because of and through its contradictions turned out to be a transformational experience both for individuals and for groups. Syntagma was the cornerstone of the expansion of commoning practices that will be described in the next chapter, and it led to the enrichment of left and anarchist political organizations with new repertoires of collective action based on commoning. At the individual level, Syntagma turned out to be a transformative experience since, in the wake of that experience, many decided to change their lives and try different approaches. Katia, an economist who used to work at the Ministry of Economics, resigned to dedicate herself to grassroots projects. Giorgos, a professional dancer and performer who used to live in Berlin, decided to abandon his career and come back to Greece to experiment with 'moneyless forms of life', as he told me. Since then, he is part of a grassroots collective in Exarcheia that distributes food and organizes social kitchens. Tonia was a manager in London and a successful businesswoman. On account of her participation at Syntagma, she decided to come back and become an organizer with the food sovereignty and Community Supported Agriculture movement, even though she would earn only a fraction of the money she was previously earning. While an increasing number of young people were leaving the crisis-stricken country because of high unemployment and a 'lack of future', the notorious Greek 'brain drain' as the media reported, a small yet dynamic section of young – and often professionally 'successful' – Greeks living abroad returned to the country to give form to the central slogan of the squares: 'let's take life into our own hands.' These types of stories, too often silenced and absent from dominant narratives, are among the tendencies I intend to capture with the present endeavour.

Chapter 4

COMMONS IN EXPANSION

How do the commons expand and multiply? How does this expansion relate to social movements?

In the relevant literature, the expansion of the commons and commoning is a relatively new subject that has been receiving increasing attention. In the first strand of literature, that of Ostrom and the institutional school, the expansion of the commons was a non-issue, as the main questions that this framework was concerned with relate to the conditions and institutions that make the commons operate well and self-sustain over time, rather than to how they expand, change or multiply. However, in recent literature the focus is on the role of the commons in societal transformation and therefore on their political aspects; hence, expansion has become a core issue. My first argument in this chapter is that, despite this recent attention, most of the aforementioned theories hold a normative rather than an analytical stance, that is to say, they explore the issue of how the commons *should expand* rather than of how they actually *do expand*.

This more politically oriented literature has given rise to a series of elaborate models on how the commons can counter and reverse capital accumulation and domination to become the predominant form of production and reproduction. However, these models have limited analytical value when studying the real conditions that favour or restrict the expansion of the commons. In other words, theoretical efforts that examine the expansion of the commons through modelling alone cannot explain why and how the commons expand in particular contexts but not in others, what are the complexities and discontinuities that follow such expansion or what are the contradictions that traverse the process.

The second argument I put forward in this chapter is that social movements constitute favourable conditions for rapid multiplication and expansion of the commons. Social movements do not form part of the theoretical framework of the institutional school, as questions of generalized political and social change were never among its priorities. In contrast, more politically oriented theories understand the commons as potential agents of social change and thus give prominence to social movements; nevertheless, studies thoroughly examining this relation based on empirical data are sparse. Therefore, in many cases, social movements are merely assigned a supplementary role in the expansion of commoning.

In contrast, my thesis is that social movements and commons can have *a co-productive relation*. In many studies of the commons, social movements are regarded as contentious mobilizations charged with the task of demanding alternatives and changes, while the commons are regarded as the social systems that bring about those changes (Harvey 2012; Bauwens and Kostakis 2014; De Angelis 2017). At best, social movements are regarded as fields of experimentation with new political practices and as generators of militant subjectivities (Hardt and Negri 2012), while it is taken for granted that even when the social movements succeed in forming commons, those die when mobilizations end (De Angelis 2017). In contrast to this view, my argument is that social movements can also create transitional forms of commoning – the liminal commons – which enact a generative process of commoning in their wake. These transitional commons that emerge within, through and because of social movements not only disseminate the ideas of the social movements throughout the social fabric but *also create a new social fabric* as an alternative social infrastructure for production and reproduction, composed of various collective ventures and networks.

The final core argument of this chapter is that the expansion of commons through social movements occurs in a *rhizomatic way*. Rhizomatic is the expansion that takes place simultaneously in different places and times in a non-linear and non-identifiable pattern. Rhizomatic expansion happens with no recognizable centre and thus without the distinction between centre and periphery. The new commons, thus, are nodes in a *rhizome* (Deleuze and Guattari 2012 [1988]); these loosely connected nodes appear and disappear very quickly.

In the previous chapter, I explored the condition of liminality and identity destabilization in social movements between 2008 and 2011; in turn, this chapter concentrates on the period following the movement of the squares. During this period, Greece has witnessed an unprecedented boom in new commoning projects; owing to its intensity, diversity, rapid explosion and eventual stagnation and shrinkage, this phenomenon constitutes an excellent case study for illustrating the issues this chapter aspires to address.

Commons and social movements

A synopsis of existing theories on commons expansion and the relation between commons and social movements is as follows.

Elinor Ostrom

The inclusion of Elinor Ostrom in the discussion on the expansion of the commons and the relation between commons and social movements mainly aims to highlight the lack of any reference to those issues in her work. Ostrom is interested in the efficient management of resources and proposes the commons as a valid alternative to the dichotomy between public and private. However, Ostrom neither has an explicit preference for the commons over the other two regimes (Ostrom et al., 2002) nor a theory of societal transformation through the expansion of the commons. Her goal is to challenge the assumption that effective solutions for the management of resources can be found only in the realm of public and private business, not to promote the displacement of the public and the private in favour of the commons. In her theory, the commons are complementary to capital and the state, and even though she argues that the commons can constitute effective alternatives for the management of resources at various scales (Ostrom et al., 1999), she does not aspire to see the commons expand and become the dominant political and social paradigm.

For Ostrom, it is the resource itself that poses 'the question of the common' and hence her focus is on resources and not on commoning; as a result, her theory of the commons is conditioned by the nature, scale and complexity of these resources, and therefore lacks the dynamic character that a theory of expansion necessitates. Ostrom does not seek to understand how commoning practices expand or how commons actually multiply or generate other commons.

However, Ostrom is interested in issues of scale. She argues that the commons can become a model for governing large-scale or even global resources (Ostrom et al., 1999), and she proposes a 'polycentric governance model' for managing 'complex economic systems' that surpass the small/medium scale (Ostrom 2010). In brief, Ostrom is interested in identifying optimal forms of governance for expanded commons but not in expanding commoning or multiplying existing commons.

The fact that Ostrom does not envisage social and political change through the commons and therefore lacks a theory of societal transformations explains why she is indifferent to the relationship between social movements and commons. In her view, the commons are social systems exclusively preoccupied with the management of resources. They do not form part of social movements and do not interact with them; they do not embody goals that go beyond the economy and do not have any projective or prefigurative function. In this vein, Ostrom never questioned two of the foundational pillars of economic theory. First, the assumption that natural elements, as well as tangible or intangible man-made creations, are mere resources to be allocated and managed. Second, the assumption that humans are rational beings who always rationally calculate and choose what is more profitable for them. Consequently, the only political notions that appear in Ostrom's vocabulary are related to the 'political environment' or 'political regime' that surrounds the commons, which can either facilitate or impede commons management (Ostrom 1990).

David Harvey

Departing from a different starting point, David Harvey seems to arrive at conclusions similar to those of Ostrom. Harvey argues that while there can be satisfying answers to the question of 'how to manage' small-scale commons, at larger scales things become more perplexing since it is impossible to transfer management techniques from the smaller scale to a larger one without affecting the nature of the commons (Harvey 2012). Harvey criticizes Ostrom's system of polycentric governance and advocates Murray Bookchin's 'confederation of libertarian municipalities' as a model for the organization of higher administrative scales at the national or international level (Harvey 2012).

Scaling up is important in both Harvey's and Ostrom's approaches. However, while for Ostrom scaling up is important due to the existence of large resources, Harvey's main concern is how to organize administration in ways that counter capital's domination. Yet, if commoning refers to anything more than decision-making or goods-distribution mechanisms, then neither Harvey nor Ostrom have a theory on how the commons *do expand*. Ostrom proposed a model for how to manage large-scale resources, while Harvey proposed a model for broader political participation in the commons; however, both models are static models of attributes and cannot address this chapter's questions on how the commons take form, multiply and expand.

In Harvey's logic, social movements play an important role, as they constitute the first element of what he terms a 'double-pronged political attack' on the capitalist system, with the commons being the second (Harvey 2012: 87). Social movements are charged with the task of forcing the state to 'supply more and more in the way of public goods for public purposes' (Harvey 2012: 87), while the commons should supplement those goods in ways that overcome capitalist relations (Harvey 2012).

Michael Hardt and Toni Negri

Hardt and Negri do not view the commons as relatively independent social systems of resource management. Instead, they focus on the more abstract level of the production of 'the common' as an inseparable social force that is already taking shape due to the informatization and 'cognitivization' of production (Hardt and Negri 2009; Federici 2010). For them, the expansion of commoning practices and of the 'common' as a distinct mode of social relations does not take the form of a counterpower or resistance to capital but is immanent in capitalism's process of evolution, as 'common space and commonwealth are created that escape the problem of defining rules of inclusion or exclusion'[1] in the contemporary organization of work and production. In other words, *a continuous expansion of the commons happens anyway* through capitalism's continuous mutation, and the main issue is how to prevent capital from capturing and 'corrupting' this immanent common production (Hardt and Negri 2009; Hardt 2012).

The main barrier they identify to toppling capitalism's domination is not related to the expansion and production of the commons but to their corruption; thus, they suggest that the core political issue is the autonomization of this ongoing expansion and the production of new autonomous subjectivities (Hardt and Negri 2009; 2012). The social movements contribute to this process because, on the one hand, they are fields of experimentation with new assemblarian practices and, on the other, they create subjectivities that 'desire and are capable of democratic relations' (Hardt and Negri 2012: 88).

Michel Bauwens and Vasilis Kostakis

Although some may argue that the inclusion of theories primarily concerned with the study of digital commons is inappropriate for this chapter, over the last years Michel Bauwens and Vasilis Kostakis

---

1. In Federici (2010: 4) referring to their work.

have attempted to offer models for commons expansion that apply to commons production at large. Like Hardt and Negri, they argue that commons-based peer production is developing already within capitalism, constituting a preliminary mode of alternative production that is substituting the old order; the main question is whether the mode itself 'can generate the institutional capacity and alliances needed' to accomplish this task (Bauwens and Kostakis 2014a: 51). Thus, they understand the commons as a model of production and economy that is antagonistic to capitalism and the question is 'which model will prevail' between the two (Bauwens and Kostakis 2014a: 60).

For Kostakis and Bauwens, the main barrier to further expansion of the model of the commons lies at the institutional and technological level, while power geometries and social movements come second. They argue that the current 'circulation of commons' leads to the 'communism of capital' (Bauwens and Kostakis 2014a; 2014b), meaning that under the current institutional framework, it is easy for capitalist enterprises to use the commons for their own profit maximization and capital accumulation. Subsequently, they propose a 'political agenda' consisting of a series of both specific and generic 'transition proposals', including the introduction of new legal licences, the linkage between digital and material production, and the introduction of communication and collaboration tools such as 'modularity' and 'stigmergy', which facilitate negotiation and co-production between commoners (Bauwens and Kostakis 2014a). In this vision, the state is not dissolved but becomes a 'partner state', which enables 'autonomous social production', while 'progressive social movements' can accelerate the transition.

Stavros Stavrides

In Stavros Stavrides' threshold analysis of common space, 'expansion' obtains a central role. Stavrides distinguishes between two distinct and opposing forms of commoning: the enclosed and the expanding (Stavrides 2016). Subsequently, he relates the two forms of commoning with different kinds of social relations. Enclosed commoning (re)produces dominant capitalistic relations and constitutes 'the death of space-commoning (and commoning through space)' (Stavrides 2016: 4). Expanding commoning, on the other hand, disrupts the normalized socio-spatial order and transforms the dominant forms of life towards an emancipatory direction in, against and beyond capitalism (Stavrides 2013; 2016).

In his effort to 'explicitly connect commoning practices with processes of opening' (Stavrides 2016: 3), Stavrides develops a theoretical framework regarding the 'institutions of expanding commoning'. He proposes that to become expanding, commoning should have four specific properties: comparability, translatability, power-sharing and gift offering. Comparability – which, in his view, is the motor of expanding commoning – refers to the comparison between different subjectivities and practices; Stavrides insists that this comparison can be liberating (Stavrides 2013). Translatability, on the other hand, 'creates the ground for negotiations between differences without reducing them to common denominators' (Stavrides 2016: 42). Power-sharing refers to the invention of specific and explicit mechanisms for the prevention of the accumulation of power. Gift offering is the social relation that transgresses 'self- or group-centred calculations and possibly hints towards different forms of togetherness and solidarity' (Stavrides 2015: 16). He emphasizes that commoners should realize that 'they often need to offer more than they expect to receive' (Stavrides: 16).

Stavrides argues against an understanding of social movements as mere dissident and 'demand-centred' mobilizations and argues in favour of social movements that operate as 'social laboratories', in which new forms of relations are developed and tested. Stavrides is inspired by the work of Raul Zibechi (2010) and emphasizes the fact that recent social movements globally 'have acquired a central role in transforming the life conditions of popular classes but also their aspirations for a different future' (Stavrides 2016: 95). Hence, Stavrides sees commoning as an indispensable part of contemporary social movements.

Massimo De Angelis

Massimo De Angelis has developed the most elaborate conceptual and theoretical framework to date to explain how the commons are produced and multiplied in current society but also how the commons can create the basis for what he calls 'a social revolution' towards a post-capitalist society (De Angelis 2017). De Angelis understands the commons and capital as two main distinct autonomous autopoietic and oppositional social systems that are composed of other molecular sub-systems and which 'both struggle to "take things into their own hands" and self-govern based on their different and often clashing, internally generated codes, measures and values' (De Angelis 2017: 103). Subsequently, he relates each social system with a social force that constitutes its particular expression and seeks 'its own reproduction [i.e., of the social system] through its operations at whatever scale of social action' (De Angelis 2017: 108). Hence, for De Angelis, the expansion of the commons happens through the expansion of their social force over the social force of other social systems.

However, the expansive social force of the commons develops in many different ways, involving different scales, processes and socio-spatial relations. Initially, De Angelis argues that the commons as micro-social systems can reproduce themselves and singles out two distinct types of reproduction: reproduction that aims at enhancing the autonomy of commons vis-à-vis capital and the state, and reproduction as the process of giving rise to more commons systems. Moving to a different scale, De Angelis refers to 'common ecologies' that are 'the interrelations among different commons and their environments' (De Angelis 2017: 287) and suggests that those interrelations are brought about by a particular type of commoning, which he calls 'boundary commoning'. Boundary commoning is a cross-boundary type of commoning that 'activates and sustains relations among commons thus giving shape to commons at larger scales, pervading social spaces and intensifying the presence of commons within them' (De Angelis 2017: 287).

Subsequently, he suggests that this 'structural coupling' between different commons systems can take two directions: 'symbiosis' or 'meta-commonality'. Symbiosis happens with 'the inclusion of the boundaries of two (or more) commons into one unit'; meta-commonality happens 'when the recurring structural coupling among the commons units maintains each common's identity and internal commoning, while at the same time establishing a new systemic coherence among two or more commons' (De Angelis 2017: 293).

In the last part of his analysis, De Angelis argues that social movements are different social systems than the commons. In his view, commons systems differ from social movement systems in that the former 'provide alternatives to the subjects who created them' while the latter 'simply demand these alternatives' (De Angelis 2017: 364). Moreover, De Angelis argues that commons and social movements have opposite cycles; social movements start with an event and finish with a deal (with the capital or the other social systems with which they interact). Commons on the other hand always start with a deal – 'a given pact with the devil' in his own words – and they finish with an event that guarantees their reproduction. He recognizes that social movements as systems can create commons, but he emphasizes that these commons are sustained only as long as movements last, and they mainly have an educational role. Finally, he completes his conceptual framework on the expansion of the commons by suggesting that the highest form of meta-commonality is what he calls a 'commons movement', which can 'mutate' the entire society through the 'commonalization' of the private and the public, by establishing 'meta-commonal' relations across the state, capital and the commons (De Angelis 2017: 332).

What are the limitations of these theories?

In Ostrom's framework, the commons are defined by the nature and scale of the resources to be governed. To this extent, commoning is bounded by the very attributes of the resources. Large-scale resources require large-scale management and small-scale resources the opposite. Hence, Ostrom does not really have a theory of expansion for the commons. In Ostrom's theory politics can either facilitate or hinder the efficient management of the commons, but, in her view, commoning does not aspire to topple capitalism. Thus, social movements are not among her interests and her theory does not offer something in the discussion about the relation between social movements and the commons.

Scale is an important issue for Harvey, too, although he mostly refers to levels of administration, not only to the scale of resources. Harvey endorses Bookchin's model of political participation as an alternative to today's decision-making system, but in effect, he has not developed a theory of how actual commoning ventures multiply and expand, either. Regarding the relationship between the commons and social movements, Harvey's logic is limited, since he only understands social movements as the contentious and demand-centred part of his dual strategy for social transformation and therefore does not reflect on the experience of the social movements of the last decade, which combined both contentious politics and forms of commoning (Hardt and Negri 2012; Stavrides 2016; Varvarousis and Kallis 2017; Varvarousis, Asara, and Akbulut 2020).

Hardt and Negri choose to speak of the 'common' instead of the 'commons', and this makes a great difference in the way expansion is perceived and theorized. The common is used by Hardt and Negri as a concept 'designating [. . .] the social relations characteristic of the dominant form of production in the post-Fordist era' (Federici 2010: 2) or as a concept defining every shared resource such as languages or metropolitan centres. The problem they draw attention to is that this 'commonwealth' is appropriated by capital, which corrupts or co-opts 'the common'. However, if the production and expansion of the common are immanent in the evolution and mutation of capitalism, then the focus is shifted towards political solutions that can guarantee the independence of this expansion from the capital and the corruption it brings.

In other words, if the focus is on the common and not on the commons, the issue of expansion becomes external to the commons, as it lies in the sphere of politics and the relation of the commons to capital. My argument is that this loose theorization of the commons in its singular form transforms commoning into an abstract force, which does not lead to the production of concrete common worlds in which one can participate or not, look after resources or not, create community bonds and live in common. The expansion of the commons as it is formulated in this chapter does not refer to the expansion of an abstract social force but to the expansion and multiplication of actual common worlds beyond their original, physical, digital or even imagined perimeter. Regarding social movements, Hardt and Negri mention the commoning character of the encampments of the so-called movement of the squares in the last decade, but they don't see the relation of these movements with the proliferation of new commons that took place in their wake in many countries. Characteristically, they refer to those movements as having 'tragically limited' outcomes (Hardt and Negri 2012: 86). Their theory lacks a systematic reflection about the role of social movements in commons' expansion and vice versa. Instead, they have developed a nuanced theory of the 'event of the commoner' (Hardt and Negri 2012), which will take place at some unknown point in the future and will lead to a radical social break after which 'a new society can be built' (Hardt and Negri 2012: 88).

Bauwens and Kostakis' framework follows an intermediate approach, as they refer both to an abstract commons-based peer production that is already developing within capitalism and to actual commoning projects. On the other hand, Stavrides' and De Angelis' theories follow a different path, since both of them understand commons as concrete social systems that can expand. However, the main issue with these analyses is that, as they are based on a political premise in which 'one should take sides' (Stavrides 2016: 8), they tend to reflect on how commons *should* expand rather than on how they do expand. Second, while their elaborate theories may offer valuable insights on how the commons can potentially expand and connect, they do not examine what the conditions that can expedite or obstruct this process are. In the expansion of the commons, however, conditions matter and thus an analytical approach should examine the histories, geographies and socioeconomic and political contexts in which expansion takes place or is hindered.

Stavrides' and De Angelis' theories follow a different path since both of them understand commons as concrete social systems that can expand. Stavrides' account is very innovative and useful for capturing the expansive force of commoning and its transformative capacity. He also offers a basic but partial set of rules on how the commons can remain open and welcoming to newcomers – thus expanding. However, because his theory is based on the political premise of permanent openness and endless expansion of commoning, he sets this dilemma as one in which 'one should take sides' and tends to reflect on how commons should expand rather than how they actually do expand. A second shortcoming, evident also in De Angelis' theorizations of commons' expansion, is that they examine the conditions that can expedite or obstruct the process mainly in theoretical terms. While this does not reduce the value of these theoretical endeavours, there is scope for more case studies that can reveal the complexity of the issue since actual conditions matter and thus an analytical approach should examine the histories, geographies and socioeconomic and political contexts in which expansion takes place or is hindered. Finally, while Stavrides stresses the point that commoning constitutes an important dimension of contemporary social movements, he has not developed a theory on the relation and interplay between the phase of more visible contention and mobilization and the phase in which commoning prevails.

Undoubtedly, De Angelis' theory on commons' expansion and the relation between the commons and social movements has a lot to offer in both normative and analytical terms. However, it would benefit from some amendments that I am trying to put forward in this chapter. First, his theoretical scheme regarding the expansion of the commons, which is based on the relations of symbiosis and meta-commonality through boundary commoning, captures very well the structural way in which many commons are forming commoning networks (commons ecologies in his terminology). However, it can neither capture the shape nor the extraordinary dynamism that the proliferation of commoning can acquire in contexts of widespread crisis and social destabilization or in combination with a major event that can fuel such a rapid expansion. In other words, there are special conditions that can break the rules of structural expansion that De Angelis describes. Indeed, the expansion that is described in the empirical part that follows cannot easily fit in De Angelis' tripartite scheme of commons' expansion. Second, while De Angelis indeed captures the dynamic interaction between the commons and social movements as separate but interrelated social systems, his theory does not fully acknowledge the co-productive relation between them. Social mobilizations do not only create 'educational alternatives' (De Angelis 2017: 368) and these alternatives (new commons) do not necessarily die when mobilizations end (De Angelis 2017: 368). Instead, they can be transmuted from liminal to more stable commons in the rhizomatic way I am explaining in the next section.

From liminal to rhizomatic

Commoning that takes place during the most contentious and visible phases of social movements does not always evaporate after mobilizations are over, but it can be disseminated within the social fabric and, at the same time, it can create a new social fabric. This expansion of the commons usually takes place rhizomatically. The commons of the social movements, thus, are not just temporal forms of commoning but liminal commons: commons that facilitate transitions and may transform into or give rise to other, more stable, forms of commoning in their wake.

In the first chapter, I explored the 'being' of liminal commons, drawing on the experience of the Syntagma Square occupation. In the present chapter, I will focus on the 'becoming' of liminal commons by looking at the aftermath of the visible phase of the mobilization. The aim is to explore how the expansion of commoning practices and the well-documented multiplication of the commons (Varvarousis and Kallis 2017; Loukakis 2018; Kalogeraki 2018) took place after the end of mobilizations. My argument is that this expansion happened following a *rhizomatic pattern*.

The concept of the rhizomatic expansion of the commons has its roots in the philosophy of Deleuze and Guattari and their concept of the rhizome, first introduced in 1980 in their book *A Thousand Plateaus*. Yet, my use of the concept does not aspire to be an exhaustive account of their work. Instead, my focus is on the expansive and ephemeral nature that the concept of rhizome implies, as well as on its capacity to constantly connect random and infinite points in a non-linear manner ('non-arborescent' in Deleuze and Guattari's terminology). Despite the non-exhaustive character of my use of the rhizome, I think that my approach is consistent with Deleuze and Guattari's own intention about the invention and use of concepts in general since for them the role of concepts is to be constantly moving, mutating and connecting (Lawley 2004). As Massumi notes at the foreword of *A Thousand Plateaus* referring to how Deleuze and Guattari want to use their concepts, 'a concept is a brick. It can be used to build the courthouse of reason. Or it can be thrown through the window. [. . .] the concept in its unrestrained usage is a set of circumstances, at a volatile juncture. [. . .] The concept has no subject or object other than itself. It is an act.' Finally, I would like to note that my use of rhizomatic expansion is also informed by the work of Manuel Castells (2012), who independently of Deleuze and Guattari has used the concept of 'rhizomatic revolution' to explain the practices of the Spanish indignados.

Hence, rhizomatic expansion describes the non-linear and simultaneous emergence and multiplication of the commoning projects that may follow the formation of liminal commons. It resembles what in biology is called 'punctuation', in which a new species appears in many different places simultaneously. Likewise, rhizomatic expansion can happen in different places and times simultaneously without any recognizable centre to fuel the reproduction and multiplication of the commons. In the words of Deleuze and Guattari, 'it is not a multiple derived from the One, or to which One is added (n+1)' (Deleuze and Guattari (2012 [1988]): 22). The nodes of a rhizome are either not systematically connected or connected through unforeseen encounters. However, every node can potentially connect to any other. Many of the new commons are liminal commons themselves, and they either evolve into more stable structures and networks or perish after a short while. Others have been directly created as more stable structures. Compatibility among emerging nodes is not checked in advance; infinite ventures can be added to the rhizome. This kind of connection, self-mutation and expansion of the commons cannot be described by the properties of the more stable nodal networking models. In non-rhizomatic networks, the connection of the nodes is the outcome not of unforeseen but of planned encounters, whose aim is to deepen a constant collaboration and not a temporal exchange of experiences. Moreover, in a network, there are usually checking mechanisms that ensure that new nodes are compatible with the existing structure and a minimum agreement is usually regarded as essential for an expansion to occur.

In the case study I am presenting here, the rhizomatic expansion of the commons was not simply related to the Greek movement of the squares but to a great extent can be regarded as its 'transmutation' (Varvarousis, Asara, and Akbulut 2020). This argument adds to the discussion on the consequences of social movements, which is perhaps more developed within social movement studies[2] (Bosi, Giougni, and Uba 2016; Fominaya 2017; Gamson 1990; Giugni 1998; Forno and Graziano 2014; and Bosi and Zamponi 2015) but remains underdeveloped in the literature on the commons.

Otherwise, with my colleagues Viviana Asara and Bengi Akbulut, we examined in detail the relationship between social movements, their outcomes and the emergence of new commons. We argued that in addition to the political, cultural and biographical outcomes of the

2. For a comprehensive review on the topic and further development of the relation between the outcomes of social movements and the commons, see Varvarousis et al. (forthcoming).

social movements, often emphasized by social movement scholars, the commons that multiplied in Athens and Barcelona in the wake of the respective movements of the squares should be conceptualized as *social outcomes* of these social movements. Social outcomes signify the alternative social infrastructure within different spheres of social production and reproduction like health and care provision, education, food production, housing, finance and others. They are characterized by their dynamic interaction with the more visible periods of the social movements, as they incarnate practices, imaginaries, collective memories and innovations that emerged and practised during such periods and disseminated through the social fabric. In this chapter, the focus is on *how* the expansion and diffusion of the social outcomes of social movements have taken place.

Lastly, the chapter explores the conditions that allowed such an extensive rhizomatic expansion to happen in Greece after the mobilizations of 2011. Such a place-bounded focus allows for further reflection on the issue of commons expansion and its relation to the social movements. Not every social movement that creates commons can give rise to such an impressive cycle of commoning in its wake. In our work on social outcomes, we show that while similar kinds of mobilization took place in Spain, Greece and Turkey, widespread social outcomes were produced in Greece and Spain but not in Turkey. How can this be explained? The Greek case highlights the importance of crisis in the destabilization of the social imaginary (Castoriadis 1975; 2010) and the emergence of new social imaginary significations that can give birth to alternative practices of solidarity and commoning.[3]

Rhizomatic expansion and new commons after 2011 in Greece

The commoning projects created after 2011 encompass a wide spectrum of ventures active in various fields of production and reproduction. We may speak of a 'boom' because unlike in other European countries (e.g. Spain: see Conill et al. 2012; Fominaya 2017), commoning was

---

3. For a full account of the social imaginary transformations and their relation to the emergence of practices related to solidarity, commons and degrowth in Greece within crisis, see Varvarousis (forthcoming).

previously marginal in Greece. Examples of these initiatives include social clinics and pharmacies, workers' cooperatives, occupied urban spaces, time banks and alternative currencies, neighbourhood assemblies and solidarity exchange networks, urban gardens, farmer or consumer cooperatives, farmers' markets without intermediaries, artist and publishing collectives and a single occupied factory. There is so much diversity among these endeavours that it is difficult to speak of a uniform movement, in terms of both their social and economic fields of operation and their political aspirations, organizational principles and networking practices. Nevertheless, all these initiatives emerged as forms of self-organization, around rules and institutions that their members themselves established to manage their common resources, and therefore, they all constitute commoning projects.

Social clinics are ventures that aim at providing healthcare services to those excluded from the public health system. Some also aim at resisting and toppling dominant public health policies, as well as developing a new model for a different provision of healthcare services. They hardly existed before 2011 but have multiplied afterwards. In 2014 there were seventy-two known initiatives. The majority of them were initiated between 2011 and 2012 (Adam and Teloni 2015).

Solidarity hubs are ventures mainly active at the local neighbourhood level, which aim at reconstructing broken social cohesion through a series of actions such as social kitchens, distribution of 'food parcels', free lessons or clothing distribution. Some appeared and disappeared quickly, while others have been more enduring and exist to this day; this fluidity makes it difficult to estimate their number. In any case, while they were non-existent before 2011 (or at least there were very few and had different names and repertoires of action), there were over 110 of them in 2014 (solidarity4all 2014).

Direct producer-to-consumer networks were also popularized after 2011, especially between 2012 and 2014. Indicatively, while they were non-existent or unknown before 2011, there were forty-seven recorded networks in 2014 (Solidarity4all 2014). Other forms of social and solidarity economy did also emerge during the crisis and after 2011. Almost 70 per cent of the existing social and solidarity economy organizations were created after 2011 (Varvarousis et al. 2017). The organizations in this economic field are both formal and informal and range from social enterprises to informal time banks and alternative currencies. In 2017 the total number of organizations across the country was estimated at 1,500 (Varvarousis et al. 2017).

Box 2. The Greek commoning movement in numbers[4]

1. A multiverse of formal and informal ventures

2. Ventures of different sizes in membership

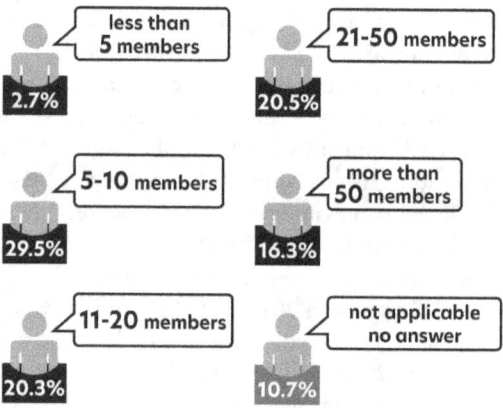

4. The graphs of 'Box 2' are derived from a quantitative analysis of a face-to-face survey research project held in 2016–17 all over Greece with 404 participants from 116 ventures (see also 'Box 1'). For a full presentation of the findings of this research project, see Varvarousis, A., Kallis, G. (2021). *Escaping Crisis. Solidarity and Cooperative Ventures in Greece during 2016-2017.* Thessaloniki. Heinrich Böll Stiftung Publications. All graphs are designed by Eleni Karafylli.

3. More women than men

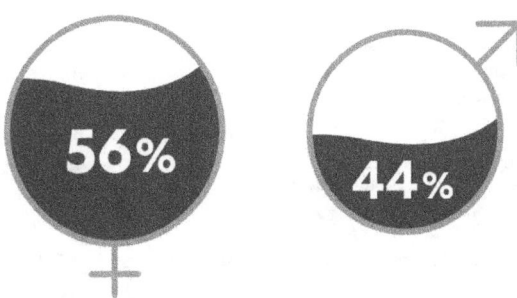

4. Mainly an urban phenomenon

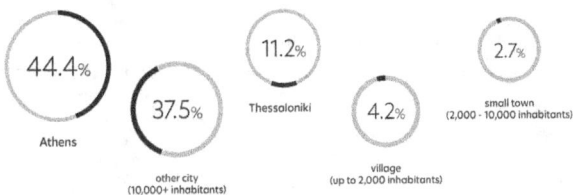

5. The participants are mainly of Greek nationality

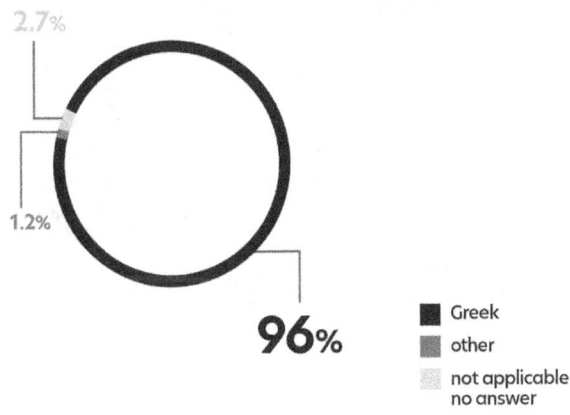

6. Most participants dedicate 2–8 hours per week to their ventures

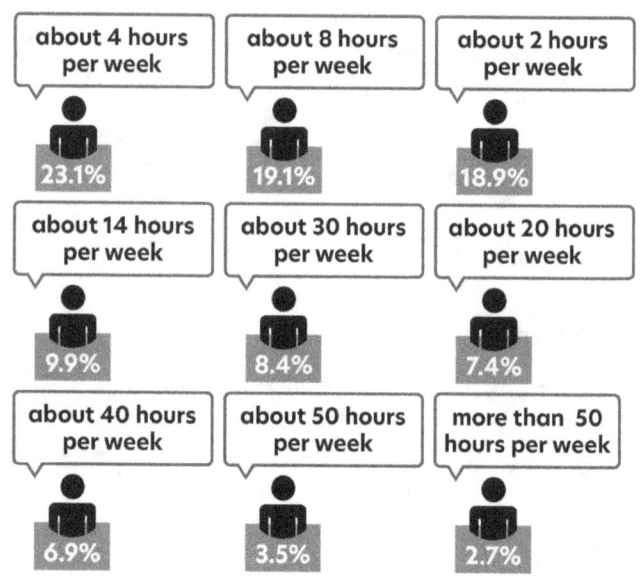

7. The majority of the ventures acknowledge their connection to the social movements of 2008 and 2011[5]

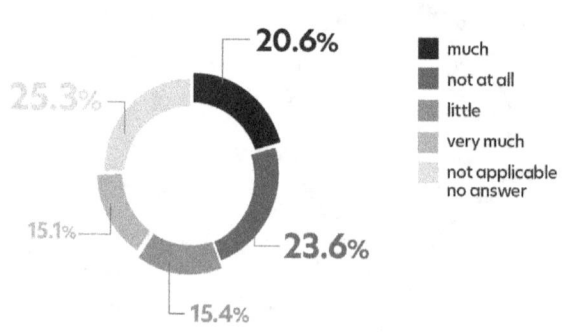

5. Original Question: To which extent do you believe that your venture's existence is related to the social movements of 2008 and 2011?

4. Commons in Expansion

8. Most of the participants claim that the overall movement will continue to exist even if economic growth returns to Greece[6]

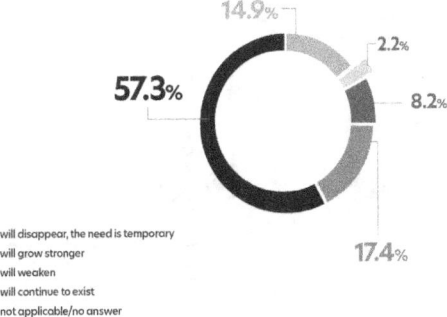

- will disappear, the need is temporary
- will grow stronger
- will weaken
- will continue to exist
- not applicable/no answer

9. Most of the ventures have a strong political and humanitarian scope, and they emphasize everyday practices[7]

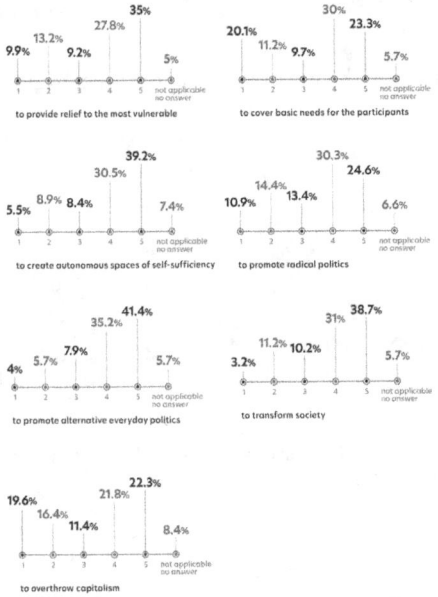

6. Original Question: What will happen to the commoning projects if economic growth returns to Greece?
7. Original Question: From a scale 1–5 (1 = not at all, 5 very important) how much important are the following goals for your venture?

10. The majority wants some sort of support from the state, but there is a strong minority that rejects it[8]

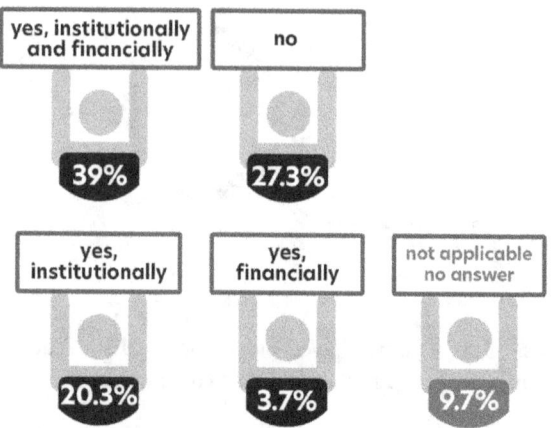

11. Nevertheless, the majority is sceptical regarding the state

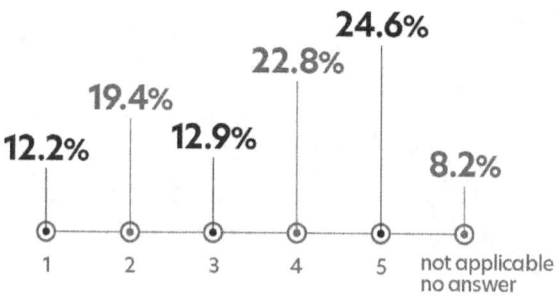

• the support of the state can be a threat to the autonomy of the ventures

8. Original Question: Do you think that the state should support the commoning ventures?

12. Most of the respondents believe that their ventures aim at transforming the state instead of replacing it or complementing it

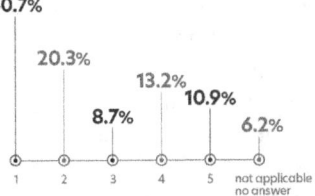

• to fully replace the state's social services

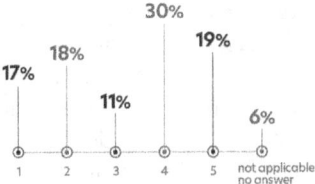

• to complement the state's social services

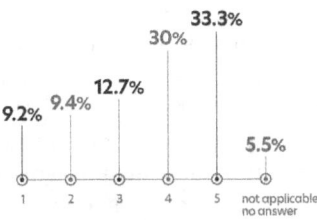

• to transform the state's system of welfare provisioning

Social movements and commons: A porous relationship

That the movement of the squares in Greece catalysed the emergence of hundreds of new commons in its wake is a sentiment not only shared by the majority of scholars in the field (Hadjimichalis 2013; Karaliotas 2016; Kioupkiolis 2014; Papapavlou 2015; Pantazidou 2013) but also reflected in our interviews. As Giovanopoulos and Mitropoulos beautifully put it: 'The shared reality that the square left behind went along with everybody to do it something in its aftermath' (2011: 14). Similarly, Katia, a woman in her forties who was an active participant in the social movement of 2011 and an organizer of the Festival of Solidarity and Cooperative Economy in the following years, told me: 'There is no doubt that the days of the squares were, and to some extent still are, a point of reference both for our lives and for the projects we are developing since then. It was like a train that came through Athens in those days, and many of us jumped on to go towards the unknown.'

Besides the shared sentiments, the testimonies and the anecdotal evidence, the explosion of new commons after 2011 and its relation to the social movements have been recorded quantitatively by the large-scale national study discussed in Box 2. Almost 51 per cent of respondents stated that the ventures in which they participate were direct outcomes of the social movements active in Greece between 2008 and 2011, while only 23 per cent consider their projects unrelated to those movements; of those, a fraction participated in projects that existed before those two movements. Similarly, a 2017 study on the condition of the social and solidarity economy in Greece showed that 70 per cent of the entities of social and solidarity economy were launched immediately after the social movements of 2011.[9] The study does not establish an explicit causal relation between the two phenomena; however, it states that 'the growth of the sector was fueled by the rising of the social movements of the period 2008-2011'[10] (p. 36).

In the statement that 51 per cent of new commons 'were direct outcomes of the social movements', what does 'direct' mean?

First, the 2011 movement of the squares, the 2008 revolt and many smaller-scale mobilizations in-between emerged and developed as forms of urban commoning. Urban commoning describes those practices that create temporal or more stable commons systems in the urban fabric, primarily by occupying public or private space to transform

---

9. This refers to the official report of the Greek Social and Solidarity Mapping and Needs Analysis project implemented between January 2017 and November 2017 by the European Village, British Council and Social Enterprise UK with the help of the Greek Ministry of Labour and the Structural Reform Support Service of the European Commission in which I was the principal investigator and main author of the report. The study was based on a survey in 250 SSE entities across Greece, 15 semi-structured in-depth interviews with key participants and stakeholders and 4 focus groups held in Athens, Thessaloniki, Crete and Karditsa. It is regarded by far the most comprehensive study of its kind until the date of writing of this chapter.

10. Own translation from Greek.

it into common space. Urban commoning can take the form of self-organized city parks, social centres, solidarity clinics and hubs for the provision of services in a horizontal and anti-hierarchical manner, temporal occupations or even mobile occupations moving from one part of the city to another within a few hours. During the December 2008 revolt, neighbourhood assemblies appeared for the first time in Athens to organize grassroots protest actions, decided in self-organized events that were public and open to all. While at first these assemblies were mostly concerned with targeting representatives of the system (attacks on police stations, occupations of municipal buildings, etc.), in later phases they expanded their actions to include the organization of screenings, social kitchens, free bazaars, concerts and small festivals (see also Stavrides 2013). When the visible phase of the mobilization ended, many of these neighbourhood initiatives continued their activity, and some developed further their commoning practices.

In Exarcheia, a group of locals transformed a parking lot into an urban park; in Petroupoli, another group occupied an abandoned botanical garden. In Patisia, when the mayor of Athens tried to transform a public square into a parking lot, locals decided to re-occupy it and manage it as a commons. In my own former neighbourhood, Holargos, through our newly formed popular assembly, we resisted the privatization of the forest, we prevented the commercialization of our town's park and we launched a campaign for harvesting the area's olive trees as a commons belonging to all. In another neighbourhood, a group of young people constructed a mobile concert stage and for many months set it up in different Athens neighbourhoods to organize street parties. The goal was to 'keep the spirit of December alive', as Parnonas, one of the organizers, told me. Some neighbourhood assemblies persisted in the next years, but most were temporarily suspended.

Despite the importance of these new collective experiences, December's impact was limited to those groups facing the impasses of crisis before the outburst of the actual crisis (Dalakoglou 2013). With the advent of the movement of the squares, which became the matrix of the commoning movement, these practices were popularized and spread all over the country. As Eugenia, one of my informants put it: 'If December was a cat's step, Syntagma was an elephant's step.' The occupation of Syntagma Square in 2011 was marked by the forms of commoning developed during the event. First, many neighbourhood assemblies of the 2008 revolt were reactivated to organize the social movements anew. Second, many new self-organized groups were formed during the occupation: the social kitchen, the cleaning commission, the technical support group, the multimedia group, the translation commission, the legal support group, the protection commission, the time bank, the commission for the unemployed, the eco-village commission, the direct democracy commission, the social solidarity group, the education commission and the self-organized health centre.[11]

At the end of June and as the Greek parliament was voting the austerity measures of the so-called Midterm Fiscal Strategy Framework, police violence was on the increase, and a series of discussions was held on what the next steps after the end of the occupation could be. There were diverse proposals; some focused on disseminating the political practices applied in the square to the rest of Athens; others on strengthening the existing neighbourhood assemblies; others yet on creating solidarity hubs of commoning practices to mitigate the effects of the adopted austerity measures in practice; finally, a minority insisted on preserving the Syntagma Square occupation at any cost.[12] While there was no consensus on what to do, these discussions directly gave birth to a series of commoning projects. For example, a group of young people who met at Syntagma created the 'Spithari Waking Life' eco-community at the outskirts of Athens. During the operation of the self-organized health centre at the square, the plan to establish the Metropolitan Solidarity Clinic was conceived, which is now run by more than 250 volunteers and treats thousands of patients.[13] As Petra, a woman in her mid-forties, says, 'it all started at the square, at the indignants; this is how we conceived it. There was that group initially just named "people's assembly" and among the many activities discussed was the initiation of a social clinic.' In addition to the groups that were explicitly conceived at the square, some of the aforementioned commissions and groups continued their activities for months or even years after the end of visible mobilizations. Among them were the multimedia group, the artist group, the time bank and the exchange bazaar, which I have followed and recorded.

Besides the aforementioned groups, the direct social outcomes of the movement include those ventures that perhaps did not have such a close and organic relation with the actual projects of the square but were created as a result of practices and discussions first practised at

11. As recorded from my own ethnographic research at the square.
12. Information obtained through active participation and participant observation.
13. Source: enallaktikos.gr.

4. Commons in Expansion 105

Syntagma and then decentralized to all Athenian neighbourhoods. 'Well, our social clinic was, at least to some extent, a demand derived from the squares. It was one among the many objectives that the citizens participating in those movements had set', says one member of a social clinic, as mentioned in a study about social clinics published by Adam and Teloni (2015: 29). Likewise, Kostas, a leading figure in Piraeus Solidarity, says about the project:

> Our project, like others that popped up in this period, was an idea related to Syntagma. My wife and I participated at Syntagma, and when that was over we came back to Piraeus and we wanted to do something similar here. It was a period when many political collectives adopted the slogans 'nobody alone in the crisis' and 'let's take our lives in our hands'. They became a source of inspiration for many emerging collectives, not only in Piraeus but also in the southern and western suburbs of Athens.

We have organized these different patterns of direct diffusion of the commons into the social fabric after the end of the visible cycle of mobilizations into three distinct categories: transplantation, ideation and breeding (Varvarousis, Asara, and Akbulut 2020). Transplantation is the process when a project decides to move from the epicentre of mobilization to the neighbourhood by keeping the same structure, repertoire of actions and probably its membership. Ideation is the process in which a project is conceived during the phase of the mobilization but is being materialized in the aftermath. Breeding refers to the process that accelerates the creation of commoning projects, directly after the end of the visible cycle, through a more random diffusion of practices, activists and ideas that are being reorganized and synthesized anew in the bosom of neighbourhood forms of collective action.

The new commons that spread all over the country in the wake of the 2011 mobilizations consisted of many highly heterogeneous practices, encompassed a variety of productive and reproductive activities, followed diverse forms of organization and embodied different world views. Some were more politically oriented and aimed at popularizing the radical spirit of the movements of the squares regarding forms of political participation. Others were mobilized against the austerity measures and the malaise of the economic crisis and tried to reconstruct the disrupted social cohesion. Others yet were largely alternative forms of employment, aiming at giving solutions to the major unemployment impasse that followed the outburst of the economic crisis in 2010. In any case, the constitutive ideas and practices of the 2008–11 social movements became, to varying degrees, the central constituent elements of these new commons. Such commonalities include, among others, direct democracy, unruliness, autonomy, self-sufficiency, solidarity and openness (Pantazidou 2013; Varvarousis 2019). Most solidarity projects have a dual purpose and therefore are agents of political transformation as well (Loukakis 2018). In many cases, through the decentralization of the actual commoning practices of the square, such elements were transmitted directly to the new projects by individuals and incipient groups formed during the occupation. Nevertheless, the 'event' of the squares created practical, imaginary and discursive resources (Khanna 2012) that gave birth to a new public culture (Pantazidou 2013), *which operated as a generator of new concrete projects, without the necessity for a direct, organic relation to the squares.*

The results of our survey seem to confirm this hypothesis. While the percentage of respondents who consider their projects direct outcomes of the 2008–11 social movements is 51 per cent, the percentage of those who believe that the 'creation of spaces of autonomy and self-sufficiency' is a top priority for their venture is 70 per cent, and the percentage of those who believe that 'the production of a different kind of politics at the everyday level' is a top priority is 77 per cent. Also, 90 per cent of these projects operate with decision mechanisms grounded in direct democracy and avoid electing representatives. These findings show that direct democracy, autonomy, self-sufficiency and the reorganization of politics at the everyday level – the cornerstones of the movement of the squares – became the groundwork for the new commons, even though a much lower number of commoning projects acknowledges a direct linkage with that social movement. This conclusion strengthens the argument that the diverse outcomes of social movements, political, cultural, biographical *and social* (Bosi, Giougni, and Uba 2016; Varvarousis, Asara, and Akbulut 2020), do not operate in silos, but rather interconnect and cross-fertilize.

The inverse is also true. Not only do social movements create social outcomes, but also social outcomes become the basis upon which new social movements may develop. This is evident in the relation between the December 2008 revolt and the 2011 movement of the squares. For instance, popular assemblies were direct social outcomes and commoning projects that sprung from the revolt; after being briefly suspended, they were reactivated to form part of the alternative social infrastructure of the commoning projects that developed out of the square. To be sure, every movement creates its own forms of organization, narratives and sets of practices; my aim here is not to promote a reductive view of the Syntagma movement as a mere continuation of the December revolt, as it was not. In this respect, my argument is different from that of Giovanopoulos and Mitropoulos (2011), Pantazidou (2013) and others who have argued that there is a cycle, a continuum of citizen action with cycles and peaks, ebbs and flows in the Greek social movement. This perception tends to emphasize continuities between mobilizations and disregard the discontinuities, disruptions, innovations and regressions that each social movement presents concerning its predecessors. However, an important element of continuity between the 2008 and 2011 mobilizations lies indeed in the practice of commoning. To conclude, there is a co-productive relation between social mobilizations and the expansion of commons, which, however, is marked not by the repetition of the same patterns but by continuities and discontinuities, affirmations and disruptions.

The a-centred rhizomatic character of this expansion

Social clinics were created all over Greece, especially after 2011. Despite their heterogeneity, their main goals include providing health services to those affected by extreme cuts and restriction of access to the public health system and resisting neoliberal public health policies, while some also aim at providing a new model of provision of health services. Liana is a woman in her late thirties and a psychologist at the Solidarity Social Clinic of Thessaloniki, one of the first and most active social clinics in Greece. When I asked her about the venture's origins, she said:

> The social clinic of Thessaloniki was established by a group of people that came together to support the hunger strike of 300 undocumented immigrants. At that moment there was only one social clinic, in Rethymno, but we barely knew about it and it definitely didn't affect our decision to start ours. To answer your question, no, neither our social clinic nor the majority of the other social clinics I know were created by other social clinics. They were launched independently. [...] At the social clinic of Thessaloniki, this is part of our written rules. We do not create annexes of our venture in other places, even if we are asked to do it. We believe that the emergence of each venture should be autonomous and independent. We are in favour of collaboration and we participate in the National Network of Social Clinics, which was created afterwards, but we want each community to decide locally about what they want to do without patronizing anybody.

The story of the social clinics is revealing of how the commons expanded in the wake of the 2008–11 social mobilizations. The Metropolitan Social Clinic in Athens was conceived autonomously at Syntagma and so were the other social clinics described in the previous section. The Solidarity Social Clinic of Thessaloniki was a transmutation of the solidarity movement towards 300 migrants who were on hunger strike. No organic relation or pre-planned agenda fuelled their expansion. No centre can be detected from which all those ventures stem. The process was not characterized by linearity. As Liana put it: 'During the years 2011-2013, Greece witnessed a boom in grassroots movements, probably the biggest in recent history. The emergence of social clinics is part of this boom. There was no organized plan or a conscious decision on our part or the part of anyone else, to my knowledge, to start creating social clinics everywhere. It just happened.'

Like in the case of social clinics, the rhizomatic pattern can be detected in almost all forms of commoning appearing in Greece in this period. The idea that people 'can take their lives in their hands' was planted either through direct participation of the people in mobilizations or through social media or even television. As Katia, who lived in a remote neighbourhood at the outskirts of Athens, said:

> I was part of the mobilization at Syntagma, but I was expecting that my neighbours here wouldn't have any idea about what's actually going on in the city centre. This neighbourhood was never very politically active. I was surprised to find out that some of my neighbours were actually more advanced than me at the local level; I even received an invitation to form a solidarity structure here. The structure itself did not last long and only did a few meetings, however, it is indicative of the whole situation. It was as if a thread had been weaved in those days; a thread that was everywhere and affected everyone.

In her ethnographic dispatch, Maro Pantazidou (2013) similarly showed how different people spontaneously started neighbourhood assemblies too. She emphasizes that in many cases 'local assemblies were born of the need to make actionable decisions, directly relevant to people's lives, something that is often limited by the scope and size of national movements that situate themselves in the central political stage' (Pantazidou 2013: 764). This quote points to the catalytic role of the conditions that allowed this rhizomatic expansion to take place. Like Pantazidou, Sofia Adam, a prominent researcher in the field of social and solidarity economy in Greece, mentions in an interview we held together:

> Solidarity economy ventures were created spontaneously after 2011 to such an extent that we can speak of a new cooperative movement. A combination of reasons allowed this rapid expansion. On the one hand, it was the rise of social movements. On the other, it was the conditions of extreme crisis and unemployment, which led people to experiment with collaborative forms of employment.

The expansion of the new commons was so rapid and unplanned that it created a very fluid environment, almost impossible to capture and analyse. In the first years after 2011, in which this boom had not been systematically documented, ventures many times made calls to come together and meet one other. The Festival for Solidarity and Cooperative Economy, the Commons Fest, the B-Fest, the Ecofests and many more gatherings were revealing of an unprecedented activity on the field, on the one hand, and a deep disintegration and fragmentation of the projects, on the other. Desperate efforts, both official and unofficial, to map them on the part of researchers, political organizations, independent organizations and even the state were unavoidably partial and fragmented, as well. Even in the case of social and solidarity economy entities, which are compelled by law to register in official registers, a combination of a volatile environment and inefficiency on the part of the state did not allow anything more than rough estimations to be made (Varvarousis et al. 2017). All this is complementary evidence to back the central argument of this section: that new commons, under specific conditions of crisis and instability and through their co-productive relation with social movements, can expand rhizomatically.

Final remarks on rhizomatic expansions

This chapter contributes to the discussion on the relationship between the commons and social movements and explains how the commons expand and multiply, as well as what is the relation of this expansion to broader, more contentious forms of social mobilization. The chapter reviews many of the existing theoretical frameworks on the commons and examines what those frameworks tell us about the research questions mentioned earlier. I argue that some of the prevalent theoretical frameworks on the field have not developed any theoretical insights on the expansion of the commons since this question is not part of their focus. I also argue that their treatment of social movements is in some cases superficial and mechanistic and does not explain in depth the porous interactions between social movements and the new commons. Moreover, I argue that even those theories that manage to address important aspects of the issue do it in a normative manner, as their theoretical arguments revolve around the question of how to expand the commons instead of how do the commons actually expand.

The chapter is anchored on a detailed examination of Greek social mobilizations in the 2008–11 period and the boom of the new commons that followed. The main point was to show how social mobilizations can operate as a matrix for the new commons to emerge and multiply; moreover, I have examined the role of liminal commons, transitional forms of commoning that may develop during social mobilization, in this expansion. I have also explored the continuities and discontinuities between different cycles of mobilization, and I have argued that not only can the commons be regarded as social outcomes of the social movements, but they can also become the foundational structures for the next cycle of social mobilization. From this theoretical perspective, social movements are not just necessary supplements for the commons to expand, nor are the commons necessary supplements for the social movements to achieve their goals.

In these contexts, and with a multidimensional crisis as an important if not a foundational parameter in this analysis, I argue that this expansion can follow a rhizomatic pattern. Rhizomatic expansion is characterized by the simultaneous emergence of various commoning projects in different places and times, a phenomenon that in biology is called punctuation. This happens within a highly accelerating spiral, in which new projects do not know each other and are very loosely connected, primarily through unforeseen encounters. Rhizomes are unstable and so are their nodes, which appear and disappear quickly. This kind of expansion adds new substance to the rules of the model suggested by De Angelis (2017), which involves a tripartite structure consisting in symbiotic/meta-commonal/boundary-commoning relations, because rhizomatic expansion highlights the openness, inclusiveness, non-linearity and diffusion pattern of the process, while it also operates as a metaphor that can capture the shape that such an expansion can take. More specifically, De Angelis' framework aims at exploring mainly the scaling-up process of a particular, already existing commons, its ontogenesis so to say, while my work aims at shedding light on the

4. Commons in Expansion

process of creation, expansion and multiplication of new commons systems.

The rhizomatic expansion of commons that I am suggesting is both a metaphor and an actual pattern of expansion with analytical value. It highlights the 'underground stem' that is created in periods of social turbulence (crisis), in which shaken subjectivities marked by collective experiences such as those of massive social mobilizations seek to create new social infrastructure and transform the urban fabric. This non-linear and often horizontal underground stem flourishes in different places and times and creates the nodes of the rhizome which is different from the more stable nodal network. The entire process is marked both symbolically and functionally by the liminal commons, these precarious forms of commoning that operate as improvised collective rituals that aim at transcending the contemporary crisis.

Chapter 5

BEYOND CLOSURE AND OPENNESS

At a meeting of the American Association of Physical Anthropology, Michael Wilson presented his theory of territoriality and lethal aggression in chimpanzees. The bottom line of his argument is that chimpanzees – especially adult males – are extremely aggressive, and this aggression is often driven by a sense of territoriality. Due to its obvious relevance for human nature, the finding caused a big cycle of discussions in the 'Twitterverse'. If chimpanzees are territorial beings that can become lethally aggressive to defend their area, humans should be similar. However, the debate heated up when someone posted the findings of a study on bonobo apes – a sister species of chimpanzees and equally related to humans – showing that they are hardly ever aggressive and territorial.

This anecdote points to the different perceptions of the role of boundaries in human settlements. This discussion is often carried out in naturalistic terms. Some try to normalize the imposition of rigid boundaries as an inevitable trait of human nature, while others condemn them as cultural artefacts of a skewed historical trajectory. In effect, the central question underlying such debates is: Is closure or openness the essence of the human being?

This chapter departs from the observation that the discussion on the commons is largely marked by this false dilemma; it goes on to deconstruct this binary opposition and reconstruct the debate around the question of the *protection of the commons*. The main argument is that *to protect their commons, commoners often invent ways that transcend the question of closure versus openness*. In light of this, I argue that it is necessary to abandon such a dichotomous polarizing debate and focus on the diverse and often contradictory strategies that commoners employ to protect their ventures.

In order to do so, the chapter starts by describing how the issue of closure and openness is addressed in the first body of literature, that of Ostrom and the theorists who followed and expanded her legacy. The rest of the chapter is divided into two sections. The first section is theoretical. It discusses issues of openness and closure in the commons literature, drawing on the thought of three prominent scholars in the field: David Harvey, Antonio Negri and Michel Hardt. The reason behind this choice is that these theorists occupy diametrically opposed positions. Harvey is in favour of closure, while Hardt and Negri are in favour of openness. In the first part of this section, the debate is explored theoretically and philosophically with a political focus. I aim to reveal the main strengths and weaknesses of each perspective and ultimately to push the discussion beyond this polarization. The second part of this section sets the basis for 'escaping' this polarization. The chapter moves on with an empirical part. It draws on the experiences of a series of new commons that were created in Greece over the last decade. It presents the multiple strategies that commoners can employ to protect their commons, overcoming the closure–openness dichotomy in practice. The chapter concludes with some reflections on the findings.

Closure and openness in Ostrom's framework

For economists, the question of closure or openness of the commons has a straightforward response: it is mainly a matter of rivalry or subtractability. To counter Hardin's theory of 'the tragedy of the commons', Elinor Ostrom emphasizes that Hardin is wrong partially because he conflates the commons with open-access goods. Following the work of Ciriacy-Wantrup and Bishop (1975), Ostrom argues that the presence of boundaries is 'the single defining characteristic' of common property as opposed to open-access resources (Ostrom 1990: 91).

Ostrom's idea is driven by scarcity. As natural resources are rival goods, the absence of clearly defined boundaries to exclude 'outsiders' will lead to overuse and, consequently, the degradation of the resource. However, more assumptions are underlying Ostrom's insistence on boundaries. First, she understands boundaries as essential for guaranteeing that those who benefit from the resource are the ones who have invested time and effort in setting up institutional arrangements and other technologies for the appropriation of resource units. In her own words, 'local appropriators face the risk that any benefits they produce by their efforts will be reaped by others who have not contributed to those efforts' (Ostrom 1990: 91).

Ostrom naturalizes possession and property through use, or in other words, the right to use is translated into the right to exclude. This is confirmed in her later work, where she asserts that besides the fact that it does not need to be divided into pieces, common property is not different, in essence, from private property (McKean and Ostrom 1995). Second, Ostrom argues that without the right to exclude 'outsiders', commoners will not have enough incentives to establish coordination procedures or put any effort into commons management (Ostrom 1990).

For all these reasons, clearly defined boundaries and exclusion become the cornerstones of Ostrom's theory on common-pool resources. Implicit in Ostrom's logic on boundaries is a perception of humans – derived from the broader neoclassical economic theory – as predominantly (though not always, as I explained in the first chapter) rational, self-interested and individualist. This depiction of humans as individualistic is generalized to apply to groups of humans as well. If self-interest is the primary motive of human activity at both the individual and the collective level, then an act of closure is essential. Property and exclusion arise as inseparable and inevitable natural pillars of social life, and scarcity is the omnipresent principle that shapes human behaviour over the commons. Commons are created only if they are compatible with group interests that reflect individual interests. Despite Ostrom's criticism of profit maximization and technocratic efficiency as central motives of human activity, her interpretation of individual and collective incentives does not escape economism.

The logic that naturalistically relates the enclosure of the commons to rivalry and scarcity is not limited to economic circles. Approaching the matter from a different angle, Stefan Meretz (2012) argues that drawing boundaries is essential for rival goods but unnecessary for non-rival goods because while the major problem in the former is overuse, in the latter it is underuse and abandonment. Likewise, Silke Helfrich (2012: 101) stresses that 'in the case of rival goods, restrictions to access are necessary [. . .] in the case of non-rival goods, only open access guarantees their development to everyone's greatest benefit'; she goes on to argue that in relation to the latter excludability is socially produced. While there is no consensus among scholars on whether digital commons and non-rival goods, in general, should be left totally unprotected from overuse[1] or be restricted to some extent, this last quote is important, as it denaturalizes the imposition of boundaries

---

1. For a more comprehensive view of the topic, see in the previous chapter the theories on commons expansion of Vasilis Kostakis and Michael Bauwens or see their papers mentioned in the references.

and grounds the question of closure or openness of the common in the contingency of the sociopolitical field.

Indeed, even though she seems inclined to leave the relation between rivalry and excludability largely unchallenged, Helfrich acknowledges that excludability 'depends *on the concrete circumstances*, on what we, as acting individuals are capable of doing, and on our decisions' (Helfrich 2012: 100, emphasis added). On the other hand, Meretz builds upon the idea that excludability is socially produced and consequently distinguishes between two main social systems: the market and the commons. 'Markets are based on and continuously create structural isolation', as in this context people cooperate only to better hold their ground in competitive situations; ultimately, markets are characterized by 'structural exclusion' (Meretz 2012: 59). He goes on to argue that, in contrast, the commons 'work only if everybody is included in the community and nobody is excluded. They are based on cooperation, and they generate cooperation', and therefore the commons represent 'structural commonality' or 'structural inclusion' (Meretz 2012: 62).

Undoubtedly, there is great merit in placing 'concrete circumstances' at the epicentre of the discussion on closure and openness in the production of the commons, as it denaturalizes the debate and opens it up to the contingency and multiplicity of real life. However, these theories are not free from dualisms and clear-cut polarizations following an either–or dialectics. Meretz clearly imbues commons with connotations of intrinsic reciprocity, inclusion, cooperation and responsibility, while the market is associated with the qualities of isolation, cut-throat competition and 'structural irresponsibility'. This juxtaposition is important, as it tries to frame the basic characteristics of two distinct social systems that certainly involve different qualities and dynamics; however, it has little analytical value for explaining the often contradictory dynamics involved in the making of any commons. As Meretz explicitly puts it, his theory assumes 'two different concepts of humanity' (Meretz 2012: 58) that are antithetical to one another. Isn't this conception a reproduction of the naturalistic discourse that it supposedly tries to overcome?

Closure and openness: A political and philosophical debate

The debate about closure and openness becomes bolder if we shift our focus from the economic dimension and the rival–non-rival dichotomy to more political and philosophical aspects. As the discussion around the common(s) has become the 'new normal' in the seeking of alternatives to capitalism, different schools of thought have emerged that try to push the debate towards different directions. These different schools often develop conflicting views on how the commons must be constructed. When it comes to the issue of openness versus closure, Hardt and Negri favour the former, while David Harvey favours the latter.

Harvey's logic

Harvey argues in favour of closure in any attempt to construct the common(s). He bases his position upon the issues of scale, complexity, state oppression and capitalist co-optation. In Harvey's logic, closure goes hand in hand with authoritarianism and hierarchy, composing together an unavoidable triptych to be taken into consideration by any attempt to create the common.

The scale is framed as the first major problem that urges for some sort of hierarchy. Drawing on Ostrom's explorations, Harvey argues that most of the cases studied by her are small and involve around a hundred users. Consequently, he argues that anything much larger than this requires hierarchy because 'direct negotiation between all individuals is impossible' (Harvey 2012: 69).

Complexity is Harvey's second concern. In the face of increasing complexity in a technological and globalized capitalism, he argues that 'a total reorganization of materialized organizational forms like New York City or Los Angeles is much harder to envisage let alone accomplish now than a century ago' because 'the fixity of structures tends to increase with time, making the conditions of change more rather than less sclerotic' (Harvey 2000: 185). This complexity renders 'the question of closure' unavoidable (Harvey 2000: 185). At this point, Harvey unfolds his perception of social change. He says that despite the confusion over the relationship between the commons and the 'evils' of enclosures, 'some sort of enclosure is often the best way to preserve certain kinds of valued commons' (Harvey 2012: 70). Here, Harvey reproduces the debate over rival and non-rival commons, but this is of secondary importance. The most important aspect of his argument is that the common is surrounded by an inherently hostile environment. The commons are perpetually endangered, and *an act of protection necessarily involves an act of closure*. Actually, in his view, protection can only be materialized through closure. The procedure goes as follows: first, the people should produce new commons, and more often than not they should enclose them in order to protect them.

Harvey further justifies his endorsement of such acts of enclosure based on the previously mentioned either–or dilemmas. He characteristically says 'at the end of it all, the analyst is often left with a simple decision: Whose side are you on, whose common interests do you seek to protect' (Harvey 2012: 71).

Furthermore, Harvey addresses the issue of state oppression: the state has the monopoly of violence and at any point can dissolve a common by the use of force. Lastly, Harvey is concerned with both the co-optation of the common and its commodification, even if the latter does not necessarily entail the transformation of the common into a commodity. Therefore, he argues in favour of autonomy, which in his view coincides with 'the demand for some kind of closure' (Harvey 2012: 71).

However, Harvey is aware that his view on the enclosure of the commons has a problematic aspect. This is evident when, in his criticism of new urbanism, he argues that 'community has often been a barrier to, rather than facilitator of, social change' (Harvey 2000: 170) or when he admits that speaking about the necessity of enclosures 'sounds like, and is, a contradictory statement, but it reflects a truly contradictory situation' (Harvey 2012: 70). In any case, he insists that it is naïve to think that closure and enforcement can be avoided (Harvey 2012).

Hardt and Negri's logic

Michael Hardt and Antonio Negri are probably the most prominent supporters of the opposite view, as they argue in favour of a 'society based on open sharing of the common' (Hardt and Negri 2012: 89). They ground their claims about openness in historical, philosophical and political assumptions whose main pillars are the concepts of *multitude* and *love*. Their analysis juxtaposes the 'exclusive, unified social body of property' to the inclusive, 'plural and open political body' of the multitude of the poor (Hardt and Negri 2009: 39). Actually, they assume that property – the foundational pillar of the 'republic' – creates individuals who are simultaneously in competition and unification, while open sharing of the common creates singularities that are multiplicities 'in the process of becoming' and are 'open to encounters with all other bodies'; most importantly, the outcome of these encounters depends on the qualities they involve and not on other preconceived static social relations.

For them, unification and property are based on identity construction, while the larger social body of the common is 'constructed by the movements of passions and languages, according to logics of both desire and rationality' (Harvey, Hardt and Negri 2009: 12) that are processes of continuous subjectification and de-subjectification. In this theoretical effort, the concept of 'love' is central; they insist that it be employed as a philosophical and political concept and consider that to cede the concept to priests, poets and psychoanalysts would be a great omission of contemporary thought (Hardt and Negri 2009).

For Hardt and Negri, love is not 'spontaneous and passive. It does not simply happen to us [...] instead it is an action, a biopolitical event, planned and realized in common' (Hardt and Negri 2009: 180). Hence, they assign to love a constitutive dimension: 'love is a process of the production of the common and the production of subjectivity' (Hardt and Negri 2009: 180); love is not only a means but also an end itself. Love is also an 'economic power' that produces networks and schemes of cooperation or, in other words, love is the ontological event that ruptures what exists to create the world anew.

At this point, Hardt and Negri elaborate their arguments against the closure of the common. If love is the constitutive force that creates the common, then why is our world characterized by malaise in almost every aspect of social life as well as in our relation with our environment at large? Hardt and Negri argue that love, like the common itself, is highly ambivalent and susceptible to corruption; they insist that today the predominant forms of love are the corrupted ones (Hardt and Negri 2009).

What corrupts love then?

For Hardt and Negri, the primary factor in the corruption of love is the shift *from the common to the same*, which reduces the production of the common to a repetitive process of unification and of production of identity. Identarian love is corrupted love, as inscribed in the mandate to love those that are more proximate, 'most like you' as they emphatically put it. Family love, love for the nation and love for those with whom one shares the same ideology are such corrupted forms of love. In contrast, 'love for the other' or 'love for alterity' is the means to reverse such corrupted forms of love (Hardt and Negri 2009: 182).

This analysis of love as both a constitutive force that produces the common and a force that composes the singularities into larger social bodies – assemblages – is diametrically opposed to Harvey's analysis on the necessity of closure in every act of emancipatory commoning. To explain this in more detail, I will now present the theoretical and political assumptions that inform these two approaches.

The foundations of the debate

David Harvey's logic on the commons is built upon two assumptions: first, that the commons must be created a priori in a hostile environment and, second, that humans are not inherently cooperative beings that tend to love 'the other' or alterity in general. Harvey takes a pragmatic stance – at least in his view – and seeks solutions that can immediately be implemented by those who actually participate in the making of the common. Moreover, he is apprehensive about the ability of capitalism to commodify goods created in common and turn them into means for expanding capital accumulation. Hence, Harvey is primarily interested in questions of how the commons can avoid being captured and co-opted by capitalism.

Moreover, Harvey insists that it is crucial for the left to engage with the issue of closure, as he believes that there is a fetishization of openness and horizontality (Harvey 2000; 2013). His aim, however, is not to start a discussion on whether the closure is necessary for the protection and expansion of the commons, as he considers any other opinion on the topic naïve; instead, his interest is in the ways those properties should be implemented. This leads to a second point about his thought: *Harvey believes that scholars ought to offer practical and concrete proposals – models – on how to solidify the commons against capitalist accumulation.* This is evident in his critique of Lefebvre and Foucault in his *Spaces of Hope* (2000), but also in his critique of Hardt and Negri, where he declares, 'enough of relationalities and immaterialities!', and 'reformism [is a] prelude to revolution' (Harvey, Hardt and Negri 2009: 9–10). In short, Harvey represents a line of thinking that focuses on the inherent 'flaws' of the capitalist system, and, additionally, he is fed up with postmodern calls for cultural change, which focus on the body, affects and social relations beyond capital-as-social-relation. Drawing on the undeniable difficulties in creating robust alternatives 'here and now' *outside* the realm of the capital, Harvey envisages a *fortification* of common production, one that will be able to counter capital's capacity to assimilate and co-opt common creation.

Philosophically, Harvey's ideas are founded on an either–or dialectic; as he admits, 'the dialectic of either/or is omnipresent' (Harvey 2000: 184). They are also founded on a *transcendental* philosophy, where different institutions and models should be put forward beforehand to be materialized afterwards.

Hardt and Negri's proposals, on the other hand, have different philosophical origins and consequently serve different objectives.

Whereas Harvey's proposals on closure and hierarchy are traversed by a transcendental philosophy, Hard and Negri's ideas are driven by a philosophy of *immanence*, as they follow a line of thought first introduced by Baruch Spinoza and further elaborated by Gilles Deleuze and Felix Guattari. This is probably the main reason that, in their analysis, *a world of the common is already here, and the only pending task is to organize it differently to transform its corrupted mutations*. They make this explicit when they claim that 'this immanent scene is the terrain – the only possible terrain – on which democracy can be constructed' (Hardt and Negri 2009: 16) and that 'a democracy of the multitude is imaginable and possible only because we all share and participate in the common' (Hardt and Negri 2009: viii). Of course, Hardt and Negri are fully aware that the process of metamorphosis they invoke cannot simply happen spontaneously; this is why they insist on the educational processes that can transform 'refusal into resistance and violence into the use of force' (Hardt and Negri 2009: 16). Central in this education process is what they call the 'struggle over the control or autonomy of the production of subjectivity' (Hardt and Negri 2009: x).

On the other hand, their belief in the immanent capacities of human societies to self-invent the future is what prevents Hardt and Negri from formulating concrete proposals and alternative models for transcending the current social condition. As they manifest, 'a book like ours should strive to understand the present but also challenge and inspire its readers to invent the future' (Harvey, Hardt and Negri 2009: 13). In contrast to Harvey's strong belief that any creation of the common today will necessarily take place in a hostile environment – and, by extension, that fortification or closure is always needed – Hardt and Negri insist on looking at the inherent multiple contradictions that traverse singularities and larger assemblages more generally; they argue in favour of an open and inclusive education process that will empower the most positive elements of these multiplicities. This is why in their theoretical endeavour they employ the concept of love: to emphasize the communicative process of commoning that can establish unpredictable connections among subjects previously perceived as separated.

Beyond polarization – Towards an analytics of openness and closure

David Harvey's insistence on the necessity of enclosure and on its positive role in the maintenance of the commons highlights a very important issue, that *of the protection of the commons*. Indeed, the commons are social systems that require a tremendous amount of creative human labour to materialize. To this extent, the commons can indeed constitute assemblages of an alternate social and spatial ordering, affective relations, values, institutions and so on. Commons are systems that strive to maintain some sort of autonomy from capital. Hence, their existence, sustainability and expansion always depend on their fragile relationship with it.

Yet, this is not the only reason why actual commoners seek to protect their common worlds. If one questions the supremacy of the economy over other aspects of social organization, one must also understand the 'threat' of capital as only one among the many threats that the commons face. Therefore, making protection identical to closure can be seen as a problematic reduction. As I will explain in the empirical part, commoners employ different methods to protect their commons, ranging from acts of closure to acts of opening, but, most importantly, commoners often invent ways to protect their commons that transcend the question of closure versus openness.

David Harvey suggests that, due to complexity, large-scale management necessarily implies hierarchical and authoritarian structures. The main problem upon which he founds this assumption is that communication between all participants in the common is often impossible. While it is true that in historical and present forms of social organization hierarchy often constitutes the only response to increasing complexity, there is empirical and scientific evidence that over the last decades, humans have experimented with and put forward exemplary methods to overcome this problem. As Frederix Laloux convincingly shows in his study on self-organized, horizontal corporate organizations (2014), there are organizations with tens of thousands of employees who have managed – to a certain extent at least – to operate without a strong hierarchy but only with a few coordinators who facilitate communication between participants. In fact, Laloux's main argument is quite the opposite of Harvey's: whereas hierarchy has been an important solution for coping with a certain degree of complexity, it could never deal with the speed and complexity of contemporary social organizations better than a structured and coordinated but non-hierarchical and self-organized apparatus (2014).

This point is crucial, not only because it suggests that well-developed models already exist – even if there are more inspiring and effective ideas than Harvey cares to admit – but also because it stresses the fact that self-organization is not necessarily as uncoordinated and unstructured as many orthodox Marxist and even anarchist thinkers and practitioners believe. Actual commoners seem to have incorporated similar views on self-organization into their everyday struggle to organize their common productive, (re)productive and recreational activities in effective ways while maintaining their structural horizontality and self-organization. Contrary to Harvey's depiction of these efforts as naïve and driven by an ideological fixation on horizontality, commoners continue to implement new forms of horizontal organization in their struggle. This is the case not only because they have repeatedly come up against the impasses of vertical and hierarchical structures, but also because they have realized that horizontality is more effective in fulfilling their needs.

On the other hand, a discourse that elevates openness to a primary element of commons constitution without seriously taking into account the multiple 'threats' the commons face in their everyday operation – and, by extension, their need to defend themselves – has little value, not only in the creation but also in the analysis of commoning processes. This is where Hardt and Negri's arguments may face harsh criticism, not because they do not incorporate the issue of closure into their analysis, but because they avoid complementing their anti-hierarchical and anti-identitary principles with a meaningful exploration of how commons systems can sustain and expand themselves. Their 'institutional decision-making', which 'allows singularities to achieve some consistency in their interactions and behaviours' (Hardt and Negri 2009: 358), is a very vague and limited concept, which, however, makes an important contribution, as it refers to a constituent rather than a constituted process. Their insistence on rejecting any form of identity creation means that they envisage 'singularity institutions that are perpetually in flux' (Hardt and Negri 2009: 358), which cannot offer even a minimum guarantee of protection to commoners.

Hardt and Negri's work is traversed by such extreme antithetical proposals that are situated in the opposite pole of what could be called 'conventional thinking'. While this has great value, as it destabilizes important pillars of the current social organization, in many cases it lacks analytical value. For instance, when they argue that property is the founding pillar of capitalism and of 'the Republic' and therefore contrast property with 'the open sharing of the common', they neglect that most commons systems need, at certain periods, to take a rest from continuous fluidity and feel secure in a relatively defined system. For that reason, the opposite of property is not necessarily absolutely free or open sharing.

Closure and openness in the post-liminal period of the Greek commoning movement

Protecting the commons: A labyrinth of strategies

In the first chapter of the book, I examine how the crisis created an ambiguous and fluid social environment, which proved catalytic for the development of the liminal commons of indignant squares and the consequent rhizomatic expansion of commoning projects throughout the Greek territory. I also explain that liminal commons, which are transitory, precarious and metastatic forms of commoning, are characterized by openness, inclusiveness, de-identification, high membership turnover, practical creation, inventiveness and social imitation. These properties are what makes liminal commons the expanding mode of commoning, as they allow them to become popular and widespread. Moreover, liminality is critical because it is the basis upon which transformative social processes unfold; these processes seek to invent new forms of sociality born within and because of the crisis of a particular social structure, but also to prefigure important characteristics of a future social structure.

In the second chapter of the book, I examine how liminal commons expanded in the wake of the squares movement. I also argue that while some of the new projects, especially those occupying and commoning urban public space, continued to be liminal, most other projects did not: they either started off as liminal and then evolved into more stable structures with permeable, but not open, boundaries or were launched as well-defined commons systems employing mechanisms of boundary setting and therefore incorporating some forms of closure. However, whether commoning projects set boundaries or not is not the only important question to ask. It is also worth exploring why they set those boundaries, how they enforce them, what these boundaries imply for their operation, how projects regulate the relations between the inside and the outside of their common world and what other mechanisms, apart from closure, they employ to protect their ventures.

Such nuanced discussion on the role of boundaries in the production and protection of the commons will allow us to move beyond a debate that seems exhausted and incapable of providing an analytical framework for explaining real-world commoning practices. In actual social systems, neither a mandatory closure linked to authority and hierarchy nor a completely open process of mutual love and open sharing prove to be effective guiding principles of organization. My main argument is that *processes of the commons protection often combine elements and mechanisms that cannot be captured by the dichotomy of closure versus openness*. On the other hand, even if it would constitute an important step forward, simply to assume that commons systems alternate between the two strategies – that is, that commons choose to either close or open their boundaries according to their needs – is not sufficient, since it downplays the contradictions that traverse every act of protection of a commons. Likewise, despite its high descriptive significance and its value as a guiding principle, the claim for 'semi-permeable boundaries' (Bollier and Helfrich 2019) has little analytical value in explaining different protection strategies.

The commons that I have studied over the years of my research seem to employ a wide spectrum of often conflicting and contradictory strategies to ensure their protection, longevity, reproduction and smooth operation. This observation is important because it reveals that while in theory, things appear to follow an either–or separation, in reality, things are more complex: an act of closure can be the consequence of an act of opening and vice versa, or an act of closure can simultaneously become an act of openness. This is because the commons are social systems that often operate at different scales and levels and include different commoning activities (i.e. they are 'manifold commons'). Therefore, an act of closure at one level may imply an opening at another one; obviously, such a case should be examined more closely, as it does not fit in rough either–or dichotomies. As it becomes obvious that the problem of openness versus closure is a complex one, a few concrete examples/patterns may help shed some new light on its many aspects.

Pattern A: Protection through 'open' regulation

Allilegyi Peiraia (Piraeus Solidarity) is a collective founded in 2012 in the port town of Piraeus, near Athens. Over the years of its operation, the collective has developed a wide range of activities in various fields of production and reproduction, including the establishment of a food bank,[2] a solidarity school,[3] a social kitchen, a workshop for clothes

---

2. A food bank is an initiative that collects food from various sources (through exchange, donations by individuals, donations by commercial shops, open-air market merchants, organizations, etc.) and stores them to (re)distribute them to the participants of the collective.

3. A solidarity school is a self-organized school that offers free courses in various fields for high school students, as well as in foreign languages for both children and adults.

and furniture manufacturing and processing, a social clinic, urban and peri-urban agriculture, and many more. At first, they started with food collection and redistribution to counter what they saw as the 'most urgent issue of the first phase of the crisis', the danger of starvation. They started off delivering food parcels[4] and free meals to whoever was in need. As the collective developed the capacity to collect large quantities of food and prepare hundreds of meals in their social kitchen, the issue of free-riding emerged: many passers-by were requesting food parcels or free meals without offering anything back to the collective. According to Katia, one of the first members of the group, 'At some point, there were only fifty of us registered members to serve eight hundred people.' This created a dual problem for the collective. On the one hand, there was a resource problem, as such a high demand could not be satisfied only through donations. On the other, they realized that this could end up becoming a charitable organization rather than a horizontal, self-organized grassroots venture, which was their objective. Thus, they looked for ways to motivate their beneficiaries to participate more actively in the commoning practices.

Against this background, they introduced a diverse set of new practices and institutions. First, they decided that for people to be able to benefit from the food distribution, they had to offer at least some hours of personal work per week to the collective. 'We want people here to believe both in themselves and in the collective, not simply to continue to passively consume whatever they are offered', as Kostas stated. To organize this system, they introduced the 'Porto', a community currency to facilitate internal transactions. The 'Porto' is a measure of the hours each member has worked for the collective. There are a minimum and a maximum of hours of 'paid' work for each person; the rest is regarded as volunteering. While this act may at first glance seem like an act of closure, since one of its purposes was to minimize free-riding, it cannot, however, be reduced to it. The introduction of the 'Porto' was followed by a conscious decision that the collective would remain open to everybody who wanted to be part of it. This was translated into a dramatic increase in registered members – from 50 to almost 200 –

---

4. Food parcels is a very popular activity among the solidary hubs presented in the previous chapter. It consists in collecting food, mainly through donations by individuals outside big supermarkets, and subsequently distributing them to families in need.

and an equally dramatic decrease in free-riding; it also contributed to opening up the collective to new fields of experimentation with new practices and processes. The shift in the relation between those who offer and those who receive created 'a dynamism that was previously unthinkable', as Evgenios, another member, mentions.

Pattern B: Protection through multiplication

This opening of the commons to new layers of activity as a means not only to expand but also to protect the venture is quite a popular practice in the Greek commoning movement, and it can be observed in different kinds of commoning projects and geographies. As Nikos, one of my informants, articulately put it, 'having only one level of activity means that your venture will last for as long as the external conditions will allow, but if you manage to create not simply a one-dimensional venture but a small universe of interconnected practices, then you may have the possibility to survive in the long run.'

The fact that a one-dimensional activity is often an unsustainable strategy for new commons is evident in the case of the solidarity hubs that I analysed in the previous chapter. Many of those ventures started off with only one goal: to collect food to support individuals and families in need by handing out 'food parcels'. The most common manner of collecting food is as follows: members of the collective go once or twice per week to big supermarkets. At the exit of the store, they place a big basket, which they often call the 'solidarity basket'. They then hand out pamphlets to entering customers, asking them to buy some basic items from an indicative list and place them in the 'solidarity basket' when they exit. After a few hours, they have usually collected the expected amount of food; they then sort it and prepare it into food parcels to deliver to families in need.

This practice was very effective in the first years of operation of the solidarity hubs, as many consumers were willing to donate products; eventually, however, it started to fade out, as fewer and fewer consumers were willing to contribute to the basket. This was confirmed by several members of the solidarity hubs I studied in 2016. Elena, an informant active in the solidarity hub of Vironas, a neighbourhood not far from the city centre, maintains: 'People got tired of this process. They stopped feeling good only by offering some products, and gradually many stopped doing it. Now we have a problem in supporting our people.' Indeed, many solidarity hubs did not manage to find new ways of action and gradually faded out or perished. At the same time, there is a strong tendency for commoning projects to evolve into what Bresnihan and Byrne (2015) call 'manifold commons', that is, commons that have more than one layer of activity. The crux of this observation is that to protect and sustain themselves, commoning ventures are often forced to multiply their activities. This deviates from the view that has dominated recent literature on the commons, which departs from a more normative and political point of view and links every act of expansion and multiplication to the broader 'autopoietic process' (De Angelis 2017) of commons systems towards social change and vis-à-vis capital. In other words, while many thinkers celebrate every commoning expansion as a strike against capitalism, my fieldwork findings suggest that in many cases new commons expand and multiply their activities as a strategy for escaping stagnation and dissolution. This, as I argue in continuation, has an important impact on their transformative potential.

One characteristic but highly controversial strategy, as it represents an act of multiplication and protection but also a big point of disagreement for more radical and anti-capitalist commons thinkers (Caffentzis and Federici 2014), is the shift of many projects towards creating employment opportunities for their members *within* capitalist economies. While the creation of employment opportunities is, by definition, foundational for cooperatives – or 'common productive assets', as we named cooperatives in the previous chapter – many other new commons that started off as independent from and antithetical to capitalist markets gradually started to consider expanding their activities to include more mainstream job creation in order to survive. As Fotini, a member of the Piraeus Solidarity hub, says:

> In the beginning, our main concern was to ensure that we have food to eat. But as food donations are on the decrease, and also because in our collective many young members really want to work and be productive, and we will lose them if we don't try to help them towards this direction, we have now shifted our focus to job creation.

The clothing and furniture workshop mentioned in my analysis of the collective along with other cooperative experiments that emerged from within Piraeus Solidarity are some examples of this dual multiplication–protection strategy.

Like Piraeus Solidarity, Plato's Academy Cooperative Café is a venture launched back in 2010 by a group of young people in order to 'create human relationships anew', to 'cultivate an alternative culture of public space use' and to become 'a cell for reclaiming a degree of autonomy and self-organization' based on synergies, as Chrys, one of the founding members, says. The venture started its operation on a volunteer basis, since the creation of employment opportunities was not among the main concerns of their members, as they explicitly mention. However, running a commoning venture is a time and energy-consuming process; this is not always taken into serious consideration by commoners when they start their ventures. This fact, in combination with very high unemployment rates among young Greeks, often creates tensions for commoners, who on the one hand invest much energy in sustaining the commons and, on the other, cannot even cover their basic needs through this participation. Indicatively, our survey showed that only 39 per cent of respondents relate their participation in the venture with the satisfaction of material needs of any sort and an even smaller 10 per cent relate their participation with monetary earnings.

This discrepancy between the time and energy that commoners devote to their ventures and the material benefits they obtain from their participation has been a key factor in the dissolution of many ventures, as for many participants it leads to a 'burnout effect' and consequently to withdrawal. In the case of Plato's Academy Cooperative Café, this observation became the grounds for modifying the operating principles of the project. As Christos says, 'after a few years, we realized that to continue operating we had to forego our volunteer status and try to create at least some jobs, for those involved more actively.' This necessity led to a collective decision to establish a minimum compensation for each member who works at the café; it also led to the creation of a parallel catering cooperative, the Nomadic Kitchen, which also employed members of the initial group. This shift allowed some of the members to secure the means of their subsistence and consequently to avoid the burnout effect caused by trying to combine their waged work outside the project with active commoning inside it. Thus, the continuation of the project was made possible.

Pattern C: Protection through networking

In the first stream of literature on the commons, that of Ostrom and her followers, networking between commoning ventures has been a neglected aspect; in the more recent, post-Marxist, literature, however, it is receiving growing attention. However, in most cases, networking is understood as a means through which commons can create 'commons ecologies' (De Angelis 2017) that will be able to counter the hegemony of the capitalist system (De Angelis 2017; Stavrides 2016; Caffentzis and Federici 2014; Kioupkiolis 2014). In this respect, very little attention has been paid to how networking operates as a source of protection for each venture participating in the network, as more often than not thinkers focus on the 'big picture'.

This reading is indeed shared by many commoning ventures since networking is perceived as a means of visibility or of intervention in the sphere of politics; nevertheless, there is growing evidence that, for many ventures, 'meta-commonal' relations (De Angelis 2017) between diverse projects also constitute a strategy of protection and sustainability.

Unlike other networking efforts that primarily aim at exchanging knowledge and know-how, the Network of Cooperative Ventures of Athens aims at creating an active support mechanism for participating cooperatives. The number of ventures participating in the network is limited, as new entrants should meet certain criteria and go through a preparatory period to become ordinary members, even though the network is, in principle, open to new members. Besides the exchange of know-how and knowledge, the mechanism includes the exchange of services and goods to create a basis for the 'circulation of commons' (Bauwens and Kostakis 2014), that is, the bases for a more robust and sustainable commoning project that can also have a greater social and political impact. In other words, although autonomous from one another, the ventures strive to create a network that will protect them and facilitate their operation. This aspect became evident when one of the collectives comprising the network experienced a mass resignation of members, becoming incapable of operating. Even though the rest of the collectives in the network did not all belong to the same economic sector, they decided to contribute during the transitional period, until the ailing collective was once more able to operate autonomously; they even relocated some of their members for several months to replace those who left. Thanks to its networking with other cooperatives, the cooperative restaurant managed to survive.

In a similar vein, the National Network of Social Clinics and Pharmacies, presented in the previous chapter, operated on several occasions as a source of stability and protection for the commoning projects participating in it. As Vaso, from the social clinic of Thessaloniki, states,

> we, as the national network of social clinics, have decided that each social clinic participating in the network should be autonomous from the rest. We do not want our ventures to create annexes, but we

want each city and each community to create their own institutions. However, our network is not merely political or informational. We intend to provide help to those collectives that do not have access to medicine or other stuff needed for their operation.

Likewise, in the cities of Rethymno and Karditsa, networking between collectives seems to have been a source of fortification and sustainability for the new commons. Karditsa has a relatively long tradition in cooperativism and commoning in comparison to other Greek cities (Varvarousis et al. 2017). This tradition is in many cases translated into robust networks of exchange between diverse projects, in an effort to ensure their longevity. The repertoire of meta-commonal relations between projects includes the provision of small community loans in cases where cooperatives cannot pay their debts, the exchange of services and goods among network members and the organization of joint seminars on aspects of the operation of the ventures. All these are protection strategies that can succeed only through networking. As Panos, one of our informants in Karditsa, noticed: 'Here in Karditsa, we know very well that our ventures cannot survive alone, not even for a minute. This is why we strive, despite the difficulties, to create a culture of cooperation and solidarity between old and new ventures in the city.' Similarly, Apostolos, from the Halikouti project in the city of Rethymno, notices: 'Here we don't aim at creating a network in the usual meaning of the term. Rather, we intend to create a broad community of communities that will be able to counter effectively the big and the small problems that each venture, each participant may have.'

Pattern D: Protection through the opening of political identities

The claim that the opening of political identities and the adoption of a heterogeneous ideological profile can be a factor of sustainability for the new commons, and a conscious strategy for their protection may sound strange. After all, in previous theoretical accounts, cultural and ideological homogeneity has usually been regarded as a source of cohesion and stability for the commons (Ostrom et al. 1999; Stavridis 2016). Indeed, during the liminal period triggered by the crisis and spatialized in the movement of the squares, a wide opening of political identities was witnessed in all politically oriented collective action. Openness, a constitutive element during the period of the squares, became a constituent element in the commons created in its wake. This new condition may be contrasted with the pre-crisis collective political action, characterized by an ideological 'purism' that was often leading collective ventures to disintegration due to ideological mismatches.

Many of the new commons I have studied have consciously chosen to abolish their recognizable ideological identity and any affiliations with particular political parties in order to sustain and protect their ventures. For instance, Trapeza Chronou Holargou-Papagou (Holargou-Papagou TimeBank) was a venture launched by Syriza members and was even hosted at a building rented by the party. When it gradually attracted newcomers who did not want to be identified with Syriza, and through a series of assemblary procedures, the venture decided to become independent from the party not only to keep those new members but also to attract more.

Other projects, which did not start with a particular ideological or political focus but as heterogeneous collectives with a focus on common practice, intentionally try to maintain this unidentifiable status to avoid ideological conflicts due to unavoidable identity mismatches. As Kostas, from Piraeus Solidarity, notices:

> Here in our group we try to avoid taking positions on issues that can threaten our capacity to act together. We are not apolitical, on the contrary, we believe that our collective is highly political, but we believe that the relations and activities that we forge here are worth more than a declaration on a specific political issue that can possibly divide us and bring us into conflict with one another.

Giota, a member of the Politeia collective, emphasizes another aspect of her collective's decision to remain ideologically unidentified; 'Our conscious decision to have and welcome ideological heterogeneity is undoubtedly a difficult one. However, I believe that, despite its difficulties, this heterogeneity is important because it gives rise to personal and collective transcendence, innovation and creativity. I believe that conflicts will exist anyway, but the conflicts that emerge in heterogeneous environments can promote dynamic development and fuel collective action.'

The cornerstone of this strategy for protecting the commons is the starting premise that effective collective action is both possible and desirable, and can be fuelled, rather than suppressed, by heterogeneity. However, differences do not remain unbridged or autonomous, but the ventures try to create ways to articulate them in a creative direction. In contrast with postmodern social theories that celebrate difference in the name of a non-conflictual and peaceful coexistence, or the so-called politics of selves (e.g. Deleuze and Guattari 2012 [1988]; Bhabha 1994; Lichterman 1996), heterogeneity in the commons we have studied is a choice, always accompanied with a conscious process to create common ground. In other words, it is not merely the opening of political identities that contributes to the protection of the commons. Rather, it is the process of creating new common ground on the basis of this opening that makes commons more sustainable. This new common ground is founded not upon pure ideologies or visionary blueprints for the future but upon common principles constructed gradually through processes of de-identification and re-identification, collective practice and visioning. This set of guiding principles, values and institutions are intentionally kept at a low or minimum level, to ensure maximum porosity that allows for membership renewal. This renewal is considered an important antidote to the previously mentioned 'burnout effect', which is a cause of dissolution for many commoning projects.

Guiding principles, thus, are different from ideologies. In many cases, they take the form of rules that express foundational and minimum agreements among commoners. For instance, in the case of the National Network of Solidarity Clinics, the list of guiding principles includes anti-fascist and anti-racist orientation, operation on a volunteer, non-waged basis, independence from the state, the church and private companies and so forth. Likewise, the Network of Cooperative Ventures of Athens has set its own principles. According to Petros, a very active member of the network:

> First, all employees should be equal members of the cooperative; no external waged worker is allowed. Second, surpluses should be used for social causes rather than be distributed among members or simply increase the capital of the collective. Third, ideological conflicts should be avoided if they are not related to practical issues, and, lastly, we do not accept any kind of 'help' from the state and the church.

While those foundational principles obviously constitute an institutional framework that puts limits to what is possible and what is not, they imply an open and porous venture that seeks to integrate and bridge differences rather than emphasize them. This self-limited openness operated as a tool for survival for many of the new commons, as they tried to involve parts of Greek society that were previously indifferent to any kind of collective action beyond the close family environment.

However, the opposite is also possible. Ideological purity and strong collective identities can also become sources of cohesion and longevity for commoning projects. It is important to stress this, as these forms of 'imaginary enclaves' (Stavridis 2013) should not be necessarily viewed as sources of unsustainability and disruption for the commons. As members of the Pagkaki collective, one of the first and most renowned ventures of the social and solidarity economy movement in the country, told me, 'we are unified ideologically and politically, and what keeps us together is our common political aims and visions'. In a similar vein, members of the Akyvernites Politeies bookstore collective in Thessaloniki clearly state that 'one of the main sources of cohesion and sustainability is our common beliefs and worldviews for a different world'.

Yet, the above is not something new. As I argued at the beginning of this subsection, ideological homogeneity is regarded in many theoretical accounts as a source of cohesion and longevity. Here, I wanted to illustrate that the opposite, namely a conscious rejection of homogeneity, does not necessarily lead to a chaotic agglomeration of differences but, if executed properly, can also operate as a source of sustainability and longevity for the commons.

Pattern E: Protection through new communication tools

I will conclude this brief description of the 'labyrinth of strategies' to protect the commons with the experimentation of many collectives with new tools for facilitating communication between both individuals and collectives. Communication practices vary from totally improvised and trial and error to organized systems that include tools deriving from non-violent communication (Rosenberg and Chopra 2015), world café methods or assemblies of feelings.

Putting communication at the epicentre of collective action and experimenting with new tools to achieve consensus are relatively new elements in Greek collective action. In many cases, the issue arose when commoners realized that despite their goodwill and their dedication to the venture, conflicts are frequent, and this may lead to the departure of members or the dissolution of the project altogether. Characteristically, at the assembly of Lampidona, a multilayered commons at the neighbourhood of Vyronas, in Athens, one member said:

> I am wondering whether we have managed to develop, throughout all those years, deep and emancipatory relations among us. My

impression is that despite our declared principles we have failed, and this is the reason behind the recent departure of our comrades (i.e. she refers to a recent break of the group). We must reexamine not only what we want to do through our venture but also how to do it in a way that cultivates strong and healthy relations that can persist. We have focused on results so intently that we have disregarded the human dimension. If we cannot do it otherwise, if we cannot improve the communication between us, the venture will perish.

Another member of the collective took the floor and said, 'I agree. In our assemblies, arguments dominate the discussion, and too little room is left for emotions to be expressed. Solidarity cannot be cultivated through the exchange of arguments, and deep relationships cannot be built only upon common targets. Fixation with targets renders humans expendable. Let me be blunt: if we don't change direction soon, we will break apart.'

Similar processes can be observed in many of the collectives I have studied. Bios Coop, one of the most notable cooperative experiments in Thessaloniki, for instance, went through such a period of mass departures and conflicts. The members of the collective decided to start a process of re-examination of the conflict by organizing a seminar on non-violent communication and a round of facilitated procedures. Likewise, Plato's Academy Cooperative Café has gone through a long process of similar experiments with new tools of communication to overcome emerging conflicts. An interesting example comes from Karditsa. There, the network of collectives organized a series of seminars on how to cooperate and communicate, in which members of more than twenty groups participated.

Resuming the argument

This chapter contributes to the literature on the commons by examining one of the perennial questions regarding their management: openness or closure? The debate has a long history. It has been conducted either in naturalist terms, that is, by building theories upon assumptions about an alleged unified human nature, or in political terms, with different thinkers trying to push towards one or the other direction.

I focus mainly on the work of David Harvey, Michael Hardt and Antonio Negri because they occupy diametrically opposite poles in the debate. After explaining and illustrating their theoretical arguments in favour of openness or closure, I propose that the debate is now exhausted and sterile and that we should move beyond it. This dichotomy does not capture the actual reality of commons formation and operation, in which the core issue is not whether commons will remain open or closed but how they will protect themselves. Subsequently, I argue that actual commons employ for their protection a labyrinth of strategies that cannot be reduced to a dichotomous logic, since within the labyrinth there are complex processes that often overlap and have dual nature, and should, therefore, be examined in more detail.

In the empirical part, I provide a few brief examples to illustrate this diversity of protection strategies. I divide these strategies according to their nature into five groups, and I explain how they contribute to the protection of the commons while deviating from the 'openness versus closure' debate.

The general value of these five strategies for the protection of commons, which cannot be categorized as strategies of closure or openness, is that they open up a plateau for investigating criteria of robustness and sustainability that often differ from those that Elinor Ostrom established. Here, the commons are examined not only as systems of resource management but also as multilayered assemblages that involve different activities, embody both (re)productive and political purposes and often connect to other projects to form networks. Moreover, this study aspires to move beyond the mere celebration of the commons as potential seeds of human emancipation and transformation, to examine them as systems that are traversed by various, and often opposing, tendencies. This is not only a theoretical exercise but also a study of ventures that have emerged in a particular context – Greece in a time of crisis and following a cycle of mobilization – and therefore it reflects on the questions, practices, possibilities and limitations that this context presents.

Besides this general contribution, this chapter tries to tackle a series of other underdeveloped theoretical issues. These include the relevance of networking, not only for the expansion of the commons but also for their protection; the simultaneous existence of tendencies both of closure and openness in a particular commons; how commons may appear open or closed in relation to different levels of activity; the multiplication of activity levels and how it affects protection strategies and the transformative potential of the commons; the role of political identity in sustaining a commons. Of course, these are important issues that cannot be exhaustively analysed in a single chapter and therefore urge for further research. Nevertheless, this chapter goes a long way in defining the agenda and exploring starting points for future discussion.

Chapter 6

TRUST, ALTRUISM AND SOLIDARITY

The self-organized refugee camp of Platanos in Lesvos

Liminal commons are often temporary and makeshift, especially the types of commons studied here, as they are created under conditions of emergency. This precariousness of liminal commons accentuates questions of openness and closure, membership and trust. It also raises questions of interest and motivation: Why do people choose to participate in a fluid project that can end at any moment, and whose returns and their distribution are unclear and subject to negotiation? The classical literature on commons has focused on questions of membership, trust and interest in ways that are not fully satisfactory, as I will argue. Rational choice models may to an extent capture the dynamics involved in more fixed types of resource commons, such as the ones studied by Ostrom, but they are inadequate for making sense of the type of commons formed in an occupied square or, in the more extreme case that I will present here, a refugee camp. The case study of the temporary commons formed for refugee reception was chosen because of its extremity. It is a limit case, and as such it intensifies and illuminates certain elements I want to emphasize in my work. In its extremity, the refugee camp lets us see more clearly how trust forms in situations where, from a rational perspective, one would least expect it – in other words, why people give without a reasonable expectation of return. My case study is the Platanos Camp on the island of Lesvos, in Greece. Before explaining why I propose to view the camp as a liminal commons, let me offer some background information.

Since 2015, the island of Lesvos became the centre of the ongoing refugee crisis. One million migrants crossed over to Greece from January 2015 to March 2016, half of them entering through Lesvos. CNN declared the island 'a war zone without the war' and *New York Times* talked of a 'full-scale disaster'. However, Lesvos has also been a global centre of humanitarianism and temporal experimentation with 'humanitarian governance' (Papataxiarchis 2016c). There was a multitude of formal and informal practices and new socioeconomic constellations, especially initially, while migrants could still cross Greece and continue their travel to central and northern Europe.

These constellations led to the emergence of diverse 'humanitarian' geographies that have shaken almost every aspect of social and economic life on the island, especially at its eastern side, which directly faces the Turkish coast, from where migrants enter Europe. From Mytilene, the capital city, all the way to the northern part, where the village of Molyvos is located, the island was 'flooded' with settlements, camps and other types of structures that tried to handle the profound 'state of emergency'. Some of those structures, such as the Moria Hotspot and Refugee Camp and the Karatepe Refugee Camp, were managed mainly by the state, the army or the municipality of Lesvos. However, during the early stages of human flows, NGOs, informal collectives and individuals were allowed to enter and act in those camps. Other structures, such as the Metadrasis Camp in Mytilene or the MSF Camp in the village of Mantamado, were coordinated exclusively by NGOs. Yet, within this universe of ventures dedicated to the management of the refugee crisis, there have also been efforts to create grassroots structures based on the principles of self-organization, solidarity, horizontality and democratic control or, in other words, on commoning. One of the most notable examples among these globally recognized grassroots ventures was the self-organized refugee camp of Platanos in Skala Sykamnias, in the northern part of the island.

Platanos' geography

Skala Sykamnias is a small fishing village situated in the part of Lesvos called 'The North' by those involved in the management of the migrant crisis. Skala has no more than 150 inhabitants and constitutes the seaport of the slightly bigger village of Sykamnia, which counts another 250 permanent inhabitants. The village is only 6 miles away from the Turkish coast. Starting in the summer of 2015 and until the spring of 2016, the coastal zone around Skala became the main entrance to Europe for the massive flows of migrants arriving from the Middle East. Over 200,000 migrants went through the area over this period.

6. Trust, Altruism and Solidarity

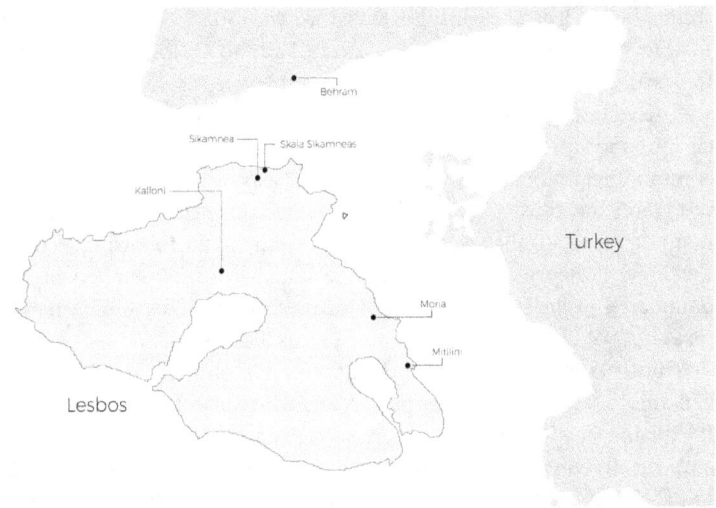

Map 1: Lesvos' map[1]

This phenomenon was not novel for the region of Sykamnia. Migrants had been crossing the sea border long before 2015. However, the scale of human flows over this last period was unprecedented. While in previous times the locals themselves were able to offer first reception services to migrants, from the summer of 2015 onwards the 'pressure' was so high that the local organization Agkalia published an open invitation online, declaring that it would cover the costs of volunteers who would travel to Skala to help with the management of the increasing migrant flows. This open internet invitation marked the beginning of the Platanos' Self-Organized Refugee Camp, a grassroots collective project that operated from 2 October 2015, until 6 June 2016. According to testimonies of both its participants and Sykamnia locals, during its 8-month operation, it offered first-aid services to a great percentage of the 200,000 migrants passing through the village and involved between 1,000 and 1,300 volunteers.

Platanos was organized and managed as a commons, and, as I will argue, it can be theorized using the incipient language of the liminal commons. However, my aim here is not just to add another case study in the liminal commons theory, even though I acknowledge that due to its infancy, this theoretical framework should be enriched with more case

---

1. Created by Eleni Karafylli for the book.

studies before it can be consolidated within the broader commons theory. Instead, through the Platanos case study, I aim to explore some research topics underdeveloped in the previous chapters, as well as to revisit and delve into issues already discussed, such as expansion, subjectivity, closure and openness. Platanos Camp was an extreme case of liminal commoning; liminality traversed almost all aspects of this project, which represents an idiosyncratic example of *collective action* that challenges many of our established views. More specifically, in the following sections, I will revisit theories of trust, benefit seeking, altruism, membership and boundaries in the making of new commons, and I will examine what the case study of Platanos can contribute to this discussion.

Due to its empirical extent and the theoretical plurality, the chapter has a manifold structure. The first part unfolds the story of Platanos in detail. It explains why it is suitable to approach Platanos as a liminal commons and details the transformations the venture both underwent and initiated throughout its operation. It also links the case study of Platanos with issues discussed in previous chapters, such as openness, closure and expansion. The focus of this section is on the relations among volunteers and between volunteers and the local community. To this extent, the chapter lacks an elaboration on how migrants perceived Platanos. This choice was made for three reasons: first and most important, the method of this study did not allow such a focus, since it was mainly based on a reconstruction of the story through interviews. Second, Platanos was only a place of transit for migrants, as they usually stayed there for a few hours. Thus, capturing their perceptions of Platanos would be a difficult, if not impossible, task. Third, my focus is on commoning practices, and therefore I am more interested in exploring those subjects and socio-spatial aspects that are relevant to this focus.

The second part focuses on participants' motives and links them with the broader discussion on why people cooperate while also offering glimpses of recent theories on altruism. This section develops an argument that contradicts the views of the institutional school, built upon utilitarianism and economic benefit, but also transcends the more recent theories on the commons, which emphasize the dimension of human cooperation. In our case, at first glance one may identify something peculiar: a community does commoning for another community.[2] The

2. Here, the term 'community' is used figuratively, to make connections with the commons literature. Neither migrants nor the members of Platanos can be regarded as a community in its more classic sense, as I will explain in more detail throughout the text.

argument is that in such emergencies, in which the crisis invades every facet of the social structure, the condition of liminality itself becomes an important drive for collective action. Thus, commoning is fuelled by both the profound loss of orientation and the sense of equality that the dissolution of the existing order brings about. People who rushed to contribute to the project, both locals and newcomers from every part of the world, were not simply driven by economic benefit, political aspirations or a pure altruistic sentiment of compassion. On the contrary, as many of them stated in interviews, their participation at Platanos gave them a chance to reorient their own ailing or problematic lives around the notions of solidarity, cooperation and equality, thus rendering the commoning project 'a healing place for all'.

The third part is dedicated to the issue of trust. After briefly presenting how trust is perceived by the dominant approaches in economics and commons theory, this section presents the concept of 'automatic trust', which constitutes a basic element of the liminal commons that arise in a 'state of emergency'.

The fourth part pushes the discussion further by acknowledging the centrality of membership in space-commoning activities. By and large – except for some digital commons – a relatively stable and defined community of commoners is considered essential for the resource or space commons to operate successfully. In the relevant literature, this is justified mainly by reference to the issue of rivalry, explained in detail in the previous chapter. However, rivalry is not the only factor. Stable membership is regarded as essential for the implementation of commoning institutions, as well as for the development of a sense of community that can make collective action successful. In the first chapter, I argued that liminal commons can operate without this limitation, as they are mainly action-based. Here I will push the argument a bit further by suggesting that, under liminal conditions, high turnover is not only compatible but also necessary for the commons to function and persist.

The liminal commons of the Platanos Self-Organized Refugee Camp

Common space

In September 2015, after a demanding summer marked by thousands of arrivals of migrants from the Middle East and Africa, a local NGO named 'Agkalia' took the initiative to publish an open call on the internet, asking everyone to join them in the management of the refugee crisis. Agkalia is a small NGO based in the town of Kaloni, the second biggest on the island, with a long record of support for local vulnerable groups. Its emblematic leader, Papa-Stratis, was an Orthodox priest. During the refugee crisis, the organization went beyond its initial scope, which was to support vulnerable Greeks, and shifted its focus towards the management of the human flows arriving primarily in Skala Sykamnias. In the call, Agkalia mentioned that they would cover the expenses of volunteers, at least for a short period.

At the same period, in Athens, many initiatives had taken action to tackle the refugee crisis. One of the most notable early examples was the self-organized initiative of 'Solidarity with Refugees and Migrants at Pedion tou Areos' and its sister initiative 'Dervenion 56 Occupation'. The two ventures made decisions in one joint assembly. Despite the openness in their discourse and everyday practice, they implemented antiauthoritarian, anarchist-oriented political procedures. These two initiatives were the first to respond to the call of Agkalia. They dispatched seven people, who went on to set up the base of the Platanos Camp at the coastal area next to Skala.

Platanos took its name from the big plane tree (πλάτανος in Greek) that stands in the area where the first tents were put up, to constitute a preliminary form of the camp. The incipient Platanos collective occupied public space to transform it into a first reception camp. In contrast to other state- or NGO-driven structures with similar aims, Platanos Camp was produced as a common space, a space shaped through commoning. Being a commons, the occupied space of Platanos was continuously made and remade, according to the specific needs defined by the host community of 'solidarians'[3] over the course of its actions. In this respect, common space can be regarded as a part of the learning experience of commoning. Platanos was fundamentally charged with the following tasks: rescuing migrants and transferring them safely to land; offering first aid, dry clothes and food; organizing their trip to registration camps. The common space of Platanos was

---

3. 'Solidarians' is a recently introduced term referring to the individuals and groups, often highly politicized, who rushed to help in dealing with the refugee crisis out of their will to stand by refugees and migrants with 'solidarity and dignity'. It is a direct translation of the Greek term 'Allilegioi', which is used by these groups and individuals to distinguish themselves from both volunteers and humanitarian workers.

shaped and reshaped to meet those needs. In the beginning, space was organized in the simplest way possible: one tent for medicines and first aid and two more for the kitchen and some basic stuff. Most clothing, shoes and other materials were kept in cardboard boxes at the nearby river shore. However, gradually, more stable constructions replaced the initial tents, and common space took a much more organized form. The camp expanded beyond the traceable perimeter of the initial occupation towards the rest of the village. According to Dimos, one of the long-time participants at Platanos and responsible for logistics, 'there was a moment when Platanos had thirteen different warehouses all over Skala and Sykamnia.'

As the Platanos Camp was such a malleable and rapidly changing space, it is difficult to pin down a 'representative' moment. As Nitsa, one of my informants pointed out:

Whenever I was away from Platanos for a few days and then came back, everything was different. I remember very clearly how one time when I came back, I couldn't find the warehouse of which I was the main member. When I entered the kiosk that was in the same place, I found an unknown guy who told me, 'we don't have shoes here' [...]. Every person and every new team was transforming and leaving their marks on the place.

Both Alexandros and Lora, two informants who stayed at Platanos for long periods, mentioned that at some point the camp obtained its 'full shape', meaning that there was a culmination in the development of the common space, followed by only smaller changes thereafter. One account of this 'full shape' is offered here. For practical reasons, this description refers only to the main stage of activity, not to the whole set of spatial relations Platanos created in the broader region of Skala and Sykamnia. The latter includes the aforementioned warehouses, the houses where solidarians stayed, and a series of more temporal spatialities that emerged through commoning to satisfy particular temporal needs and initiatives that are explained in more detail in the following pages.

Having been created primarily by highly politicized individuals in its first steps, Platanos Camp was exclusively managed by the general assembly. The assembly was not meeting regularly but whenever an issue arose. Yet, all informants confirm that assemblies were very frequent (about twice per week), and there were very few issues – mostly urgent and practical ones – that were not discussed and decided there. The assembly arrived at resolutions by consensus or wide consent, after extensive discussion and synthesis.

Agkalia NGO funded the venture only for the first few weeks of its operation. Thereafter, Platanos became a self-funded project, based on donations from all over the world. Unlike an NGO, however, the camp operated on a very small budget (considering its scale of activity) and donations in money were discouraged. To succeed in both maintaining its operation and minimizing monetary donations, Platanos members urged donors to either fund its suppliers directly or send donations in kind. 'Platanos' assembly has been looking for a pattern that would keep the euros away from our hands (as much as possible), as we are mostly interested in increasing the level of transparency and in the same time to decrease the necessary energy for administration and accounting', reads the organization's announcement regarding donations. Subsequently, they asked donors to contribute their ideas on how to improve this 'pattern' to become even more transparent and participatory for those who were not physically present at Skala.

This process gave rise to an impressive cycle of e-commoning, which became one of the cornerstones of Platanos' success. The communication team of Platanos was regularly publishing a list of needs online. They were also publishing the project's accounting spreadsheets for everyone to access and check that their contributions were used for the intended purposes. Occasionally, as in the previous quote, Platanos' assembly asked its followers to contribute their ideas for the resolution of specific problems.

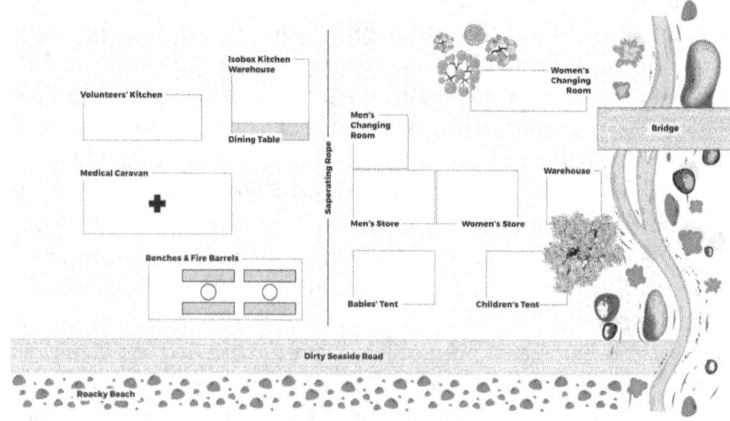

(*Source*: My drawing based on testimonies and drawings of my informants)[4]

4. Illustrated by Eleni Karafylli for the book.

A liminal commons at its extreme

In the introduction and the first chapter, I introduced the concept of liminal commons through the case study of the Syntagma Square encampment in Athens during the movement of the squares. In that case, liminality stemmed from the perplexed subjectivities of Greeks affected by the multidimensional crisis. However, my analysis of liminal commons went further than that. I argued that the collapse of the commoners' previously rigid identities is not the only factor that leads to the creation of liminal commons; liminality is also apparent in a series of spatial and social relations. As a necessary condition, I emphasized the negotiation between previously unconnected groups, which takes place in, through and because of liminality and is driven by crisis. I also explored how emerging temporal spatialities weave together the fluid landscape of the liminal commons.

Liminal commons are not simply liminal spaces. They are products of conscious commoning practices that do not aim at creating stable and enduring common constellations; instead, they constitute transitional forms of commoning that create passages and facilitate social, temporal and spatial transitions. The aim of this chapter is dual: first, to explain Platanos Camp using the language of liminal commons and, second, to further develop the theory of liminal commons through the study of Platanos.

Subjects and places in crisis

Let me start with the basics. A first reception camp and its surroundings constitute an ad hoc liminal space. The transformation of the rigid boundary into a sea passage creates a contested 'borderscape' and thus a liminal zone. Refugees and migrants are by definition liminal subjects. Their forced displacement is followed by an identity destabilization linked with the psychosocial trauma of living in a state of ambiguity. A first reception camp in Europe, then, is not just another stop in their journey but represents – at least symbolically – the passage to the future they are seeking.

On the other hand, Skala will never be the same place again. The collapse of the boundary brought dramatic changes to the place. 'Nothing is the same since then. Not even the sea. When I am looking at it, I swear I can still see boats coming', says Nitsa, a middle-aged woman from Sykamnia and one of the few locals actively participating at Platanos. The thousands of solidarians, volunteers and commoners who rushed to Platanos or other NGO-driven structures at Sykamnia contributed equally to the 'liminalization' of the place, either directly, by leaving the mark of their individual and collective performances, or indirectly, by investing it with new meanings and imaginaries that affect its dominant identity. Moreover, as I will explain in more detail in the upcoming section on the motives of Platanos' participants, contrary to their depiction by the media as 'heroes' driven by a pure sentiment of compassion for fellow humans, many of the solidarians were also going through a liminal phase, and their actions at Skala were underpinned by their loss of identity and their agony to reorient both their lives and their collective dreams. As Papataxiarchis (2016b: 7) puts it, referring to this period in Skala Sykamnias, 'displacement becomes a general condition.'

The encounter with the 'other'

Liminality characterizes not only the subjects who operated at Platanos but also the socio-spatial relations of the commoning project more broadly. Platanos was founded to facilitate transitions, both literally and metaphorically: the camp was helping migrants reach the seashore and, after receiving first aid, continue their travel to the registration centres. At the same time, Platanos was intended as a means of constructing a social bond with the newcomer 'other', based on equality, solidarity and dignity. Taking place as a crucial part of a commoning project and not as a standardized service of a humanitarian agency, this mutual encounter was often taking the form of an act of negotiation between cultural differences. Such a negotiation is often experienced as an in-between reality, marked by the suspending qualities of liminality (see also Stavrides 2013).

Platanos was an improvised space shaped by liminality. The learning experience of Platanos as inscribed in its socio-spatial relations was continuously informed by the encounter between different 'others', thus rendering the very idea of otherness a relative and contestable term. As Tara, a young woman who spent over three months at the site, put it:

> In neighbouring NGO camps, you could see an orderly world shaped from the top down and replicating the same model everywhere. The important thing for them was to follow the rules. For us, instead, the important thing was not to apply a model but to invent those ways that would give the migrants a sense of dignity and true welcoming. In this process, we tried to learn from them and modify the camp and the services according to what they needed, based on what they say and on what we could observe that they don't like. Of course, the fact that

migrants were normally spending no more than a few hours at the camp was not allowing much time for deep interaction. However, through the observations of long-time solidarians and Hasan, who is Syrian and was there to help almost constantly, I think we succeeded in formulating services that were really appropriate for the refugees.

When I asked her to specify some of the spatial transformations that were planned through actual interaction with refugees, she answered:

> Well, first of all, I remember that we tried to understand what would be suitable for them to eat, and I think that their feedback counted a lot. Second, I remember that we tried to find Syrian tea to offer. The issue of how to approach women was always an important one. In the beginning, we didn't have separate dressing rooms. Then, we decided to separate them and put them in diametrically opposite places in the camp to maximize a sense of safety and discretion.

On this subject, Lora added: 'The dog issue was also an important thing to deal with. Many of the volunteers had brought their dogs, but we realized that some of the migrants were afraid of them. So, the assembly decided that they should either be leashed or not brought to the camp. Unfortunately, not all dog owners respected this decision.' Lastly, the creation of the 'children's corner' was a direct outcome of this interaction and allowed kids to calm down and forget the difficult moments of the sea passage.

A liminal human composition

The suspending qualities of liminality do characterize not only the relations between Platanos and its 'outside' but also the operation and composition of the camp itself. Platanos was initially a relatively coherent venture. However, it went through a series of transformations of its identity and function that rendered liminality one of its permanent characteristics. Most importantly, Platanos was characterized by a diverse human composition.

More than a thousand[5] individuals participated in the activities of Platanos over its eight-month operation. However, the average

---

5. All numbers presented in this section are approximations based on the testimonies of different participants, including those of Dimos, the person

workforce available varied between five and fifty people. Out of these thousand people, only around twenty spent more than one month at the camp, and only three spent more than four months. The vast majority of individuals stayed at Skala for only a week or two. As mentioned earlier, the initial group that arrived at Skala to create the structure was highly politicized. However, from early on it became obvious that maintaining a rigid political identity would be difficult, if not impossible. The very first encounter of the incipient Platanos group with the members of Agkalia NGO, which was founded by an Orthodox priest and consisted of people of diverse ideological and political backgrounds, became the first setting in which negotiation of differences would take place.

The group that first occupied the Platanos' space raised a red and black flag to manifest the anti-fascist character of the venture; this flag later became a source of both conflict and inspiration. Platanos was stigmatized by the local community as an anarchist encampment, which, as I will explain, became a source of intense conflict with parts of the local community and the authorities. Yet, as the reputation of the venture was growing, both locally and globally, Platanos soon became a heterogeneous organization. Its initial political identity was contested, as it could not express the majority; thus, the assembly decided to abolish it and open itself up to a liminal stage of ambivalence. 'Whoever walks up the small slope leading to Platanos should leave his political identity behind', says Nitsa referring to that decision.

In the first phase of its expansion, the initial group opened up to include more people, primarily Greeks, who came from all over the country. A small group of locals also got involved, in varying degrees. Nitsa was probably the only local person who was fully involved and who also participated in assemblies. Other locals, while contributing regularly to the venture, preferred to stay away from its assemblary processes because as Nitsa puts it:

> People here cannot afford to be organized. They want to help when they want and when they can, but they can never commit to organized action. That was evident also before the construction of

charged, for a certain period, with the task of logistics, Nitsa, a long-time member and permanent resident in Skala, and Telis, a leading figure at Agkalia NGO who was keen on doing accounting for Platanos. Therefore, numbers are not accurate but constitute, I believe, representative figures to help tell the real history of Platanos.

Platanos when we were trying to cope with the situation alone. You could see people offering everything on one day and doing nothing on the next one. Especially when locals found out that Platanos' members are anarchists, their involvement in the project became almost impossible.

Besides the locals who regularly participated in the camp, two other 'special' groups had occasional involvement: the famous 'grannies' of Skala and the equally famous 'fishermen'. Their images became so globally recognizable that members of both categories were proposed to be nominated for the Nobel Peace Prize. The grannies were usually sitting on a bench near the camp, mainly to observe, but also to occasionally help by doing what they always do: looking after babies. In the same vein, the fishermen kept doing what 'has to be done': rescuing people and getting them to the shore. As Thomas, one of the fishermen, told me, 'in comparison to human life, my daily wage is not worth anything'. These groups maintained an 'external' relation with Platanos, yet their presence was crucial for the project because it was an important link with the local community. This became apparent during an incident in which Platanos' members had a conflict with the local authorities over the construction of a new first-aid building at the camp. Thomas' and Nitsa's interventions were catalytic for the resolution of the conflict, as they convinced the assembly to change its original decision and reach a compromise with the authorities.

Now, if we extend 'locality' to also include the rest of Lesvos, one may find more groups that were involved at Platanos. The 'Lesvian Initiative of Solidarity with Migrants' was created to support Platanos, first, against the threat of evacuation by the local authorities and, second, by providing an additional workforce. About five to ten people were making the trip to Skala every day, while in some cases the two ventures held joint assemblies. Besides this initiative, many other individuals from all over Lesvos were frequently participating in the structure: from independent university students to members of local cultural organizations and even members of organizations associated with the Orthodox Church from Mytilene and beyond.

After a few weeks of operation and the creation of a blog and Facebook page that rapidly attracted almost 8,000 followers, Platanos became a venture of global radiance. Hundreds of volunteers rushed to take part in this collective effort. Their motives and levels of participation, however, varied. For some, 'the only thing they were doing was to help', as Alexandros mentions, while others were enchanted by 'the magic of self-organization' as Tara, a foreign woman, told me.

To the groups actively shaping Platanos Camp, one should add the agents of *e-commoning*. I am introducing the term 'e-commoning' to describe a process of commoning that takes place through the web but differs from processes aiming at producing digital goods, such as peer-to-peer (P2P) production (Bauwens and Kostakis 2014; Benkler 2007). E-commoning takes place online but is related to the production, expansion and management of a place-based commons. In other words, e-commoners collaborate with space-commoners to accomplish a commoning task related to a particular commons. E-commoning does not aim at creating digital goods (even if the production of digital goods may be part of it). Furthermore, e-commoning is not a form of e-volunteering (Papataxiarchis 2016a; 2016b) and does not limit its scope to fundraising or crowd-funding. E-commoners are conscious agents of the production of the common; they participate in the making of its institutions, in its democratic control, and they are even accountable to the rest of the community of commoners for their actions. E-commoners are not simply donors; they have an active rather than a passive role in the shaping of the common.

Indeed, Platanos was embraced by thousands of social media followers worldwide. One can single out three categories among them: first, those who were only watching and perhaps commenting on the day-to-day activity of Platanos. Second, the e-volunteers that Papataxiarchis (2016a) mentions. E-volunteers are individuals who aim at volunteering via the web. This involves 'all activities that are undertaken on the Web, done in a voluntary and non-paid way'.[6] E-volunteers can share knowledge, donate or even produce goods online. They can do this either on their own or under the umbrella of big international organizations, such as the UN, which recently set up an e-volunteering platform. For Papataxiarchis, however, e-volunteers take a different role; they are those who may also physically participate in the field, but they are driven by their concern with their own 'e-career [. . .] before a global audience on the internet'. They publicize their actions online to find funding to continue travelling as 'disaster specialists'; they act in a highly performative manner (Papataxiarchis 2016a). Third, e-commoners are those who are deeply concerned with the sustenance and facilitation of the commoning project. There may be various motives behind their actions and many reasons why they prefer to do e-commoning instead of space-commoning for the project.

---

6. Retrieved from http://e-volunteering.eu/ (accessed April 2018).

The important thing, however, is that they prioritize the common over their own public exposure, and they act in communication with the host community while simultaneously shaping and transforming it. For example, in the case of Platanos, e-commoners were all those people who, despite being far from the site, were regularly informed of the specific needs of the project and were rushing to collect supplies and send them to the structure. They were shaping some of its institutions, as in the case of the 'pattern' of resource management described earlier, and they were even running campaigns in their own regions to support Platanos with supplies and new members.

The social body of the project was very diverse and far from homogeneous. Yet, the project was always operating under horizontal principles and procedures, which rendered equal participation and democratic operation of the venture a challenging task. Liminality, thus, the condition of in-betweenness, signifying here the temporal gestures that can erect bridges to each other's otherness (see also Stavrides 2013), was not just an outcome but also an absolute prerequisite for the operation of this democratic stage of negotiation of differences. In other words, commoning in Platanos was possible only through and because of liminality.

Participants in Platanos were well aware of this condition. Being in such a liminal zone where *everyone was a foreigner*, all groups learned to step back and listen to one another, learn from one another and show patience to one another. First, the president of Sykamnia, who was against the creation of Platanos from the very beginning, concerned that newcomers 'will transform our village into Exarcheia'[7], was initially declaring that 'they have no place there' and that 'we will throw them at sea'. Despite remaining critical of Platanos until the deconstruction of the site, he ultimately stepped back and accepted its existence in Skala, as in effect the local authorities never attempted to evacuate the camp.

Second, while the initial anarchist group started with a more 'hardcore' political stance, for example manifesting its radical political identity through the red and black flag, it gradually decided to open up to newcomers with different political backgrounds and ideas. To do this, it adopted a minimum and mostly practice-based set of guiding principles, such as horizontality, self-organization and respect towards migrants, and it eliminated – or at least renegotiated – parts of its original 'hardcore' discourse and practice. In a few cases, even some of the 'red

---

7. An Athenian neighbourhood marked by anarchism due to the existence of many anarchist squats.

lines' upon which Platanos was founded were 'violated'. For instance, while Platanos remained independent of NGOs or state institutions throughout its eight-month life, in some cases it collaborated with them to achieve specific goals. For example, collaboration with the neighbouring Lighthouse Camp, managed by a Swedish NGO, was frequent; another NGO, called Adventists, stationed a bus operating as a mobile clinic near Platanos Camp. It is worth noting that this 'transformation' of the group towards more open and less 'pure' forms of organization and operation was an issue of concern for the Athenian 'parent organization' that first decided to respond to the call of Agkalia; this led to conflicts between Platanos and the Dervenion 56 Occupation, with the latter accusing the former of 'watering down' its radicalism.

However, the inverse dynamic also developed. Platanos was a radical project, founded not only to save human lives and counter the effects of the crisis but also to promote an anti-war, anti-government and often anti-capitalist agenda, by proving that self-organization is an effective answer to the malaise of the contemporary world. Despite any modifications, the basic elements of this discourse remained dominant until the conclusion of the project and became a source of inspiration and self-transformation for many of the less politicized participants. For Tara, Platanos was a life-changing experience.

> I was not an activist or anti-government at all. I was sceptical of institutional politics, but this was often leading me to apathy. I had a few connections with the Black Lives Matter or the Occupy movement, but I had no concept of what self-organization is about. When I was thinking about politics, I was always thinking about how I can get the government to do things better; here, I learned that self-organization and not working with the government is a way of protesting against what big governments decide and do.

Like Tara, Lora notices: 'Platanos was my first actual experience of self-organization, and it was very intense. It made me eager to think about the possibilities of expanding it in the future.' But it was not only foreign solidarians who were affected by their participation in Platanos and their encounter with a culture of self-organization. Nitsa, the previously mentioned local woman, stated:

> I was always a leftist and I was always helping my husband with the refugees; he was rescuing them and I was offering them first aid on land. But I heard the term self-organization for the first time in my

life at Platanos. [...] This experience helped me understand better who is who in the village, and I think it created the basis for self-organized responses to future crises.

Dimos admitted: 'I was always hearing leftists and anarchists calling each other "comrade" and, to be honest, it sounded a bit ridiculous to my ears. Here, I understood what being a comrade means.'

Platanos consisted of a highly heterogeneous mosaic of subjects, yet it managed to function as a commons without hierarchies. There was a frequent rotation of coordinator roles and, despite the emergency character of the structure, most decisions were taken democratically by the general assembly. Liminality became the cornerstone of this heterogeneous organization and the driving force behind the effective communication of difference. The organizational structure remained intentionally loose because 'each person should discover on their own where they fit better and what work they do more effectively', as Lora says. Platanos challenged almost everyone and everything and triggered changes at various levels.

The expanding character of Platanos

I have already argued that liminal commons constitute the 'expanding mode of commoning', and I suggested that their expansion often happens in an unplanned and unpredictable *rhizomatic* manner. I also proposed that this expansion can be of two types: surface expansion and internal multiplication. The former refers to an expansion, either spatial or in membership, that can be externally observed. The latter refers instead to the internal multiplication of the common, which is a process of metamorphosis. This may take the form of a multiplication of the commons' activities or of a deepening of the levels of common production. This kind of expansion is often externally invisible. Let us now see how these theoretical arguments can inform the Platanos case and, in turn, draw from it.

We previously saw that Platanos started as a small project with the mutual approach between the self-organized initiative of Solidarity with Refugees and Migrants at Pedion tou Areos and its sister venture Dervenion 56 Occupation with Agkalia NGO. The expansion of the venture was unprecedented, both spatially and in terms of a new membership. Moreover, the sphere of operation of the project extended much further than the actual site of the camp. Platanos became the main first reception structure in the whole of northern Lesvos, and after January, when the arrivals at the north diminished and refugees were channelled towards other parts of the island, Platanos members decided 'to expand their activities in every part of the island where there is need for help' as they published on their Facebook page. During this metastatic phase, Platanos created numerous micro-commoning projects all over the island: from the port of Mytilene to the coastal zone of the southern part and beyond. Those projects, which often involved cooking meals, dissemination of information and distribution of clothing, lasted from a few hours to a few days, appearing and disappearing in their fleeting transitoriness.

Besides the expansion of Platanos' common space itself, the venture catalysed the creation of many other initiatives, both during its period of operation and in its wake. The aforementioned Lesvian Initiative of Solidarity with Migrants is but one example. To an extent, this was intentional. The creation of the blog and the Facebook page was partially driven by the fact that, as Dimos says, 'we believed that what we did had some value, and therefore we decided to communicate it in order to inspire more people to do the same'. 'One, two, a thousand Platanos' was a slogan often used by Platanos' members and supporters. Various posts on the venture's Facebook page are characteristic of this tendency towards expansion: 'The progress of this initiative (Platanos) permits us to dream of an alternative future: a society of active solidarity and self-organization; a world where *common* struggles will no more be individual, but collective'; 'Platanos is a continuous experiment which through its development and dissemination searches for the realization of a free, consciously defined society'; 'Platanos has established channels of communication and cooperation with collectives from all over Greece.' The networking of Platanos in Greece, as manifested in this last quote, allowed the venture to operate at much larger scales by sending clothes, food and other first-aid materials from its accumulated surplus to every part of the country. 'Platanos was a phenomenon on its own', says Lora, 'people were excited about what Platanos signified for self-organization and solidarity in general and believed that it can be a model for self-organization elsewhere. In that period some people were proposing to do the same in Eidomeni for instance'.

While some of the ventures whose creation was catalysed by Platanos had an organic relation with it and were collectively conceived in the camp, the experience of Platanos gave birth to a cycle of rhizomatic expansion, in which new ventures were popping up in unplanned ways in Greece and beyond. As Tara says:

> After leaving Lesvos, many people tried similar things back in their countries or in other places they went. I had news of some of them through our network [...] For instance, I remember a woman called Naria, who, after leaving Platanos, went to the US and started a self-organized project inspired by Platanos. In the beginning, she was collecting things and raising funds for Platanos, but then, to my knowledge, the project became independent.

A similar story comes from my own experience. In September 2017, I participated in the organizing committee of an international conference in Lesvos called 'Contested Borderscapes'. I was excited to hear a young Spaniard in the introductory activists' panel say: 'I am here because of Lesvos. Last year, I came to Platanos and it was a striking experience for me. The project I will describe to you now has been inspired by Platanos to a large extent.'

While these examples represent instances of mainly surface expansion, Platanos' group also undertook a series of new tasks that pointed to an inner multiplication of the project. This internal expansion primarily refers to a series of initiatives that the project took to expand commoning activities towards the Greek local community. Dimos, a leading figure in this process, confirms:

> After a certain moment, some of us had the idea to expand our activities to include Greek people as well. We wanted to show that solidarity does not limit its scope only to refugees and migrants but is unlimited. Moreover, we wanted to show our real face to the local community and help them overcome their suspicion of us. The idea arose because we had a surplus of many things, from clothes to food. Some proposed that we burn the clothes, but I came up with the idea to distribute them in Sykamnia, Skala and neighbouring villages. In the beginning, this happened through a local person, but then we realized that this resembles charity. So, next time, we decided to do it personally and urged people to open their houses to solidarity. We had a dual aim. First, to support those in need and, second, to allow them to reciprocate the solidarity and become active participants in our effort. We did this several times, maybe ten or fifteen. I think that the initiative had great potential, but not all members of Platanos actively supported it, so it stopped at some point.

A consciously precarious commons

Liminal commons are always precarious forms of commoning; they either become passages to more stable commons projects or disappear leaving behind a series of social, biographical, cultural and even political outcomes. This means that what matters most for a liminal commons is not its longevity and endurance but its effectiveness in facilitating transitions, physical and metaphorical, tangible and intangible ones. To this extent, liminal commons challenge the very criteria for successful commoning specified not only by Elinor Ostrom and her colleagues from the institutional school but also by scholars from different schools of thought who evaluate commons primarily in terms of their capacity to endure.

Platanos is an example of a commoning project that was intentionally temporary. It was created, first and foremost, to facilitate the safe transition of refugees and migrants to Greece and Europe and to establish a new culture of self-organization and solidarity in a social field in which humanitarianism and charity were previously predominant. Therefore, it was geared towards promoting sociopolitical transition, too. When, after the March 2016 EU–Turkey deal, arrivals stopped and for many weeks no boats were landing in northern Lesvos, Platanos' members decided to dismantle the camp in an organized and collective way that would be in line with its life up to that point. The following quote is from the project's Facebook page:

> We want the closing and the removal of the material to be fully aligned with its months-long operations: we want it to be in consistency with our principles, with dignity, with a sense of responsibility towards refugees & migrants and the local community of Skala Sykamnias. We have, therefore, already initiated communication with structures of support to refugees & immigrants in Greece, in order to check the running needs [sic] for materials and equipment.

Thus, commoning characterized not only the initiation and operation but also the epilogue of the structure.

The liminal character of the commons is made evident. In fact, the call was an invitation to recreate a temporal community for the dismantling of the camp, since Platanos never had a stable community. As with its initiation and development, the dissolution of the commons was carried out by a fluid community always-in-the-making. E-commoning practices were also prevalent, especially in securing economic support for the group and in finding equivalent structures to distribute the remaining material. However, for some members of Platanos this epilogue was not an endpoint but a point of suspension. Part of the material was stored in situ at Sykamnia, to leave open the possibility of 'set[ting] up the camp and the rescue team again', as they wrote on Facebook.

Beyond utility and altruism

Elinor Ostrom showed that people can effectively cooperate to meet collective needs and that, under specific conditions, commoning institutions are preferable to private property or state regulations. However, her work has been criticized for focusing excessively on economic aspects of the commons and for assuming that economic benefit is the most important motive for commoning (e.g. Stavrides 2016; De Angelis 2017; Lieros 2016). Ostrom's subjects of commoning are divided into stable, clear-cut categories according to their degree of profit-seeking at the expense of others and their willingness to cooperate, which is also considered fixed. The very conditionality of cooperative habits follows a simplistic logic in her analysis and, despite her rich references to other human motives, the *homo economicus*, the prototype of the rational individual who seeks to maximize profit and socialize costs, remains the core unit of her theory. In Ostrom's view, the commons are successful only when individuals are persuaded that commoning can be more beneficial than other types of resource management.

However, commons literature about human motives has advanced since. Studies on conditional cooperation have shown that individuals are affected by many factors other than economic benefit and have problematized the connection between 'preference for reciprocity' and 'actual reciprocal behaviour' (Velez et al. 2009). Hence, conditionality becomes a non-linear and complex set of relations that doesn't fit in a stable and clear-cut categorization. Motives are distinct from incentives, and this opens up the discussion to input from other disciplines, including phycology, anthropology, sociology and evolutionary theory.

From an evolutionary perspective, research has shown that people are not selfish by nature. Until recently, based on Darwin's principle of natural selection, biologists used to believe that humans are intrinsically competitive and selfish (Wilson 2015). Yet, this is valid only if the individual is taken as the privileged unit in the biological hierarchy of nature (Bollier 2014). By contrast, when the focus is shifted towards the competition among groups, it becomes clear that intra-group collaboration and altruism become stronger sources of sustainability than selfishness and competition (Wilson 2015; Bollier 2014; Benkler 2011).

In his book *The Penguin and the Leviathan*, Yochai Benkler (2011) offers a very comprehensive account of the diverse motives that make people cooperate rather than compete, drawing on findings from a wide range of disciplines. Benkler argues that empathy, shared values, group identity, conformity, beliefs, moral codes and social norms are drives for action equally powerful with self-interest, while creativity, learning and innovation are equally important with efficiency. Benkler challenges the view – often held by economists – that inevitably most people are free-riders and argues instead that they are consistently pro-cooperative. He deconstructs the narrative of humans as essentially rational beings and emphasizes their emotional dimension. Like Wilson (2015), Benkler distinguishes between two kinds of altruism: altruism in actions and altruism in thoughts and feelings. While economists and most psychologists typically believe that there is no genuine altruism and that every altruistic act is connected to utility, both these thinkers suggest that it is meaningless to think in this way and instead propose focusing on the fact that humans are physiologically and psychologically 'wired' to receive pleasure from helping others.

Following a different path, social anthropologist Katerina Rozakou (2016; 2017) tries to untangle the construct of the disinterested volunteer in contemporary Western societies and Greece in particular. In her analysis, she distinguishes between two distinct and even opposing types of volunteerism. The first constitutes 'the epitome of the modern citizen; a disinterested subject working voluntarily for the common good' (Rozakou 2016: 81). This is the subject of apolitical humanitarianism (Rozakou 2016: 81). Volunteers of this type become involved in altruistic practices in the name of democracy and citizenship (Paley 2001[8]) and are often driven by an abstract sentiment of 'love' for fellow humans and their country (Rozakou 2016). For Rozakou, crafting this type of volunteer is part of the broader neoliberal biopolitical project, which is founded on the commercialization of care and the construction of the 'responsible' citizen. The second type of volunteerism is stemming from different ideological backgrounds, is

---

8. Quoted also in Rozakou (2016).

grounded in alternative forms of sociality and challenges the neoliberal biopolitical project and ultimately the very idea of volunteerism. The subject of the second type of volunteerism draws upon leftist ideology, the notion of solidarity and active participation in governance.

I have briefly introduced the debate on self-interest versus cooperation and the two opposing types of volunteerism to familiarize the reader with the theoretical background of these important and still open questions. However, my aim here is not to take sides or to argue that my study of Platanos can enrich one or the other approach. In contrast to the ontological nature of these debates, my focus is on transitions from self-interest to altruism and from one type of volunteerism to the other, and vice versa. My main argument is that in periods of intensified crisis, the very experience of liminality can become the main drive for participating in commoning and solidarity projects, and volunteerism can be regarded as a vehicle for the reorientation and reconstruction of a broken life. Given the fluid and rapidly changing environment created by the state of emergency, subjects are moving back and forth, and the performance of temporal individual and collective identities can lead to diverse and often opposing futures. Contradiction becomes a general condition.

Platanos as 'healing place for all'

Platanos was the child of crisis, more specifically of a crisis that broke out within another big and multidimensional crisis. As explained in detail in the previous chapters, since 2010, if not before, Greece has been amid an extensive crisis which, along with the emergence of social movements, catalysed the rise of hundreds of commoning projects across the country. Within this multifaceted crisis, which also led to a generalized crisis of identity, solidarity became the cornerstone of new emerging kinds of sociality that tried to repair the fractured social cohesion. Those types of sociality became the foundation for the practices framed as 'solidarity to refugees'.

The connection between the two solidarity movements, the one towards refugees and the second against austerity measures, was evident throughout the country. After 2015, most of the ventures I had been studying expanded their repertoires of action to include direct or indirect activities related to the 'solidarity to refugees' movement. Lesvos was not an exception. The informal organization Village of Altogether was created in 2012 in Mytilene to coordinate a collective response to the devastating consequences of the economic crisis. It was this collective that in 2014 created PIKPA Self-organized Refugee Camp at the outskirts of the city and later created the larger organization Lesvos Solidarity, which is now one of the most important grassroots initiatives dedicated to refugees in the country.

Fuelled by the so-called refugee crisis, the 'solidarity to refugees' movement launched a new cycle of liminality and liminal commoning in the country and constituted a vital source of inspiration for the existing anti-austerity solidarity and commoning movement, which, as I argued in the second chapter, from early 2014 onwards was showing signs of stagnation.

However, these macro-observations can only partially and superficially capture the real liminal condition that drove many of the volunteers at Platanos. As liminality is necessarily experiential, only a closer look at the participants' different stories can shed light on the issue. The following quotes tell the stories of real people who participated in Platanos. They diverge from dominant narratives, which talk about heroes, middle-class Westerners driven by guilt and duty or humanitarian professionals driven by economic benefit and technocratic efficiency. These stories may not typify the entire membership of Platanos, but they do not describe marginal phenomena; in any case, they have been excluded from dominant representations.

Dimos, who spent over four months in Platanos, was a great source for the thoughts presented here. We met several times during my research, and I was able to observe the evolution of his answers to my questions. The first time I asked him why he went to Platanos was only a few months after the actual experience, and he was 'still perplexed', as he told me. After a few weeks, when I asked him the same question again, he said:

> Well, if I had to answer this question a few months ago when I first went to Platanos, I would have told you, as most of the volunteers, that I came here to help. Now, I really understand my motivations better. Going to Platanos was an expression of my desperation due to my total disorientation. I went to find new meaning.

Dimos was a successful businessman before the crisis. At the age of thirty-five, he decided to give up, owing both to economic troubles brought on by austerity and to a total lack of fulfilment in his job. For several years he remained at a stage of suspension, which he tried to overcome through his participation in Platanos. When I asked him for insights into the motives of other participants, he said:

Talking about people's motives is difficult since in Platanos there was a condition of emergency, and there was little time for meaningful verbal interaction. However, as I was there during the most intense months, I met hundreds of people. I could say that there was a small minority, about ten per cent, which was impenetrable and was only interested in practical things. They had gone there just to help people and they operated mechanically, a sign that they knew what they were doing. But there were many people whose restlessness was evident in all their actions. When I was talking to those people, I was getting the same impression. They were unsatisfied with their lives and had come to Platanos to create anew what I call a sense of self.

Thanasis was a long-time volunteer who ended up in Platanos after volunteering in different places on the island, such as Moria. His testimony was revealing: 'Look, I had spent much time being depressed back in Athens. I had gone through several jobs and had never felt like I felt here. For the first time in my life, I was doing something that gave me some meaning.' Like Thanasis, Robin from Ireland said: 'This is the first unpaid job in my life and yet the only one that gives meaning to it.' Tara, who also spent many weeks at Platanos, says:

> I was ready to leave Atlanta behind and do something else. I was in an identity crisis, and I believe that many people participating in Platanos were in a similar situation. I tend to believe that people who enter this condition of exploring new possibilities with their personal crisis prefer to go to such conflict sites, where they can be a person of help; it is a life-affirming experience.

'It is a character-rebuilding opportunity', says Lora. 'It was a period of soul-searching for me. I was not satisfied with my life back in my country. This is why I came here.' Antonis, one of the leading figures at the camp and a member of the rescue team, admitted: 'Some of the people are focused only on food and clothes but, for me, emotional healing is equally important.' I retrieved the following quote from a video[9] that some Platanos' members shot together:

> Platanos is a healing environment for both migrants and volunteers. The main reason is behind what we suffer from. I think we suffer

---

9. The video was handed to me personally by one of its creators.

from division, primarily internal, which is reflected upon our surroundings creating conflicts, whether trivial or bigger ones, even wars. Instead, Platanos is a place of compassion and love, which is a remedy for the division that afflicts us all equally.

Platanos was marked by liminality, and liminality became a source of action. However, it is interesting to see the transformations and contradictions of the process and link them to the theories presented at the beginning of this section. Many of the volunteers who rushed to Platanos could belong to the first category, which Rozakou describes as 'the epitome of the modern citizen'. As Tara mentions: 'In the beginning, many people coming to Platanos believed that the refugees are only Syrians, as they only knew about the war in Syria. They came to Platanos without knowing what Platanos is. Those people didn't care about whether they participated in Platanos or Lighthouse.'[10] However, as many of my informants mentioned, this gradually changed. Many of those who came to Platanos as volunteers of the first category described by Rozakou left Platanos as activists and supporters of self-organization, incorporating a radical anti-volunteering culture informed by the values of social change and solidarity, which characterize the second category of volunteers Rozakou describes. In Skala, during 2015 and 2016, these categories became fluid through and because of the profound liminality of the whole situation. 'Many people experienced life-changing transformations here', says Tara. 'I remember a French couple who just came to help for a few days, as they said, and stayed for about a month. They advanced from asking for instructions about everything to taking the initiative to reconceive and remake the kindergarten space entirely.'

'Holidarity' is a term unknown in the scientific literature but well known in places where volunteerism is common. Holidarity signifies an 'attitude' that combines holidays with some humanitarian work. However, owing to the striking reality of Platanos and the liminality associated with it, what for many started perhaps as holidarity was transformed into a genuine and enduring politicization process based on the values of self-organization and solidarity. This view challenges the moralism of popular conservative critiques of solidarity, which seek to taint the 'providers' of solidarity as self-interested, post-material party-goers.

10. The neighbouring, NGO-managed camp.

However, the opposite also occurred. Many highly politicized people took a break from their jobs and came to Platanos to support migrants with dignity and demonstrate that self-organization can be effective in addressing such emergencies. In the course of their participation, however, many of them realized that working with migrants and refugees was more fulfilling than their previous jobs. Given that Platanos was a precarious project that could not constitute a permanent source of income for its participants, many supporters of self-organization ended up getting hired by humanitarian NGOs as professionals. For instance, Virna abandoned her job as a university teacher to be as close as possible to what gave meaning to her life; she ended up working for the Metadrasis NGO. The same happened to Petros, who was previously a leading figure in relative social movements and is now the financial manager of a local NGO in Lesvos. This is not a marginal phenomenon, as it describes the trajectories of many people I met during my one-and-a-half-year stay on the island.

Rethinking trust in times of emergency

Along with the destabilization of the *homo economicus*, which for several decades was – and to some extent still is – the dominant model of human agency both in policymaking and in the public discourse (Bollier 2014; Benkler 2011), there is another key concept that was neglected for years but now receives increasing attention in many fields of social theory, including that of institutional economics: trust. This neglect stemmed from the fact that in most economic research trust was considered to be 'on the soft side', and thus economists and managers doubted its relevance (Reina, Reina, and Hudnut 2017). Trust was examined mainly by psychologists, mostly as a property of interpersonal relationships and therefore as belonging to the realm of family, friendship and erotic life (Simpson 2007).

However, in the twenty-first century and particularly in its second decade, trust has become fundamental in any attempt to speak about successful collective action, whether in the field of business or in the world of grassroots ventures and even in the realm of the virtual digital communities. Horizontality, or at least a specific 'domesticated' version of it, is gaining ground in management theory. *Forbes* declares: 'Leaders can no longer trust in power; instead, they rely on the power of trust.' In the hundreds of websites that offer advice on how to build cohesive teams, trust is referred to as the most important element in creating '*harmonious synergistic and efficient work environments*'. The word 'empowerment' has become the key for effective work, while with respect to leadership styles, fear, top-down control, incentives and sanctions are being replaced – at least in theory – by trust, shared goals and community building. Trust is suddenly everywhere.

Commons scholars have criticized early game theory experiments for artificially creating conditions in which no bonds of trust and communication could be forged among participants (Bollier 2014). Ostrom showed that within the commons, trust and the institutions of commoning can replace systems of top-down monitoring and heavy sanctions, as she insists that graduated and light sanctions can work well within the communities of commoners (Ostrom 1990).

However, in both business and commons theories, this explosion in the use of the concept of trust is informed by certain common assumptions. First, trust is always regarded as something that can exist mainly in groups of small size with specific membership (Laloux 2014; Ostrom 1990). Second, it takes much time to build trust, and this can only be the outcome of a gradual, evolving and largely linear process. Third (and this applies to business theory only), despite empowerment, horizontality and trust among employees, leadership is still needed, but its content and role must be redefined. Fourth, trust cannot develop in conditions of emergency, in which people become instinctively selfish and rush to save themselves, usually at the expense of others. This last point is often accompanied by the conviction that such states of emergency urge for a concentration of power, strengthening of leadership and even temporal suspension of democratic control over decisions and resource management.

The Platanos' case is interesting because it challenges all the aforementioned assumptions. Initially, the group consisted of similarly minded individuals with a common vision, political trajectories and world views, who also shared common past experiences. Thus, trust was created through the well-known processes based on repetition, shared values, common vision, shared experience, deep interpersonal interaction and collective memory. However, the group eventually expanded and became very heterogeneous. Its new characteristics were unstable membership, diversity of approaches, varying political and cultural backgrounds, absence of any sort of collective memory, lack of past shared experiences and even diversity of objectives. Yet, the group continued to be very effective in its actions, expanded its field of operation, maintained its horizontal and grassroots orientation

6. Trust, Altruism and Solidarity

and intentionally institutionalized a series of mechanisms against the accumulation and crystallization of any form of power. What does this imply for trust-building within groups in extraordinary conditions of crisis and emergency?

Without trust, self-organization is impossible, and any venture based on volunteerism collapses. However, in cases like Platanos, in which emergency and crisis are constitutive, there is hardly ever the time for people to get to know each other in depth, create a collective memory, weave a common political vision and mitigate the apparent cultural differences between subjects. Hence, trust should develop from different sources than usually, in ways that go beyond the underlying principles of linearity, slowness and scalability that usually accompany its creation. Trust must become almost *automatic*. It is within this context that I am examining the Platanos' case. I am not interested in challenging the validity of known mechanisms of creating trust, nor am I claiming that this *automatic trust* I am presenting here has the same potential as trust relations that are forged through long-lasting relationships and commoning. Instead, I aim to bring to light the processes that enable commoning in times of crisis and emergency, which directly challenge the assumption that democracy is ineffective under conditions of scarcity of time and resources and thus crises should be managed 'with an iron fist'. Specifically, I am interested in the conditions that make automatic trust flourish, the strengths and limitations of this process, what it leaves behind and whether it enacts processes of enduring commoning or not.

First, horizontal self-organization based on open assemblary processes, in which everyone is welcome to participate, creates a sense of equality, an important precondition of the 'sense of trust', as Dimos mentioned in his description of Platanos. A decision mechanism based on open and direct democracy eliminates the distance between the centre of decisions and the 'troops' and enables everyone to be part of the decision, without any trial periods. Hence, it contributes to the creation of automatic trust because everyone can instantly feel both important and part of the group. In other words, instant membership strengthens automatic trust.

Second, a shared goal considered fair or 'noble' by a majority, if not everyone, creates a non-competitive environment in which trust can develop organically in a short time. In contrast, when the common objective is limited to profit maximization or puts the group in competition with other groups, it is very likely that a mentality of 'what is in it for me (or her/him/us/the others)' will emerge, which restitutes the calculative logic of the *homo economicus* and prevents automatic trust from flourishing.

Third, weaving a common vision that can be embraced by the vast majority is important because it allows for a temporal identification of everyone with the group and hence creates a sort of community bond, even if an actual stable community is absent. In the story of Platanos, this became apparent when the original group suspended its initial anarchist identity to allow hundreds of people to accommodate themselves within the project in a constructive and self-determined way.

Fourth, loose organization and the semi-binding character of decisions allowed people in Platanos to 'find their place' in the camp. The semi-binding character of decisions, that is, absence of sanctions and tolerance in their occasional violation, minimized conflict in assembly meetings and promoted a culture of cooperation rather than competition. Given the enormous number of people involved in the project, this created a tradition of goodwill that facilitated the automatic creation of trust bonds.

Fifth, the extreme and often self-sacrificing character of the common activity created a sense of instant comradeship that enabled the 'sense of trust' to which Dimos referred. As he mentioned in another discussion: 'When at two o'clock in the morning you see your fellow beings throwing themselves selflessly into the freezing-cold sea trying to help, it is indeed very difficult to think about their selfish aspects – or yours.' Emergency urges for togetherness, and this contributes to the creation of an immediate trust. Emergency also creates an 'automatic filter', as Dimos mentions, making it easier to distinguish who is trustworthy and who is not.

Sixth, studies have suggested that feeling helpful is self-rewarding since it raises the levels of dopamine and oxytocin in our bodies (Benkler 2011). My own participation in structures similar to Platanos confirms that, especially when this self-rewarding joy is shared in a group, it creates a social bond characterized by fulfilment and satisfaction, both of which contribute to the creation of automatic trust. As Manos, a dentist who went to Platanos for two distinct periods, told me: 'The general feeling was that we enjoyed it very much. Since you are interested in collectives and such, you must visit the place for sure. Of course, many times the conditions were so difficult that we were crying; it went beyond us. But we all like it very much.' Likewise, Tara mentioned: 'It is very different than what usually happens in life when we are all told not to trust anybody. You almost become a child and, as you know, children can trust immediately.'

Seventh, 'peripheral' collective experiences – especially celebrative ones – create a widespread sense of trust and reinforce a sense of belonging, even if this does not translate immediately into a concrete community. Platanos' members often had celebrations together. Nitsa, the only 'full member' of the project who was a permanent resident of Sykamnia, said:

> They (the members of Platanos) organized a surprise party for my birthday. They did the same for my husband, for Yiannis (the other local who helped with electric facilities) and for some other people. We also had a great party for New Year's Eve. These celebrations were very important for us locals to feel part of the group, and they strengthened Platanos in many ways.

Lastly, constant creativity becomes a strong source of group cohesion. Within its condition of liminal flux, Platanos inspired people to become creative and collectively invent ways to overcome their common problems. Thus, collective inventiveness (Stavrides 2016) becomes another source of automatic trust. When, after the EU–Turkey deal, the emergency was over and hence the most creative part of Platanos came to an end, the absence of creativity led to the emergence of several conflicts between solidarians who remained inactive at the camp. Creativity is an absolute prerequisite for liminal commons to function and endure.

The big advantage of the automatic trust is that in a given context and under specific conditions, such as the ones described earlier, it can become the foundation of crisis management without authoritarianism and without establishing an undemocratic 'state of exception'. The case of Platanos proves that liminal commons can play an important role in the management of emergency in extreme situations. Moreover, automatic trust creates a zone of experimentation with emergent forms of sociality that were previously inconceivable. The major disadvantage is that this kind of emergency-driven trust can also mask differences and artificially bridge them in a fragile manner; this fragility prevents the emergence of robust and sustainable social bonds, and thus automatic trust can easily be reversed. However, my study suggests that very rarely do these temporary bonds completely disappear. On the contrary, they contribute to the creation of common sense, collective experiences and even concrete ventures that continue to exist in the wake of the crisis. Some examples have been already presented, but I am certain that many more implicit and explicit outcomes of Platanos can be identified in its 'afterlife'. As Nitsa and Dimos said in a joint interview: 'The seed of solidarity was planted in Platanos to flourish everywhere in its wake.'

Rethinking membership

The idea that stable membership is an absolute prerequisite for a horizontal group or for a commons to operate successfully is deeply rooted in our thought. High participant turnover automatically translates into a chaotic agglomeration of individuals, a crowd, incapable of acting in common, respecting rules or cooperating efficiently. A rapid change in group membership can only be imagined in a Fordist-Taylorist context, where the worker is regarded merely as an easily replaceable tool.

After having presented insights into people's motivations and automatic trust, in this brief last part of the chapter, I will argue that we must rethink the above assumptions on membership as well. The case of Platanos demonstrates that in liminal situations, high participant turnover not only is compatible with horizontal and meaningful commoning but may also be necessary for the successful operation of liminal commons. I will also argue that while exhaustion and 'burnout' indeed necessitate high turnover, there are more reasons that make a rapid change in membership valuable. These reasons have to do with issues of creativity, interconnectivity and expansion, and obviously do not point to the Fordist-Taylorist model and the reduction of humans to interchangeable tools.

First and foremost, Platanos was a very efficient venture, especially regarding its main activity, that is, offering first reception services to migrants. Platanos operated for eight consecutive months and serviced the vast majority of migrants arriving on the island. According to estimations by both locals and volunteers, Platanos had an operational capacity many times greater than the neighbouring Lighthouse Camp, which was offering the same services plus overnight accommodation, and was managed by a much better funded Swedish NGO. Despite its minimum funds, Platanos managed to become a global point of reference regarding self-organization in times of emergency, appearing in the global media and even being mentioned in the Nobel awards.

Second, everyday life in Platanos was very hard and demanding in terms of the energy, both physical and psychological, needed for carrying out its tasks. As Dimos says: 'We were sleeping in shifts for four hours maximum, and we were keeping watch all night. In the winter this was often unbearable, especially for those of us who are not that young anymore.' People often needed to take some distance before they could come back and act again. Besides, Platanos was a project developing at the margins of many participants' 'normality'; it was, therefore, difficult to have members stay for many consecutive weeks or months. For many, Platanos was a life-changing experience, as their participation in the project helped them change their life trajectory. Yet, Platanos was always *a transitional structure for both migrants and non-migrants*. High turnover, then, is an essential element of this extensive transitoriness.

Such a highly demanding venture requires a good amount of creativity and inventiveness to function. Also, its effectiveness is threatened by a fixation on roles and institutions that do not allow the collective to rethink and reinvent the whole structure through improvisation with new practices. To be sure, fresh energy and ideas are always needed, but they should be accompanied by a loose organization that allows space for those new ideas to arise and be put into practice.

As previously described, the operation of Platanos was to a large extent based on processes of e-commoning. High membership turnover proved essential for increasing remote and digital contributions. People coming to Platanos had a first-hand experience of the venture's value. After getting identified with it, they were returning to their homes, but actually operated as the global extension of the camp and continued to support it economically, materially and politically. A concrete membership would never be able to promote such a rapid internationalization of the commons.

On the other hand, a loose organization often translates into an absence of any organization. While, as I argued earlier, transitoriness can be a source of strength for liminal commons, finding the functional balance between openness, flexibility, institutionalization and effectiveness is not an easy task. In Platanos, the collective experimented with various forms of operational rules to find a balance between the two opposing tendencies. For instance, a volunteer coordinator was charged with the task of familiarizing newcomers with assemblary and self-organizational processes, and of course with the tasks to be carried out when a new boat was arriving. However, in some cases, things were not very well communicated and the decision-making process failed to offer a solution. In such cases, where consensus failed and there was no decided-upon alternative, some long-time members independently decided what had to be done. Translation and facilitation were present in every assembly, yet more politicized or 'core' members often spoke more than newcomers. While, on the one hand, this situation is to be expected, on the other, it can demotivate people to continue participating in decision-making.

Resuming the argument

This final empirical chapter revisited the theory of liminal commons through the emblematic case of Platanos Self-Organized Refugee Camp, which constituted a liminal commons par excellence. Through close examination of its operation, I tried to elucidate important dimensions of the framework that I have been developing throughout this incipient theoretical effort. Liminal commons are transitional forms of commoning that do not aim to endure or to become fixed but emerge to facilitate transitions of some kind and then consciously dissolve after completing their aims (or even after failing to complete them). This perspective differs from established approaches on the commons, which try to set down the criteria that make commons enduring and their institutions stable. Instead, this new approach shifts the focus to processes of transformation, reversion and transition. Thus, success is measured not only in terms of sustainability but also in terms of expansion, management of emergency and crisis, and reversion of dominant taxonomies and established ways of thinking and acting. In other words, the liminal commons theory does aspire not to replace theories of more long-lasting commoning but to destabilize and expand them, simultaneously complementing them with a new theoretical tool that allows us to express and conceptualize processes that have commoning at their core but share little else with the common-pool resources studied by Ostrom and her followers.

The case of Platanos allowed us to revisit issues related to subjectivity in times of crisis and further develop insights on the subjects of commoning, presented in more detail in the first chapter. We saw that liminal commons emerge as heterogeneous multiplicities driven by crisis and emergency and further fuel the negation and reversion of established identities at the personal and collective levels. In this chapter, we also examined the emerging spatialities of this widespread liminality and observed how a generalized encounter with the 'other' can be the cornerstone of a type of sociality in which *everyone is a foreigner*.

This chapter also made an important contribution in the re-examination of processes of expansion of the commons in both surface and internal ways. By introducing the concept of *e-commoning*,

6. Trust, Altruism and Solidarity

I aim to bridge various levels and scales of the commoning present in liminal commons in an innovative way that diverges from studies on digital commons and e-volunteering and goes beyond them. By exploring the conditions of emergence and dissolution of the liminal commons of Platanos, I put forward that there are consciously temporal commons, which pay more attention to their capacity of creating new ventures than of enduring for a long time. This is an entirely new approach to collective action, which is inherent in the theory of liminal commons.

Besides revisiting insights first presented in previous chapters, this chapter expanded the theory of liminal commons by shedding light on important pending questions of commons theory. Trust, utility, altruism and membership were closely re-examined under conditions of crisis and emergency, and a series of innovative arguments was presented.

First, departing from essentialist and ontological perspectives and focusing on the transformation of the reasons that make people engage with commoning practices, I tried to problematize narratives that ascribe to humans a natural tendency to compete or collaborate. Furthermore, I argued that the condition of liminality is not only an outcome; rather, it can also be a source of activity and experimentation with alternatives, which contributes to the reorientation and reconstruction of broken lives and places. Second, I argued that in conditions of emergency and crisis, a peculiar kind of trust may emerge: *automatic trust*. Subsequently, I examined in more detail the necessary conditions for this kind of trust to emerge and whether – or how – this automatic trust translates into more stable relations. Third, in contrast to dominant narratives, I argued that high participant turnover in commoning projects can be a major strength in conditions of emergency and should not be treated de facto as a shortcoming.

Chapter 7

EPILOGUE
RITUALS AND TRANSFORMATIONS

All societies perform rituals to demarcate transitions (Thomassen 2009). Yet, many scholars suggest that in contemporary societies rituals have faded away and lost their central function in processes of transformation, both individual and societal (e.g. Turner 1982; Thomassen 2014). As Mary Douglas beautifully put it, 'ritual has become a bad word signifying empty conformity. We are witnessing a revolt against formalism, even against form' (Douglas 1996: 1).

Victor Turner (1982), in his exploration of the rituals of modern civilizations, suggested that we may no longer speak about liminality but mostly about *liminoid* experiences. Liminoid signifies an 'out-of-the-ordinary' experience or a 'break from normality', which many people seek in activities related to sports, leisure, theatre, holidays and arts. These can range from using drugs at a trance party to practising a dangerous or even life-threatening extreme sport; in effect, it can be any activity that pushes the subject to temporarily forego his or her established views and habits. Liminoid experiences have many of the qualities that can be found in liminal experiences, but they no longer involve the perhaps most crucial characteristic of liminality: transition. They are 'as-if-liminality' (Turner 1982; Thomassen 2014).

This narrative about how such liminoid experiences today have replaced liminality to become the performative equivalent of archaic rituals is often accompanied by theoretical observations about the prevailing social relations in modern societies. First, scholars associate the replacement of the liminal with the liminoid with the increasing individualization and fragmentation of contemporary society. Such accounts are produced by both anthropologists and geographers, who, however, emphasize different aspects of this fragmentation. From an anthropological perspective, Thomassen (2014: 186) argues that post-industrial society is much too fractured for such 'unified' ritual experiences; specialization and rationalization have splintered the social fabric alongside a general process of individualization. Meaning has become personal. Expressive culture develops into several specialized fields and genres, and nobody is any longer forced to undergo the same ritual passages. Rather, individuals themselves seek such liminoid experiences on a voluntary basis. Liminoid phenomena develop within relatively independent genres, and the engagement with these phenomena becomes tied to the individual consumption of the out-of-the-ordinary as a commodity.

From an urban studies perspective, as Stavrides (2013) argues, fragmentation is manifested in the contemporary metropolis as 'an urban archipelago of enclosures'. These enclosures are materialized in a series of unconnected urban enclaves, spaces that are 'defined by specific recognizable boundaries within the city and are explicitly connected with specific protocols of use' (Stavrides 2016: 18) and behaviour. Individualization, fragmentation and commodification characterize these enclaves, in his view. These theoretical accounts highlight the tendency – prevalent in many parts of modern society – to 'consume differently' by simultaneously eradicating the distance between the known and the unknown, the familiar and the 'other'. This is often accompanied by the tendency to celebrate all that is different, all that is 'other' and to celebrate every break from normality and order. Turner himself was in the habit of celebrating every experience of 'as-if-liminality' as a possible source of renovation and as a positive 'survival of the playful'. As Turner's friend Richard Schechner writes in the preface to Turner's last book, *The Anthropology of Performance* (1988): 'Turner was keen on passing the threshold and he was always urging for opening one more door and living one more liminal experience.'

A second important note on the transition from liminal to liminoid has to do with the changes in the domains of work, leisure and play between the tribal and the (post)industrial societies. In his famous essay on the topic, Victor Turner (1974) argues that work in its current form is an artefact of the Industrial Revolution and so does the distinction between work and leisure.[1] In tribal and agrarian societies, work and

---

1. Leisure in this theoretical perspective is differentiated from the aristocratic idleness since the latter is not defined by work (which is done by slaves, peasants or servants).

7. Epilogue

leisure are blended into a continuum that begins 'at sunrise to finish only at sunset' (Turner 1974: 67) and contains all the elements of social life: the sacred, the profane, the play, as well as moments of rest. Rituals in tribal societies are submerged in this continuum and blend work with play[2] in an indistinguishable form. To this extent, rituals in general and rites of passage, in particular, are deeply embedded in the social structure of the tribal societies. In fact, they often operate as a mirror of this rigid structure; they not only invert its image but also reflect it. As Turner (1974:72) put it, 'a mirror inverts but also reflects an object. It does not break it down into constituents in order to remould it, far less does it annihilate and replace that object.'

Against this background, liminality in the context of tribal societies signifies a period of aberration from the norm rather than a period of genuine transformation, at least at the social level. Liminal entities are carefully guided during the rites of passage to accomplish a predefined transition, and the figure of the master of ceremony is central in this process. Even the emergence of the so-called *anti-structure*, which constitutes the dissolution of social structure along with its established social roles, statuses, duties and so on, happens in an otherwise rigid and unchangeable context. Even more importantly, the liminal phase in the archaic rites of passage is *obligatory* for its subjects, both individuals and collectives. Transgression, play, the inversion of the status quo, as well as the breaking of rules is, in fact, part of the social structure and is demanding and compulsory. The liminal is part and parcel of the normativeness of the tribal society; it inverts it but cannot subvert it.

On the other hand, liminoid experiences develop in contemporary societies as leisure experiences, Turner argues. Since leisure is defined only in relation to work, one can associate it with the realm of play, freedom from obligation and free choice. In this sense, liminoid phenomena are removed from the context of the rites of passage and become a set of individualized, fragmented and experimental activities that are primarily conceived as a matter of choice, not an obligation. 'One works at the liminal, one plays with the liminoid', as Turner said (1974: 86). Thus, liminoid phenomena can be very subversive, in both form and content,

---

2. While leisure is an artefact of the Industrial Revolution, play exists throughout the history of human society. However, play in archaic societies is indistinguishable from work both in the daily routine and in the ritual context. In (post)industrial societies leisure includes but exceeds play; it is a non-work or even an anti-work phase in the lives of those who also work (Turner 1974).

but because they often develop as commodities to be consumed on the margins of people's structured lives (i.e. work), they have limited capacity to provide the means for collective or even societal transformations. One could even argue that in modern societies the liminoid became a privileged ally of what Zygmound Bauman (1998) framed as 'sensation gathering', which characterizes what he calls the era of 'liquid modernity'.

The earlier observations are important in the effort to understand transformative processes in the contemporary world, as well as examine the role of rituals in these transformations. In this context, some very crucial questions emerge: Is it necessary for transitions and transformations to be symbolically marked and ritualized in the contemporary world? What can be the value of rituals in contemporary radical politics? What role does crisis play in rendering rituals and liminal phenomena again necessary for a society, rather than performing just a break-from-normality role?

There is a nascent literature that tries to make sense of the role of rituals in general, and liminality in particular, in contemporary societies and which tries to link again the concept with its fundamental attributes described by Van Gennep one century ago. In this respect, liminality has been linked to contemporary political, social and cultural transformations. In a recent article, Dorothea von Hantelmann (2020) asks what could be the new ritual space of the twenty-first century. In her thoughtful analysis, she examines how ritual spaces have been transformed throughout history. She argues that the theatre was the ritual place of Greek antiquity, the church that of European medieval times and the museum that of industrial societies. Subsequently, similar to Turner, she associates the prevalence of the latter with the increased individualization of the industrial society, the need for separation from the stringest traditional social ties, the elevation of plurality as an important characteristic of contemporary art and lifestyle, and the shift from the predominance of the linguistic encounters to the visual ones. However, she argues that if separation was the central quest of the (post)modern era, the central question nowadays is how to connect what has been disconnected. By using Bruno Latour's words on the topic, she claims that the task of the twenty-first century is not one of critique but of composition, not of emancipation but of care. Then she tries to conceptualize the specific elements that should be connected by the new ritual spaces and she gives a preliminary road map about how to design them.

Dorothea von Hantelmann's work is important as it poses a series of crucial questions about the future of rituals and their potential role in contemporary societies. Yet, she treats rituals and the ritual form more broadly as a sort of homeostatic apparatus whose sole aim is to keep society together, to weave social ties and to affirm and solidify the social structure and social order. But rituals and rites of passage in particular, as Van Gennep and Turner have shown, can also become transgressive machines, not only affirmative but also subversive for the social structure and order. Especially in the context of the exploration of this book, rituals are examined mostly as 'portals', whose role is to facilitate individuals and cohorts of individuals to move from a problematic personal and social situation to a new one; as 'pilots', which help people experience and compare their new everyday practices to their former ones; and as 'navigation tools', which allow individuals and collectives to experiment with new forms of being in common and come up with new conceptualizations and everyday practices concerning forms of social organization.

The following two authors approach the topic with an approach similar in scope and content to mine, the one presented here. Bjørn Thomassen is a key figure in the process of reclaiming ritual and liminality as tools for approaching societal transformations and radical politics. In his work, he links liminality with political events and tries to develop what he calls an 'anthropology of political revolutions'. His exploration is both theoretical and historical; he points out a series of dimensions that should be taken into account if liminality is to be used in this context. Most notably, Thomassen insists that 'liminality must somehow come to an end' and that liminal periods are not only associated with positive creativity and possibility but also with danger and suffering. He goes on to develop a series of arguments about the role of the 'trickster' in contemporary liminal periods of revolution and layout an agenda with research questions to be further explored (Thomassen 2009; 2014).

The other fundamental contribution to the field comes from Stavros Stavrides, whose work has been referenced in several parts of this book. Stavrides uses liminality mostly as a spatial metaphor for conceptualizing common space and his 'city of thresholds'. In fact, Stavrides' focus is not on the experience of liminality and its many contradictory and even opposing tendencies but on the connecting qualities that the spatiality of threshold possesses, since 'considering common spaces as threshold spaces opens the possibility of studying practices of space-commoning that transcend enclosure and open towards new commoners' (Stavrides 2016: 5). Therefore, the 'threshold' comes first, and the theory of liminality is sporadically used to supplement and complete his arguments. Nevertheless, his theoretical project is important and relevant for the study of liminality as well, since it tries to link liminality with a theory of common space from an explicitly political and emancipatory angle.

What can the liminal commons add to this discussion?

Throughout this book, an effort has been made to explicitly link liminality with processes of transformation at various levels and scales, from the molecular level of the individual to the broader level of an entire country. This endeavour is informed by a careful examination of collective experiences that take the form of improvised rituals of commoning or, in other words, liminal commons. To be sure, the fact that this theoretical exploration is anchored in specific case studies limits the generalizability of its findings; on the other hand, it has allowed me to reveal the complexities and contradictions of 'real life' and, by extension, to enrich the existing literature with new theoretical questions and observations.

Scholarship on societal transformation may belong to one of two currents. The first tries to understand the malaise in current social organization in terms of its institutions, forms of governance, economy, social relations and human–nature relations; subsequently, it tries to address these issues by promoting alternative views. These alternative views can take the form of general guiding principles or new models for the reconstitution of the aforementioned 'parameters' of social life. In any case, they try to provide a positive prototype of a future social structure. In the second current, scholars try to decipher the mechanisms that underlie transformation and examine the conditions that may facilitate or hamper such change. The present work is a modest attempt belonging to the second stream.

A process of individualization, commodification and fragmentation such as the one described by the scholars mentioned earlier did take place in Greek society from the late 1980s until the early 2000s, as I explained in detail in Chapter 3. By securing high consumption levels for large parts of the population, this process gave rise to a state of *doxa*, the ancient Greek term that according to Bourdieu (2013 [1977]: 161) signifies a period when 'the natural and social world appears as self-evident', and therefore many things are taken for granted. It was this fixed state of doxa that after 2008 was shaken by the multidimensional crisis and gave way to a stage of suspension, of liminality.

7. Epilogue

One of the main arguments of this book is that the multifaceted Greek crisis led to improvised collective responses in the form of commoning projects, which I call 'the liminal commons'. Liminal commons differ from other types of contemporary liminal experiences in that they have the commons as their focal point, rather than the individual 'break from normality' of liminoid experiences. On the other hand, liminal commons differ from the more 'conventional' commons studied by Elinor Ostrom and other scholars in that they do not aspire to endure for long periods but, on the contrary, to facilitate transitions. Yet, liminal commons do not only facilitate transitions but also mark them; therefore, they often acquire a highly symbolic dimension, as well as a highly performative and ritualistic function. Liminal commons are the improvised collective rituals that aim at transcending the contemporary crisis.

Anthropologists argue that every transition requires a symbolic ritual (Van Gennep 1960 [1908]; Thomassen 2014). Thus, the role of liminal commons is crucial in a society in crisis. Liminal commons can become social laboratories where new collective meanings and societal orientations can be born and put into practice, and new connections can be established between the heterogeneous and unconnected individual and collective subjects. In this respect, as liminal commons are improvised socio-spatial processes with no recognizable 'master of ceremony', they often become a stage of experimentation with practices that facilitate equality, identity transgression and re-subjectification. Liminal commons promote an inclusive 'togetherness'.

In the relevant literature, liminality is presented either as something obligatory for all members of the collective, as in the organized rituals of archaic societies, or as a condition in which individuals freely choose to disrupt their routine, as in the case of liminoid experiences. This view is quite simplistic and does not correspond to the reality of the liminal commons, in which liminality is both the outcome and the prerequisite of human agency. In other words, while crisis is a favourable condition for the creation of liminal commons, liminal commons are in turn a factor of further expansion of the crisis, rendering it contagious and metastatic. Thus, liminal commoners are neither passive receivers of liminality nor sense-gatherers that seek a 'genuine' extraordinary experience. Rather, they are people who, on the one hand, are affected and disoriented by crisis and, on the other, are active agents who create and recreate liminal spaces, institutions and relations to facilitate their collectively desired transitions.

The degree of liminality can vary in the formation of liminal commons. Some instances are characterized by 'extreme' liminality; this is the case with the Platanos Self-Organized Refugee Camp, presented in Chapter 6, where 'everyone is a foreigner' and thus liminality and flux mark all dimensions of the venture, including spatial, social, institutional and membership ones. However, liminality may only characterize a fraction of a particular commoning project. For example, in the Akadimia Platonos neighbourhood in Athens, some people set up a collectively owned café called 'Plato's Academy Cooperative Café'. The project has set a series of goals. On the one hand, it is a cooperative business that aims at providing an income to those working there. In this respect, the project can be characterized as a commons but, obviously, not as a liminal one. On the other hand, the project was created to change how residents use the nearby green park. The park was previously abandoned, as residents considered it dangerous and avoided using it. The group wanted to make the park usable and safe for all residents again. To facilitate this transition, they took a series of initiatives. For many years, they organized festivals, concerts and even specific rituals for the transition from winter to spring and from summer to autumn. All these self-organized practices of commoning were highly performative and had a strong liminal dimension; therefore, they can be regarded as the liminal part of an otherwise non-liminal commons.

In this book, I have explored different aspects of the liminal commons, including issues of operation, subjectification, institutions, expansion, transformative potential, protection, openness, closure, trust-building, motivations, membership, networking, multiplication and political identity. Owing to the flux of liminality, this has been a difficult task; nevertheless, I have tried to avoid simplifications and general claims and to theorize my observations carefully and rigorously. Most importantly, I have tried to relate each one of my theoretical propositions to both the actual experience in the field and the respective literature on commons and liminality. My intention is not only to propose a new analytical tool for approaching contemporary collective performances that emerge in contexts of crisis but also to create a new field for further exploration and future research.

In each of the empirical chapters, I have attempted to explore one or more key issues related to specific qualities and characteristics of the liminal commons. I have aimed to render this incipient theoretical language understandable and useful for approaching similar phenomena beyond the context of this study. The second chapter, which was the first

7. Epilogue

of the four empirical chapters, dealt primarily with issues of subjectivity in the formation of the commons and subsequently elaborated on the ontological characteristics of liminal commons. It revealed that in contexts of crisis, predefined categories of fixed subjects as perceived by previous commons theories lose their analytical value since liminality becomes the main catalyst of commoning. The new collective performances that unfold in the public space 'secrete' new social and spatial relations and blur clear-cut dualisms and dichotomies. They tend to be open to everyone, very malleable and rapidly changing, yet they strive to keep some core symbolic elements unaffected as the most important part of their collective invention. The new common space is porous and expanding and tends to connect with other newly shaped common spaces in other parts of the city and the country. Sustaining the common space is not an end in itself but is important for as long as the space remains open to experimentation and possibility. Then it dissolves and is diffused in the urban fabric while simultaneously creating new urban fabric. Thus, the experience of liminal commoning can be transformative – and in the Greek case, it has, indeed, been transformative both for the participants and for the city at large. The commons itself may have perished, but it has left an important legacy in the cultural, social, infrastructural and political field and has catalysed many socio-spatial processes in the ensuing years. A part of the intended transitions was successfully accomplished.

The fourth chapter addressed a specific question: What happens when a liminal commons comes to an end? In doing so, it addressed issues of re-aggregation, which is the last stage in the liminal process as described by Van Gennep and Turner. The empirical evidence revealed that liminal commons can create an expansion dynamic in their wake. The expansion of commoning after the movement of the squares – which I approached as a contemporary commoning ritual – was unprecedented by Greek standards. This chapter explored the role contemporary social movements can play if they adopt commoning as a core dimension of their repertoires of action. I argued that social movements and commons can have a co-productive relation, in which they fuel each other. Such interaction can lead to a sweeping rhizomatic expansion of cells of commoning. This expansion is unplanned, a-centred and non-linear. In the Greek case, this expansion put to practice the new elements created within and through liminality. In other words, it attempted to involve wider parts of Greek society in the re-aggregation process and become the matrix for a broader societal transformation.

The fifth chapter explored issues of openness, closure and protection of the commons in the post-liminal phase of Greek commoning movements when the new commons were not aiming to facilitate transitions but to constitute viable alternative social systems of production and reproduction. This focus partially deviates from the main theme of this book, that is, the study of the relation between crisis, commons and liminality. Nevertheless, it is important because it allows exploring how elements that are constitutive in liminal commons can become constituent – yet implemented in a different manner – in the ventures that succeed the liminal ones. Openness was constitutive in the liminal commons of the squares, and this tendency characterized many of the new commons of the next years. Yet, as the new commons went beyond the liminality and precarity exhibited by liminal commons, sustainability and survival became important; therefore, new rules and methods were employed for their protection. After examining these methods of protection, this chapter concluded that they do not fit in the dichotomy of openness versus closure, popular in commons theory. Instead, it presented a series of strategies of protection that transcend this dualism. The chapter went on to detail five different strategies commoners employ to protect their ventures.

The last empirical chapter of this book examined an extreme case of liminal commons: the self-organized camp of Platanos in Lesvos, which operated for eight months to facilitate the safe transit of migrants from Asia to Europe. Besides this literal transition, the chapter explored how the liminal commons of Platanos operated as a modern ritual that facilitated various transitions and transformations: personal, spatial, collective, political and social.

However, the main purpose of this chapter was to define what makes a liminal commons function and meet its goals, since liminal commons violate almost all criteria of success Elinor Ostrom laid out for the commons. Building upon the findings of the first chapter, I explained how liminality, understood as the condition of in-betweenness, became an absolute prerequisite for the democratic operation of such a heterogeneous project. Moreover, the chapter offered a reflection on issues relevant to all commons, namely trust, the commoners' motives and membership. My argument was that in conditions of emergency, trust is created and sustained in ways other than the well-known processes based on repetition, shared values, common vision, shared experience, deep interpersonal interaction and collective memory. Trust becomes automatic. Additionally, I argued that in such liminal conditions the calculative logic of the rational individual collapses, and along with it the notions of self-interest and incentive become deeply problematized and questioned. In this context, liminality becomes the main drive for participating in commoning. It is often accompanied by a desire for a meaningful transformation at the personal and the collective level and for a reconstruction of a broken past upon new foundations.

Conclusions and possible topics for future research

This book has set the foundations for the study of a series of phenomena that unfold in modern societies as contemporary commoning rituals and play an important role in the transformation of individuals, collectives, places and even entire societies. However, this is a preliminary effort and, as such, it is inevitably incomplete. This is reflected also in my own theoretical journey, which started with a fragmented and partial observation I did in a context totally different from the commoning projects presented in this work. While in the beginning I thought that this observation only applied to that particular case, I am now confident that the idea of the liminal commons describes a widespread and common process, which takes place in modern societies more often than I initially expected. Therefore, I no longer believe that the scope of this book is limited to a small niche of extraordinary and rare socio-spatial processes. Individuals and groups all over the world very often – especially when enduring crises destabilize the 'doxa' of established truths and patterns – attempt to collectively transform their everyday realities and advance to another state of being. In this process, they often employ transitional strategies in which previous roles and identities are contested and reversed, and new identities and practices are temporally performed. These improvised contemporary rituals are often marked by a commitment to equality and balanced participation. The theory of liminal commons may prove illuminating and useful in the context of such collective performances.

Having said this, it seems evident that the possible lines of development of the theory of liminal commons are multiple and cannot be exhausted by a single person in a single text. It is worth mentioning that I have only used a fraction of my empirical data in this book, and, therefore, there already exists a big pool of information and primary data that could be further tapped into for future works. What follows is the formulation of a basic research agenda that includes topics I have intentionally left out of the present work and which I am planning to develop in the future.

First, in this book I have repeatedly argued that in the case of liminal commons, due to the temporary suspension or delegitimization of pre-existing categorizations and taxonomies, many things that are taken for granted in the study of collective action are challenged and reversed. One of those things has to do with the inversion of power relations and the questioning or collapse of pre-existing leaderships. However, such abolition of leadership is always incomplete and fragile. Undoubtedly, liminality is a source of equality; yet, at the same time, the loss of frame that follows liminal periods is conducive to the emergence of new hierarchies and relations of power and domination. In this work, I have intentionally focused more on the practices that commoners employ to avoid such accumulation of power, and I have given some hints on how trust and cooperation may flourish in such conditions. However, I think that future work on the topic should more carefully examine these opposing tendencies and theorize when, how and why one prevails over the other.

Second, the present work constitutes only a small first step in the exploration of the outcomes of liminal commons. Throughout the book, I have made the case that, despite their precarious and temporary nature, liminal commons can have important aftereffects: in the first place, they have an expansive and metastatic character and can become the matrix for a rhizomatic multiplication of commoning practices. Moreover, participation in liminal commons affects people at the individual level; Chapters 3 and 6 include many references to the interviewees' life stories that demonstrate such major shifts. Further, liminal commons affect groups; we saw how the liminal commons of the movement of the squares affected pre-existing political groups, which were compelled to change their repertoires of action to integrate new elements that were practised on the squares. Lastly, liminal commons affect and transform places and invest them with new symbolic meanings, as in the case of Sykamnia in Lesvos.

To assess the depth and range of the above changes, more studies are needed, especially diachronic research projects that follow the evolution of subjects and places to observe the long-term effects of liminal commons. Such an approach will not only be useful in theorizing the transformation trajectory of subjects and places but will also allow for a fruitful exploration and comparative analysis of how diverse experiences of liminal commoning can coexist and intersect in this transformative process. Moreover, it will allow us to reflect on the

7. Epilogue

factors that facilitate or hinder such long-lasting transformations. For instance, the role of ideology, political identity, previous participation of subjects in collective ventures and other aspects not sufficiently analysed in the present work should be revisited and further explored.

Third, since all cases I have examined in the present work belong to a particular context and geography, I consider it crucial to investigate how individual and collective subjects in other parts of the world respond to similar cases of generalized crisis. It is vital to examine how the constitution of each dominant social imaginary affects the creation and performance of such modern collective rituals and how this social imaginary is imprinted in how liminal commons are conceived, performed, institutionalized, managed and finally dismantled. It is also important to study how and why liminal commons in different parts of the world that employ similar structures and repertoires of action can have diverse outcomes or, in other words, to relate the specific content of performed rituals with the contexts in which they develop. Different world views, cultures and societal trajectories can lead to the development of different apparatuses for balancing the individual and the collective, gender power dynamics, class differences and other social divisions. Such a polyhedric observation from the viewpoint of different societies will allow us to draw links between the diverse responses to similar triggers; by extension, it will help us extract patterns for better understanding the tripartite relation between crisis, liminality and commoning.

Lastly, I think that future research will benefit from an exploration of the role of liminal commons in what Hardt and Negri (2009: x) have called 'struggle over the control of the production of subjectivity'. I have previously explained how liminal commons differ from older accounts on liminality regarding the role of the subject in the liminal situation. In studies of liminality in archaic societies, we saw that rites of passage were mandatory for all members of society. This means that the identity transformations one would have in his or her life were predefined and sanctioned by elaborate rituals and explicit masters of ceremony. In contemporary instances of liminality in the form of liminoid experiences, while the subject may have the capacity to choose his or her own rituals, these rituals are deprived of their transformative potential. My argument is that liminal commons involve both passive and active dynamics; while crisis creates a favourable environment, human agency is crucial for their materialization.

Crisis figures as a core element in this theoretical effort. Indeed, liminality is always linked to a state of crisis. Yet, crisis here is not perceived as a bad spell or as an eschatological limit/end but as a period in which perplexity, ambiguity and destabilization arise. In my work, crisis is neither demonized nor celebrated; rather, it is utilized as an analytical tool for approaching transformative processes at various scales. The liminal commons presented here are all related to crisis; they are outcomes of crisis. However, as I have previously pointed out, while liminal commons are outcomes of crisis they can also give rise to new crises and they can further expand crises by rendering them contagious.

Despite this innovative approach to contemporary commoning rituals as forms that include both passive and active elements, one can identify a primary and a secondary force in the process. Crisis is something that occurs to a collective subject due to a rapid change in core fields of social life; accordingly, liminal commons constitute a possible response, a collective probing for an escape from the state of crisis, materialized through commoning. While this order has been central in my work and reflects with satisfactory accuracy the commons I studied for this book, in the last months of my inquiry I have come up with a new question: Can people consciously decide to go through such a liminal commoning ritual to pursue a collective transition towards the desired direction? In other words, do liminal commons develop only in response to rapid external changes that create conditions of crisis? Or is crisis something that can be intentionally created through the performance of rituals of commoning that maintain their transitory and transformative character? Can we have real transformative collective experiences that will not end up being mere liminoid aberrations from 'normality' but will be constituent of new structures and realities?

These questions are new and therefore not adequately theorized, yet they are linked to the broader discussion on individual and collective transformation. For Greek-French philosopher Cornelius Castoriadis, a crucial element of any project of autonomy is the establishment of a more conscious and reflective relationship with the unknown. For Castoriadis, an autonomous individual is one who creates a different relationship with his or her unconscious, a relation in which the unconscious is not completely mystified but becomes the object of inquiry and reflection. Likewise, an autonomous society is one that is able to have a reflective and critical relation with its social imaginary – a notion explained in more detail in the first chapter – that is, a society that is able to challenge, rethink and recreate its own institutions and norms (Castoriadis 1975). My argument, thus, is that liminal commons can potentially play an important role in this process of collective and societal transformation. In this respect, the way in which subjects respond to crises is very important. Some may repress the thought and pretend that it is not happening or that it is a bad spell that will quickly go away. Others may welcome crisis as an important element and as an opportunity for a meaningful reconstitution and renewal. The hypothesis is that once people get accustomed to collective performances of commoning practices to transcend a crisis, they may be able to employ similar procedures, not necessarily in response to an external threat or factor of destabilization but as part of a conscious strategy for societal transformation towards a desired direction. In other words, the liminal commons may be a key element in the process of claiming awareness and control over the mechanism of individual, collective and societal subjectification.

BIBLIOGRAPHY

Adam, S., and D. D. Teloni (2015) *Social Clinics in Greece in a Time of Crisis*. Athens: GSEE Publications.
Agamben, G. (1998) *Homo Sacer: Sovereign Power and Bare Life*. Stanford: Stanford University Press.
Androulidakis, A. (2016) *The Greek Trauma*. Athens: Nisides (in Greek).
Arenas, I. (2014) 'Assembling the Multitude: Material Geographies of Social Movements from Oaxaca to Occupy'. *Environment and Planning D: Society and Space* 32 (3): 433–49.
Athanasiou, A. (2014) *Precarious Intensities: Gendered Bodies in the Streets and Squares of Greece*. Paper Presented at the Comparative Perspectives Symposium: Gendered Bodies in the Protest Sphere.
Bauman, Z. (1998) *Globalization: The Human Consequences*. Cambridge: Polity Press.
Bauman, Z. (2013) *Liquid Modernity*. New York: John Wiley & Sons.
Bauwens, M., and V. Kostakis (2014) 'From the Communism of Capital to Capital for the Commons: Towards an Open Cooperativism'. *TripleC* 12(1): 356–61.
Benkler, Y. (2007) *The Wealth of Networks: How Social Production Transforms Markets and Freedom*. London: Yale University Press.
Benkler, Y. (2011) *The Penguin and the Leviathan: How Cooperation Triumphs over Self-interest*. Danvers: Crown Business.
Berardi, F. (2009) *Communism Is Back but Should Call It the Therapy of Singularization*. Conference Paper. London: The Idea of Communism.
Bey, H. (2003) *TAZ: The Temporary Autonomous Zone, Ontological Anarchy, Poetic Terrorism*. New York: Autonomedia.
Bhabha, H. (1994) *The Location of Culture*. London: Routledge.
Bollier, D. (2014) *Think Like a Commoner: A Short Introduction to the Life of the Commons*. Gabriola: New Society Publishers.
Bollier, D., and S. Helfrich (2019) *Free, Fair, and Alive: The Insurgent Power of the Commons*. Gabriola Island: New Society Publishers.
Bookchin, M. (1995) *Social Anarchism or Lifestyle Anarchism. An Unbridgeable Chasm*. Stirling: AK Press.
Bosi, L., M. Giougni, and K. Uba (2016) *The Consequences of Social Movements*. Cambridge: Cambridge University Press.
Bosi, L., and L. Zamponi (2015) 'Direct Social Actions and Economic Crises. The Relationship between Forms of Action and Socio-Economic Context in Italy'. *PArtecipazione e Conflitto* 8(2): 367–91.
Bourdieu, P. (1977) *Outline of a Theory of Practice* (Vol. 16). Cambridge: Cambridge University Press.

Bresnihan, P., and M. Byrne (2015) 'Escape into the City: Everyday Practices of Commoning and the Production of Urban Space in Dublin'. *Antipode* 47(1): 36–54.

Brighenti, A. (2013) *Urban Interstices: The Aesthetics and the Politics of the In-between*. Farham: Ashgate.

Bryman, A. (2016) *Social Research Methods*. Oxford: Oxford University Press.

Butler, J. (1997) *The Psychic Life of Power: Theories in Subjection*. Stanford: Stanford University Press.

Butler, J. (2015) *Notes Toward a Performative Theory of Assembly*. Boston: Harvard University Press.

Caffentzis, G. (2004) *A Tale of Two Conferences: Globalization, the Crisis of Neoliberalism and Question of the Commons*. Available at http://www.globaljusticecenter.org/papers/caffentzis.htm (22 November 2015).

Caffentzis, G. (2010) 'The Future of "The Commons": Neoliberalism's "Plan B" or the Original Disaccumulation of Capital?' *New Formations* 69: 23–41.

Caffentzis, G., and S. Federici (2014) 'Commons Against and Beyond Capitalism'. *Community Development Journal* 49: 92–105.

Castells, M. (1983) *The City and the Grassroots: A Cross-cultural Theory of Urban Social Movements (No. 7)*. Berkley: University of California Press.

Castells, M. (2004) *The Power of Identity*. Malden: Blackwell Pub.

Castells, M. (2012) *Networks of Outrage and Hope*. Cambridge: Polity.

Castoriadis, C. (1975) *The Imaginary Institution of the Society*. Athens: Kedros (in Greek).

Castoriadis, C. (1985) 'On Rationality and Development'. *Thesis Eleven* 10: 18–36.

Castoriadis, C. (1991) *Philosophy, Politics, Autonomy – Essays in Political Philosophy*. Oxford: Oxford University Press.

Castoriadis, C. (2000) *The Rising Tide of Insignificancy*. Athens. Ypsilon (in Greek).

Castoriadis, C. (2010) *A Society Adrift*. New York: Fordham University Press.

Castoriadis, C. (2011) *Postscript on Insignificance. Dialogues with Cornelius Castoriadis*. London: Continuum.

Ciriacy-Wantrup, S. V., and R. C. Bishop (1975) '"Common Property" as a Concept in Natural Resources Policy'. *Natural Resources Journal* 15(4): 713–27.

Conill, J., M. Castells, A. Cardenas, and L. Servon (2012) 'Beyond the Crisis: The Emergence of Alternative Economic Practices'. In *Aftermath: The Cultures of Economic Crisis*, edited by M. Castells, J. Caraça and G. Cardoso, 210–51. Oxford: Oxford University Press.

Dalakoglou, D. (2013) 'The Crisis before "the Crisis": Violence and Urban Neoliberalization in Athens'. *Social Justice* 39: 24–42.

D'Alisa, G. (2013) 'Bienes Comunes: Las Estructuras que Conectan'. *Ecología Política* 45: 30–41.

De Angelis, M. (2001) 'Marx and Primitive Accumulation: The Continuous Character of Capital's Enclosures'. *The Commoner* 2(1): 1–22.

De Angelis, M. (2007) *The Beginning of History: Value Struggles and Global Capital*. London: Pluto Press.

De Angelis, M. (2012) 'Crises, Movements and Commons'. *Borderlands E-Journal: New Spaces in the Humanities* 11(2): 4.

De Angelis, M. (2013) *Crises, Commons and Social Movements: Problematising the Diffusion of Alternatives*. Conference Paper. San Francisco: ISA.

De Angelis, M. (2014) 'The Commons: A Brief Life Journey'. *Community Development Journal* 49(suppl_1): 68–80.

De Angelis, M. (2017) *Omnia Sunt Communia. On the Commons and the Transformation to Postcapitalism*. London: Zed Books.

De Angelis, M., and S. Stavrides (2010) 'On the Commons: A Public Interview with Massimo De Angelis and Stavros Stavrides'. *e-flux Journal* 17.

Deleuze, G., and F. Guattari (2010) *Nomadology: The War Machine*. Seattle: Wormwood.

Deleuze, G., and F. Guattari (2012 [1988]) *A Thousand Plateaus*. London: Bloomsbury.

Demertzis, N. (1994) *The Greek Political Culture Today*. Athens: Odysseas (in Greek).

Dikeç, M., and E. Swyngedouw (2017) 'Theorizing the Politicizing City'. *International Journal of Urban and Regional Research* 41(1): 1–18.

Dobry, M. (2015) 'Critical Processes and Political Fluidity: A Theoretical Appraisal'. In *Breaking Boundaries Varieties of Liminality*, edited by A. Horvath, B. Thomassen and H. Wydra, 93–111. New York: Berghahn.

Douglas, M. (1996) *Natural Symbols: Explorations in Cosmology*. London: Routledge.

Douzinas, C. (2013) *Philosophy and Resistance in the Crisis*. Cambridge: Polity Press.

Doxiadis, E., and A. Placas (2018) *Living under Austerity. Greek Society in Crisis*. New York-Oxford: Berghahn.

Durkheim, É. (1967) *The Elementary Forms of Religious Life*. New York: Free Press.

Economou, M., M. Madianos, L. Peppou, C. Theleritis, A. Patelakis, and C. Stefanis (2013) 'Major Depression in the Era of Economic Crisis: A Replication of a Cross-sectional Study across Greece'. *Journal of Affective Disorders* 145(3): 308–14.

EL.STAT (2009) *Labour Force Survey, 4th Quarter*. Available at: www.statistics.gr.

EL.STAT. (2012) *Report on Suicide Rates 2012*. Available at: www.statistics.gr.

EL.STAT. (2013) *Labour Force Survey, 3rd Quarter*. Available at: www.statistics.gr.

EL.STAT. (2014) *Hellas in Numbers – 2014*. Available at: www.statistics.gr.

EL.STAT. (2015) *Hellas in Numbers – 2015*. Available at: www.statistics.gr.

Federici, S. (2010) 'Feminism and the Politics of the Commons'. In *Uses of a WorldWind: Movement, Movements, and Contemporary Radical Currents in the United States*, edited by C. Hughes, S. Peace, and K. Van Meter, 285–93. Oaskland: AK Press.

Foramitti, J., A. Varvarousis, and G. Kallis (2020) 'Transition within a Transition: How Cooperative Platforms Want to Change the Sharing Economy'. *Sustainability Science* 15(4): 1185–97.

Fillipidis, C. (2011) 'The Polis-jungle, Magical Densities, and the Survival Guide of the Enemy Within'. In *Revolt and Crisis in Greece: Between a Present Yet to Pass and a Future Still to Come*, edited by A. Vradis and D. Dalakoglou, 59–76. Oakland: AK Press and Occupied London.

Floros, C., and I. Chatziantoniou (2019) *The Greek Debt Crisis: In Quest of Growth in Times of Austerity*. London: Palgrave Macmillan

Fominaya, F. C. (2017) 'European Anti-austerity and Pro-democracy Protests in the Wake of the Global Financial Crisis'. *Social Movement Studies* 16(1): 1–20.

Forno, F., and P. Graziano (2014) 'Sustainable Community Movement Organisations'. *Journal of Consumer Culture* 14(2): 139–57.

Foucault, M. (1991) 'Governmentality'. In *The Foucault Effect: Studies in Governmentality*, edited by Graham Burchell, Colin Gordon and Peter Miller, 87–104. Chicago: University of Chicago Press.

Foucault, M. (2009) *Security, Territory, Population: Lectures at the College de France, 1977–1978*. Basingstoke: Palgrave Macmillan.

Foucault, M., P. Rabinow, and R. Hurley (1997) *The Essential Works of Michel Foucault, 1954–1984*. New York: The New Press

Gamson, W. A. (1990) *The Strategy of Social Protest*. New York: Wadsworth Pub Co

García López, G. A., I. Velicu, and G. D'Alisa (2017) 'Performing Counter-hegemonic Common (s)Senses: Rearticulating Democracy, Community and Forests in Puerto Rico'. *Capitalism Nature Socialism* 28(3): 88–107.

Garsten, C. (1999) 'Betwixt and Between: Temporary Employees as Liminal Subjects in Flexible Organizations'. *Organization Studies* 20(4): 601–17.

Giovanopoulos, C., and D. Mitropoulos (2011) *Democracy under Construction: From the Streets to the Square*. Athens: Asynexeia.

Giugni, M. (1998) 'Introduction: Social Movements and Change: Incorporation, Transformation and Democratization'. In *From Contention to Democracy*, edited by M. Giugni, C. McAdam, and C. Tilly, ix–xi. Oxford: Rowman and Littlefield Publishers.

Goutsos, D., and G. Polymeneas (2014) 'Identity as Space: Localism in the Greek Protests of Syntagma Square'. *Journal of Language and Politics* 13(4): 675–701.

Hadjimichalis, C. (2011) 'Uneven Geographical Development and Socio-spatial Justice and Solidarity: European Regions after the 2009 Financial Crisis'. *European Urban and Regional Studies* 18(3): 254–74.

Hadjimichalis, C. (2013) 'From Streets and Squares to Radical Political Emancipation? Resistance and Lessons from Athens during the Crisis'. *Human Geography* 6(2): 116–36.

Hadjimichalis, C. (2017) *Crisis Spaces. Structures, Struggles and Solidarity in Southern Europe*. London: Routledge

Hardin, G. (1968) 'The Tragedy of the Commons'. *Science* 162(3859): 1243–8.
Hardt, M. (2011) 'Reclaim the Common in Communism', *Guardian.co.uk*. Available at: http://www.guardian.co.uk/commentisfree/2011/feb/03/communism-capitalism-socialism-property.
Hardt, M., and A. Negri (2005) *Multitude: War and Democracy in the Age of Empire*. London: Penguin.
Hardt, M., and A. Negri (2009) *Commonwealth*. Boston: Harvard University Press.
Hardt, M., and A. Negri (2012) *Declaration*. Self-published and Distributed by Argo Navis Author Services.
Hardt, M., and A. Negri (2017) *Assembly*. Oxford: Oxford University Press.
Hardt, M., A. Negri, and D. Harvey (2009) 'Commonwealth: An Exchange'. *Artforum* 48(3): 210–21.
Harjunen, H. (2003, August) 'Obesity as a Liminal and Marginalized Experience'. In *Gender and Power in New Europe: The 5th European Feminist Research Conference, Lund University, Sweden*.
Harvey, D. (1996) *Justice, Nature and the Geography of Difference*. Oxford: Blackwell.
Harvey, D. (2000) *Spaces of Hope*. Edinburg: Edinburgh University Press.
Harvey, D. (2004) 'The "New Imperialism": Accumulation by Dispossession'. *Actuel Marx* 1: 71–90.
Harvey, D. (2009) 'Opening Speech at the Urban Reform Tent, World Social'. *Forum, Belem*, 29 January.
Harvey, D. (2011) 'The Future of the Commons'. *Radical History Review* 2011(109): 101–7.
Harvey, D. (2012) *Rebel Cities: From the Right to the City to the Urban Revolution*. London: Verso.
Helfrich, S. (2012) 'The Logic of the Commons & the Market: A Shorthand Comparison of Their Core Beliefs.'. In *The Wealth of the Commons: A World beyond Market and State*, edited by D. Bollier and S. Helfrich, 76–7. London: Levellers Press
Herzfeld, M. (2002) *Ours Once More: Folklore, Ideology and the Making of Modern Greece*. Athens: Aleksandreia (in Greek).
Hess, C., and E. Ostrom (2007) *Understanding Knowledge as a Commons*. Boston: The MIT Press.
Holloway, J. (2005) 'Change the World Without Taking Power'. *Capital & Class* 29(1): 39–42.
Holloway, J. (2014) *Change the World without Taking Power: The Meaning of Revolution Today*. Morrisville: Lulu Press, Inc.
Holloway, J., K. Nasioka, and P. Doulos (2020) *Beyond Crisis: After the Collapse of Institutional Hope in Greece, What?* Oakland: PM Press.
Horvath, A. (2013) *Modernism and Charisma*. London: Palgrave Macmillan.
Horvath, A. (2015) 'The Genealogy of Political Alchemy: The Technological Invention of Identity Change'. In *Breaking Boundaries Varieties of*

Liminality, edited by A. Horvath, B. Thomassen and H. Wydra, 72–92. New York: Berghahn.
Insurgenta, I. (2014) 'Transforming Crisis to Krisis. The #Festival4sce: A Hub of Networks towards the Alternative Route in Greece'. *Revolution News*. Available at: https://revolution-news.com/transforming-crisis-krisis-%CE%A4he-festival4sce-hub-networks-towards-alternative-route-greece/.
Kaika, M. (2012) 'The Economic Crisis Seen from the Everyday: Europe's Nouveau Poor and the Global Affective Implications of a "Local" Debt Crisis'. *City* 16(4); 422–30.
Kaika, M., and L. Karaliotas (2014) 'The Spatialization of Democratic Politics: Insights from Indignant Squares'. *European Urban and Regional Studies* 23(4): 556–70.
Kallis, G. (2017) *In Defense of Degrowth*. Brussels: Uneven Earth Press.
Kallis, G. (2014) *The Tigers That Became Pigs and the New Development Plan (published online)*. Available at http://greeklish.info/gr/greece/economics/302.
Kalogeraki, S. (2018) 'Socio-political Responses during Recessionary Times in Greece: An Introduction'. *Partecipazione e conflitto* 11(1): 1–11.
Kaplanis, Y. (2011) 'An Economy That Excludes the Many and an "Accidental" Revolt'. In *Revolt and Crisis in Greece: Between a Present Yet to Pass and a Future Still to Come*, edited by A. Vradis and D. Dalakoglou, 215–28. Oakland and London: AK Press and Occupied London.
Karaliotas, L. (2016) 'Staging Equality in Greek Squares: Hybrid Spaces of Political Subjectification'. *International Journal of Urban and Regional Research* 41(1): 54–69.
Karamichas, J. (2012) 'Square Politics: Key Characteristics of the Indignant Mobilizations in Greece'. In *62nd PSA Annual International Conference*.
Khanna, A. (2012) 'Seeing Citizen Action through an Unruly Lens'. *Development* 55(2): 162–72.
Kioupkiolis, A. (2014) *The Commons of Freedom*. Athens: Exarcheia (in Greek).
Klein, N. (2007) *The Shock Doctrine: The Rise of Disaster Capitalism*. Toronto: Random House of Canada.
Khasnabish, A. (2014) 'Review of the book *Anti-Crisis*, by Janet Roitman'. *Anthropological Quarterly* 87(2): 569–77. doi:10.1353/anq.2014.0021.
Koselleck, R. (1988) *Critique and Crisis: Enlightenment and the Pathogenesis of Modern Society*. Boston: MIT Press.
Koselleck, R., and M. Richter (2006) 'Crisis'. *Journal of the History of Ideas* 67(2): 357–400.
Kostakis, V., and M. Bauwens (2014) *Network Society and Future Scenarios for a Collaborative Economy*. New York: Springer.
Laloux, F. (2014) *Reinventing Organizations: A Guide to Creating Organizations Inspired by the Next Stage in Human Consciousness*. Oxford: Nelson Parker.
Latouche, S. (2015) 'Disaster, Pedagogy of'. In *Degrowth a Vocabulary for a New Era*, edited by G. D'Alisa, F. Demaria and G. Kallis, 94–96. New York: Routledge.

Lawley, S. (2004) 'Deleuze's Rhizome and the Study of Organization: Conceptual Movement and an Open Future'. *Tamara: Journal for Critical Organization Inquiry* 3(4): 36–49.

Lefebvre, H. (1996) *Writings on Cities* (Vol. 63). Oxford: Blackwell.

Leontidou, L. (2012) 'Athens in the Mediterranean "Movement of the Piazzas" Spontaneity in Material and Virtual Public Spaces'. *City* 16(3): 299–312.

Lichterman, P. (1996) *The Search for Political Community*: Cambridge: Cambridge University Press.

Lieros, G. (2016) *Commons, Communities, Common Property and Communism*. Athens: Ekdoseis ton Synadelfwn (in Greek).

LIFO (2016) 'Athens the City of Xanax'. Published on 19 February 2016. Available at: https://www.lifo.gr/various/athina-poli-toy-xanax (in Greek) (accessed 24 February 2022).

Linebaugh, P. (2009) *The Magna Carta Manifesto: Liberties and Commons for All*. Berkley: University of California Press.

Loukakis, A. (2018) 'Not just Solidarity Providers: Investigating the Political Dimension of Alternative Action Organisations (AAOs) during the Economic Crisis in Greece'. *Partecipazione e conflitto* 11(1): 12–37.

Mair, V. H. (2009) 'Danger + Opportunity ≠ Crisis'. Available at: http://www.pinyin.info/chinese/crisis.html.

Marcuse, P. (2011) *The Purpose of the Occupation Movement and the Danger of Fetishizing Space*. Available at: http://pmarcuse.wordpress.com/2011/11/15/the-purpose-of-the-occupation-movement-and-the-danger-of-fetishizing-space/.

Massey, D. (2013) *Space, Place and Gender*. New York: John Wiley & Sons.

Matsaganis, M. (2013) *The Greek Crisis: Social Impact and Policy Responses*. Berlin: Friedrich Ebert Stiftung.

McKean, M., and E. Ostrom (1995) 'Common Property Regimes in the Forest: Just a Relic from the Past'. *Unasylva* 46(180): 3–15.

Meretz, S. (2012) 'The Structural Communality of the Commons'. In *The Wealth of the Commons: A World beyond Market and State*, edited by D. Bollier and S. Helfrich, 67–74. London: Levellers Press.

Midnight Notes Collective and Friends (2009) *Promissory Notes – From Crisis to Commons*. Kingston: Jamaica Plain.

Mountian, I. (2009) 'Some Questions around Social Imaginary and Discourse Analysis for Critical Research'. *Annual Review of Critical Psychology* 7: 205–22.

Mylonas, Y. (2019) *The 'Greek Crisis' in Europe. Race, Class and Politics*. Leiden: Brill.

Ostrom, E. (1990) *Governing the Commons: The Evolution of Institutions for Collective Action*. Cambridge: Cambridge University Press.

Ostrom, E. (2009) 'A General Framework for Analyzing Sustainability of Social-Ecological Systems'. *Science* 325(5939): 419–22.

Ostrom, E. (2010) 'Beyond Markets and States: Polycentric Governance of Complex Economic Systems'. *American Economic Review* 100(3): 641–72.

Ostrom, E., J. Burger, C. B. Field, R. B. Norgaard, and D. Policansky (1999) 'Revisiting the Commons: Local Lessons, Global Challenges'. *Science* 284(5412): 278–82.

Paley, J. (2001) *Marketing Democracy: Power and Social Movements in Post-dictatorship Chile*. Berkley: University of California Press.

Pantazidou, M. (2013) 'Treading New Ground: A Changing Moment for Citizen Action in Greece'. *Development in Practice* 23: 5–6, 755–70.

Papadopoulos, D., V. Tsianos, and M. Tsomou (2012) 'Athens: Metropolitan Blockade – Real Democracy'. *Journal of the European Institute for Progressive Cultural Studies*. Available at: http://eipcp.net/transversal/1011/ptt/en.

Papageorgiou, N. (2017) 'Secularization and Gender in Greece: The "Resistance" of the Orthodox Church'. *Epitheorisi Koinonikon Erevnon* 148: 1–19 (in Greek).

Papakonstantinou, G. (2016) *Game Over: The Inside Story of the Greek Crisis*. Scotts Valley: CreateSpace.

Papapavlou, M. (2015) *The Experience of the Syntagma Square*. Athens: Ekdoseis ton Synadelfwn (in Greek).

Papataxiarchis, E. (2016a) 'Being "There": At the Front Line of the "European Refugee Crisis" – part 1'. *Anthropology Today* 32(2): 5–9.

Papataxiarchis, E. (2016b) 'Being "There": At the Front Line of the "European Refugee Crisis" – part 2'. *Anthropology Today* 32(3): 3–7.

Papataxiarchis, E. (2016c) 'Unwrapping Solidarity? Society Reborn in Austerity'. *Social Anthropology* 24(2): 205–10.

Papataxiarchis, E. (2016d) 'A Great Inversion. The Refugee Crisis and the New Patriotism of Solidarity'. *Synchrona Themata* 132–133: 7–28.

Pennington, M. (2012) *Elinor Ostrom, Common-Pool Resources and the Classical Liberal Tradition in the Future of the Commons: Beyond Market Failure and Government Regulation*. London: iea-The Institute of Economic Affairs.

Petropoulou, C. (2010) 'From the December Youth Uprising to the Rebirth of Urban Social Movements: A Space–time Approach'. *International Journal of Urban and Regional Research* 34(1): 217–24.

Pettifer, J. (2015) *The Making of the Greek Crisis*. London: Penguin

Pickerill, J., and J. Krinsky (2012) 'Why Does Occupy Matter?' *Social Movement Studies* 11(3–4): 279–87.

Polletta, F., and J. M. Jasper (2001) 'Collective Identity and Social Movements'. *Annual Review of Sociology* 27(1): 283–305.

Portwood-Stacer, L. (2013) *Lifestyle Politics and Radical Activism*. New York: Bloomsbury Publishing USA.

Pritchard, A., and N. Morgan (2006) 'Hotel Babylon? Exploring Hotels as Liminal Sites of Transition and Transgression'. *Tourism Management* 27(5): 762–72.

PROLEPSIS (2013) *Results from the Survey on 'Dietary Habits'*. Available at Http://diatrofi.prolepsis.gr/en/what-we- do/the-need/food-insecurity/.

Rancière, J. (1992) 'Politics, Identification, and Subjectivization'. *October* 61(Summer): 58–64.

Rancière, J. (1999) *Dis-agreement: Politics and Philosophy*. Minneapolis: University of Minnesota Press.
Rancière, J. (2006) *The Politics of Aesthetics*. London: Continuum.
Reason, P., and H. Bradbury (eds) (2008) *The Sage Handbook of Action Research: Participative Inquiry and Practice*. California: Sage.
Reina, D., M. Reina, and D. Hudnut (2017) *Why Trust Is Critical to Team Success?* Research Report. Center for Creative Leadership.
Rifkin, J. (2014) *The Zero Marginal Cost Society: The Internet of Things, the Collaborative Commons, and the Eclipse of Capitalism*. New York: St. Martin's Press.
Roitman, J. (2013) *Anti-crisis*. Durham: Duke University Press.
Rosenberg, M., and D. Chopra (2015) *Nonviolent Communication: A Language of Life: Life-Changing Tools for Healthy Relationships*. San Diego: PuddleDancer Press.
Rozakou, K. (2016) 'Crafting the Volunteer: Voluntary Associations and the Reformation of Sociality'. *Journal of Modern Greek Studies* 34(1): 79–102.
Rozakou, K. (2017) 'Solidarity# Humanitarianism: The Blurred Boundaries of Humanitarianism in Greece'. *Etnofoor* 29(2): 99–104.
Simiti, M. (2015) 'Rage and Protest: The Case of the Greek Indignant Movement'. *Contention* 3(2): 33–50.
Simmel, G. (1994) 'Bridge and Door'. *Theory, Culture & Society* 11(1): 5–10.
Simpson, J. A. (2007) 'Psychological Foundations of Trust'. *Current Directions in Psychological Science* 16(5): 264–8.
Sohn, H., S. Kousoulas, and G. Bruyns (2015) 'Introduction: Commoning as Differentiated Publicness'. *Footprint*, 1–8.
Solidarity4all (2014) 'Building Hope against Fear and Devastation'. Available at: https://www.solidarity4all.gr/en/news/solidarity-all-building-hope-against-fear-anddevastation (accessed 1 October 2019).
Sotirakopoulos, N., and G. Sotiropoulos (2013) '"Direct Democracy Now!": The Greek Indignados and the Present Cycle of Struggles'. *Current Sociology* 61(4): 443–56.
Stavrides, S. (2013) *The City of Thresholds*. Trento: Professional Dreamers.
Stavrides, S. (2015) 'Common Space as Threshold Space: Urban Commoning in Struggles to Re-appropriate Public Space'. *Footprint*, 9–19.
Stavrides, S. (2016) *Commons Space*. London: Zed Books.
Steins, N., and V. Edwards (1999) 'Platforms for Collective Action in Multiple-Use Common-Pool Resources'. *Agriculture and Human Values* 16: 241–55.
Szakolczai, A. (2000) *Reflexive Historical Sociology*. London: Routledge.
Taylor, V., N. Whittier, A. D. Morris, and C. M. Mueller (1992) 'Collective Identity in Social Movement Communities: Lesbian Feminist Mobilization'. *Social Perspectives in Lesbian and Gay Studies: A Reader*, 349–65.
Thomassen, B. (2009) 'The Uses and Meanings of Liminality'. *International Political Anthropology* 2(1): 5–28.
Thomassen, B. (2014) *Liminality and the Modern Living through the In-Between*. Farnham: Ashgate.

Tsafos, N. (2013) *Beyond Debt: The Greek Crisis in Context*. North Charleston: CreateSpace Independent Publishing Platform.

Tsaliki, L. (2012) *The Greek 'Indignados': The Aganaktismenoi as a Case Study of the 'New Repertoire of Collective Action'*. Speech at the "In/compatible Publics: Publics in Crisis-Production, Regulation and Control of Publics" Panel, Transmediale Media Art Festival, Berlin.

Tsavdaroglou, H. (2016) *Commons and Enclosures*. Doctoral Thesis (in Greek).

Tsigganou, I. (1999) 'Family as Mechanism of Social Control in the Contemporary Greek Society'. *Epitheorisi Koinonikon Erevnon* 98–99: 121–36 (in Greek).

Turner, V. W. (1967) *The Forest of Symbols*. New York: Cornell University Press.

Turner, V. (1974) 'Liminal to Liminoid, in Play, Flow, and Ritual: An Essay in Comparative Symbology'. *Rice Institute Pamphlet – Rice University Studies* 60(3): 53–92.

Turner, V. (1977) *The Ritual Process*. New York: Cornell University Press.

Turner, V. (1982) *From Ritual to Theatre: The Human Seriousness of Play*. New York: PAJ.

Turner, V., and E. L. Turner (1978) *Image and Pilgrimage in Christian Culture*. New York: Columbia University Press.

Turner, V. (1988) *The Anthropology of Performance*. New York: PAJ.

Tzogopoulos, G. (2013) *The Greek Crisis in the Media. Stereotyping in the International Press*. London: Routledge.

Vaiou, D. (2014) 'Tracing Aspects of the Greek Crisis in Athens: Putting Women in the Picture'. *European Urban and Regional Studies* 23(3); 220–30.

Van Gennep A (1960) *The Rites of Passage*. London: Routledge.

Varoufakis, Y. (2017) *Adults in the Room: My Battle with the European and American Deep Establishment*. New York: Farrar, Straus and Giroux.

Varvarousis, A. (2019) 'Crisis, Liminality and the Decolonization of the Social Imaginary'. *Environment and Planning E. Nature and Space* 2(3): 493–512.

Varvarousis, A. (2020) 'The Rhizomatic Expansion of Commoning through Social Movements'. *Ecological Economics* 171: 106596.

Varvarousis, A., and G. Kallis (2017) 'Commoning against the Crisis'. In *Another Economy Is Possible. Culture and Economy in a Time of Crisis*, edited by Castells et Alter, 128–59. Cambridge: Polity Press.

Varvarousis, A., N. Temple, C. Galanos, G. Tsitsirigos, and G. Bekridaki (2017) *Social and Solidarity Economy Report*. Athens: British Council Publications (in Greek).

Varvarousis, A., V. Asara, and B. Akbulut, (2020) 'Commons: A Social Outcome of the Movement of the Squares'. *Social Movement Studies* 20(3): 292–311.

Velez, M. A., J. K. Stranlund, and J. J. Murphy (2009) 'What Motivates Common Pool Resource Users? Experimental Evidence from the Field'. *Journal of Economic Behavior & Organization* 70(3): 485–97.

von Hantelmann, D. (2020) 'What Is the New Ritual Space for the 21st Century?'. *Multitudes* 79(2): 123–32.

Vradis, A. (2011) 'Breaking the Spatial Contract'. In *Democracy under Construction: From the Streets to the Square*, edited by C. Giovanopoulos and D. Mitropoulos, 211–18. Athens: Asynexeia (in Greek).

Vradis, A., and D. Dalakoglou (2011) *Revolt and Crisis in Greece: Between a Present Yet to Pass and a Future Still to Come*. Oakland, CA and London: AK Press and Occupied London.

Wilson, D. S. (2015) *Does Altruism Exist?: Culture, Genes, and the Welfare of Others*. New Haven: Yale University Press.

Zibechi, R. (2010) *Territories in Resistance. A Cartography of Latin American Social Movements*. Edinburg: AK Press.

Zizek, S. (2020) *Pandemic!: COVID-19 Shakes the World*. Cambridge: Polity Press.

INDEX

Adam, S. 105, 108–9
Adventists 152
aganaktismenoi ('indignant') 62
Akbulut, Bengi 93
Allilegyi Peiraia (Piraeus Solidarity) 105, 125, 128
altruism 157–63
  in actions 158–9
  in thoughts and feelings 158–9
Antiauthoritarian Movement 77
anti-capitalist commons 22, 32–3, 51–2
apofasismenoi ('determined') 62
Asara, Viviana 93
Athanasiou, A. 71
automatic trust 141, 165–8

Bauwens, Michel 85–6, 90
'being-in-common' 46
Benkler, Yochai 158
Bey, Hakeem 36–9
Bhabha, Homi 27
Bios Coop 135
Bishop, R. C. 114
bonobo apes 113
Bookchin, Murray 84
Bookchin's model of political participation 89
boundaries 114–15, 124–5
breeding 105
Bresnihan, P. 128
'Bridge and Door' (Simmel) 28
Brighenti, A. 68
Butler, Judith 68–9, 71
Byrne, M. 128

Caffentzis, G. 22
Castells, Manuel 46, 59, 75, 92
Castoriadis, Cornelius 30–1

Chatterton, Paul 47
chimpanzees, aggression in 113
Ciriacy-Wantrup, S. V. 114
city of thresholds 33
climate camps 3
closure/openness of
  commons 113–36
  analytics of 121–3
  in Ostrom's framework 114–16
  political and philosophical debate about 116–23
  analytics 121–3
  foundations of 120–1
  Hardt and Negri's logic 118–19
  Harvey's logic 117–18
  in post-liminal period of Greek commoning movement 124–35
  multiplication, protection through 127–9
  networking, protection through 129–31
  new communication tools, protection through 134–5
  opening of political identities, protection through 131–4
  'open' regulation, protection through 125–7
  protection of commons 124–35
clothes, workshop for 125–6
commoning 3–4, 9–12, 22–3
  communitas in 26
  destabilization of identity relate to 71–3
  dynamism of 10–12
  as learning process 12
  liminal subjects of 45–79

Index

movement in numbers in Greece 96–101
new business model 10
post-capitalist futures 10
role of 6
social movements and 8–9
common-pool resources 48, 48 n.2, 115
commons 1–4, 9–12
  anti-capitalist 22, 51–2
  in autonomous Marxists' approaches 19–23, 51–2
  Bollier's and Helfrich's patterns of 3
  closure/openness of 113–36
  communism of 51
  distorted 22
  dynamism of 10–12
  in expansion 81–111
  as governance system 49
  knowledge/information 48–9, 48 n.3
  liminal 4–5, 31–45
  manifold 128
  movement of squares and 45–8
  new business model 10
  Ostrom's rules for managing 3
  peer-to-peer production and 10–11
  political dimension of 19–23
  post-capitalist futures 10
  protection of 7, 113
  range 4
  research on 3
  role of 6
  social movements and 8–9, 22–3, 82–94, 101–7
  for societal transformation 22
  strength of 10–12
  struggle for 46
  as systems 18–19
  who/why interested in 9–10
  'Commons and Democracy' Plan 20
commons' expansion 81–111

Bauwens's on 85–6, 90
commons and social movements, relation between 82–94
  De Angelis's on 87–91
  Hardt's on 85
  Harvey's on 84–5
  Kostakis's on 85–6
  from liminal to rhizomatic 92–4
  limitations of theories on 89–91
  Negri's on 85
  new commons after 2011 in Greece 94–111
  Ostrom's on 83–4, 89
  rhizomatic expansion 92–111
  Stavrides's on 86–7, 90
commons fix 22
common space 46
communication practices 134–5
Communist Manifesto 52
communitas 26
  in commoning practices 26
  versus community 26
communities 140–1, 140 n.2, 166
  versus communitas 26
  fixed *versus* open 31–2
  and identity 32–5
  liminal commons and 31–5
  in movement 33
contemporary movements 46
Covid-19 pandemic 5–6
crises 6, 10–11, 26–8
  in autonomous Marxists' approaches 19–23, 51–2
  as calamity 13
  common narrative of 15–16
  concept of 12–13
  contemporary literature on 13–14
  inhabiting 12–15
  and liminality 26–9
  as limit 15–16
  as opportunity 13–14
  Ostrom's work through 16–19
  Roitman's argument 14–15
  and subjectification 52–4

De Angelis, Massimo 20, 22, 46–7, 74–5, 87–93
de-identification of subjects 70
Deleuze, Gilles 38, 92, 121
'Dervenion 56 Occupation' 152–3
deterritorialization of subjects 70
digital commons 141
Dikeç, M. 46
dis-identification 53
dispossessed 51–2
distorted commons 22
Durkheim, É. 25

e-commoners 150–1
e-commoning 150
economics 18
'Eight Design Principles for Successful Commons' (Ostrom) 17, 49
e-volunteers 150
exclusion 114–15
expansion, commons in 81–111
 Bauwens's on 85–6, 90
 commons and social movements, relation between 82–94
 De Angelis's on 87–91
 Hardt's on 85
 Harvey's on 84–5
 Kostakis's on 85–6
 from liminal to rhizomatic 92–4
 limitations of theories on 89–91
 Negri's on 85
 new commons after 2011 in Greece 94–111
 Ostrom's on 83–4, 89
 rhizomatic expansion 92–111
 Stavrides's on 86–7, 90

Federici, S. 22
food bank 125, 125 n.2
food parcels 126–7, 126 n.4
Foucault, Michel 31

free meals 126
Free State (or Republic) of Fiume 37 n.4
furniture manufacturing, workshop for 126

game theory 18
Giovanopoulos, C. 101, 107
Goutsos, D. 75
Greece 5
 commoning movement in numbers 96–101
 crisis 14–15
  bailout agreement of 2010 58
  in economic terms 55
  first cracks 58–61
  GDP decline 55–6, 55 n.5
  memorandum trauma 61
  in numbers 54–6
  Olympic Games 58–9
  revolt in 2008 59–60
  slogans 61
  social imaginary before 56–8
  socio-spatial inequalities 58–9
  stock market crash of 1999 58
 history 56
 movement of squares in 6, 45–8
 new commons after 2011 in 94–111
 social imaginary in 56–8
Greek Social and Solidarity Mapping and Needs Analysis project 102 n.9
Guattari, Felix 38, 92–3, 121
'Guerrilla Gardening' movement 9

Hardt, Michael 20, 22, 33, 46, 85–6, 89–90, 114, 117–21, 123, 135, 185
Harvey, David 53, 84–5, 89, 114, 117–23, 135
Helfrich, Silke 115–16

holidarity 162
Holloway, J. 61
homo economicus 157, 163
humanitarianism 138
humans 28
hybridity 68

IAD; *see* Institutional Analysis and Development
ideation 105
in-betweenness 68
individualism 69
information commons 48–9, 48 n.3
Institutional Analysis and Development (IAD) 17
internal multiplication 76–7
interstitiality 68

Jameson, Frederic 16

Kaika, M. 46
Karaliotas, L. 46
Karamichas, J. 66
Karditsa 131
King, Martin Luther 14
Kioupkiolis, A. 46
knowledge commons 48–9, 48 n.3
Koselleck, R. 12
Kostakis, Vasilis 85–6
Kostas 105, 126, 132
Krinsky, J. 46
KRRS (Karnataka Rajya Raitha Sangha) union of fishermen, India 9

Laloux, Frederix 122
Latouche, Serge 14
Les Rites de Passage (Van Gennep) 24
Lesvos Island 1, 138–9
liminal commons 4–5, 31–45
   basic characteristics of 6
   Bey's temporary autonomous zones 36–9

community and 31–5
expansion of 6
Greek case 42–4
identity and 31–5
membership turnover in 7
motivation in 7
of occupied squares 61–77
ontology/operation of 73–6
Platanos as 137–57
of Platanos Self-Organized Refugee Camp 141–57
and temporality 35–6
trust in 7
liminal human composition 147–53
liminality 23–31, 68
   Bhabha's usage of 27
   in context of (post) modernity 27–8
   and crises 26–9
   normality and 29
   social imaginary 29–31
   social normalization 31
   social structures 29
   Turner on 25–7
   Van Gennep on 24–6, 34
liminal subjects of commoning 45–79
   anti-capitalist commons 51–2
   crisis and subjectification 52–4
   Greek memorandum trauma 54–61
   movement of squares 45–8
   occupied squares, liminal commons of 61–77
   in Ostrom's theory 48–51
liminoid 27
Linebaugh, Peter 4
liquid modernity 27–8
living-in-common 46
love 118–19

magma 30 n.3
manifold commons 128
Marcuze, P. 46

Marxists, autonomous 19–23,
    51–2
membership in space-commoning
    activities 141, 168–71
Meretz, Stefan 115–16
Metapolitefsi 56, 56 n.6
Metropolitan Solidarity Clinic 104
migrants 1–2
Mitropoulos, D. 101, 107
Molyvos 138
movement of squares 6
    commons and 45–8
    counter-hegemonic politics
        theory and 47–8
    empirical approach, merit
        of 47–8
Movimento dos Trabalhadores Sem
    Terra 9
multiplication, protection
    through 127–9
multitude 118–19

National Network of Social Clinics
    and Pharmacies 130–1
National Network of Solidarity
    Clinics 133
Negri, Antonio 20, 22, 33, 46,
    85–6, 89–90, 114, 117–21,
    123, 135, 185
neoliberalism 69
networking, protection
    through 129–31
Network of Cooperative Ventures of
    Athens 130, 133
Noborder Camp 1–2
    effervescence of 3
    experience of 3
Nomadic Kitchen 129
nomadology 38
non-rhizomatic networks 93
normality 29

Obama, Barack 14
occupied squares, liminal commons
    of 3, 61–77

assemblies 65–6
common space 62–6
first rally 61–2
human composition and diverse
    repertoires of action 66–8
identity, destabilization of 71–3
internal multiplication 76–7
liminal commons, ontology and
    operation of 73–6
liminality for subjects, role
    of 68–70
surface expansion 76
occupy movements 9, 33, 61–77
    Butler on 68–9
openness 131–2; *see also* closure/
    openness of commons
Ostrom, Elinor 3, 16–19, 31–2,
    34–5, 47, 157
    on economic theory 17–18
    'Eight Design Principles
        for Successful
        Commons' 17, 49
    on expansion of commons 83–4
    framework in closure/openness
        of commons 114–16
    on game theory 18
    liminal subjects of commoning,
        theory on 48–51
    logic on boundaries 114–15
    social movements and commons,
        relationship between 84,
        89–91
    theory of subjectivity 47–51
    theory *versus* framework
        by autonomous
        Marxists 20–1, 51–2
    view on commons 47–51

Pagani detention centre 1–3
Pantazidou, Maro 107–8
Papapavlou, M. 66, 68
Papataxiarchis, E. 150
peer-to-peer (P2P) production 150
Penguin and the Leviathan, The
    (Benkler) 158

peri-urban agriculture   126
Pickerill, Jenny   46-7
PIKPA Self-organized Refugee
    Camp   160
'Plan C&D'   20
Platanos Self-organized Refugee
    Camp in Lesvos   7,
    137-41
    common space   141-4
    expanding character of
        Platanos   153-5
    as 'healing place for all'   159-63
    liminal commons of   141-57
    liminal human
        composition   147-53
    'other,' encounter with   146-7
    Platanos' geography   138-41
    precarious commons   156-7
    subjects and places in
        crisis   145-6
Platform Capitalism   10
Plato's Academy Cooperative
    Café   128-9, 135
political identities, opening
    of   131-4
political subjectification   53
politics   53
polycentric governance model   83
Polymeneas, G.   75
'Porto,' community currency   126
producer-to-consumer
    networks   95
property   114-15, 123
protection of commons   124-35
    labyrinth of strategies   124-5
    through multiplication   127-9
    through networking   129-31
    through new communication
        tools   134-5
    through opening of political
        identities   131-4
    through 'open' regulation   125-7

Rancière, J.   53
'Reclaim the Streets' movement   9

refugees
    camps   3, 137-57
    crisis   1, 159-60
    Platanos Self-organized Refugee
        Camp in Lesvos   7,
        137-41
    solidarity to refugees
        movement   160
Rethymno   131
rhizomatic expansion of
    commons   92-111
    a-centred rhizomatic character
        of   107-9
    and new commons after 2011 in
        Greece   94-111
    social movements and
        commons   101-7
rhizomes   41, 66, 82, 92-3,
    110-11
Rifkin, Jeremy   10
rites of passage   4-5, 24-5, 175,
    177, 185
rituals   4, 7, 25, 173-83
Roitman, Janet   14
Rozakou, Katerina   158, 162

schizophrenia   34
self-esteem   69
self-organization   60, 122-3, 162-6
self-organized street parties/
    festivals   3
self-reflection   69
self-reliance   69
Simmel, Georg   28
Skala Sykamnias   138
social clinics in Greece   9, 95, 105,
    107-8, 126
social imaginary, in Greece   29-31,
    56-8
social kitchen   125
social mobilizations of
    2008 revolt   6
social movements   81-2
    Bauwens's on   85-6, 90
    commoning and   8-9

and commons 8–9, 22–3,
    82–94, 101–7
  De Angelis's on 87–91
  and emergence of new
    commons 93–111
  Hardt's on 85
  Harvey's on 84–5
  Kostakis's on 85–6
  Negri's on 85
  Ostrom's on 84
  outcomes 93–4
  in rhizomatic way 94–111
  social outcomes of 94
  Stavrides's on 86–7, 90
  urban 59–60
social normalization 31
social structures 17–21, 26, 29–31,
    52, 74, 124, 141, 175–8
solidarity basket 127
solidarity economy 102
solidarity hubs 95
solidarity school 125, 125 n.3
Solidarity Social Clinic of
    Thessaloniki 108
solidarity to refugees
    movement 160
Spaces of Hope (Lefebvre and
    Foucault) 120
Spinoza, Baruch 121
'Spithari Waking Life' eco-
    community 104
Stavrides, Stavros 32–4, 46, 86–7,
    90–1
subjectification 52–4
summer camps 3
surface expansion 76–7
Swyngedouw, E. 46
Syntagma (Constitution)
    Square 48, 61–77, 103

Tao Te Ching (Tzu) 38
TAZs; *see* temporary autonomous
    zones (TAZs)
Teloni, D. D. 105
temporary autonomous zones
    (TAZs) 36–9
temporary commoning 3
theory of territoriality 113
Thousand Plateaus, A
    (Deleuze and
    Guattari) 92
transformations 7, 173–83
transplantation 105
Trapeza Chronou
    Holargou-Papagou
    (Holargou-Papagou
    TimeBank) 132
trust 141, 163–8
Turner, Victor 25–7, 61, 71
Tzu, Lao 38

urban agriculture 126
urban commoning 103
urban social movements 59–60
utility 157–63

Van Gennep, Arnold 24–6, 34
Via Campesina 9
volunteerism 158–9

Wilson, Michael 113
Wilson, Peter Lamborn; *see* Bey,
    Hakeem

Zapatista movement in
    Mexico 9, 33
'Zeitgeist' movement 63
zero marginal cost society 10
Zibechi, Raul 66

www.ingramcontent.com/pod-product-compliance
Lightning Source LLC
Chambersburg PA
CBHW051810230426
43672CB00012B/2680